THE MEXICAN OUTSIDERS

The Mexican Outsiders

A COMMUNITY HISTORY OF MARGINALIZATION AND DISCRIMINATION IN CALIFORNIA

Martha Menchaca

UNIVERSITY OF TEXAS PRESS

AUSTIN

Copyright © 1995 by the University of Texas Press
All rights reserved
Printed in the United States of America
Second paperback printing, 1996

Requests for permission to reproduce material from this work
should be sent to Permissions, University of Texas Press,
Box 7819, Austin, TX 78713-7819.

∞ The paper used in this publication meets the minimum
requirements of American National Standard for Information
Sciences—Permanence of Paper for Printed Library Materials,
ANSI Z39.48-1984.

Library of Congress Cataloging-in-Publication Data

Menchaca, Martha.
    The Mexican outsiders : a community history of
marginalization and discrimination in California / Martha
Menchaca. — 1st ed.
        p.   cm.
    Includes bibliographical references and index.
    ISBN 0-292-75173-7 (alk. paper). — ISBN 0-292-75174-5
(pbk. : alk. paper)
        1. Mexican Americans—California—Santa Paula—Social
conditions.   2. Mexicans—California—Santa Paula—Social
conditions.   3. Discrimination—California—Santa Paula.
4. Racism—California—Santa Paula.   5. Santa Paula (Calif.)—
Race relations.   6. Mexican Americans—California—Social
conditions—Case studies.   7. Mexicans—California—Social
conditions—Case studies.   8. California—Race relations—
Case studies.   9. Discrimination—California—Case studies.
10. Racism—California—Case studies.
I. Title.
F869.S53M46 1995
305.868'72079492—dc20   94-46190

For my family
and the Mexican-origin people
of Santa Paula

Contents

Illustrations

PHOTOGRAPHS

MAPS

TABLES

Acknowledgments

The following ethnographic history attempts to advance information about how past social injustices have affected the people of Mexican descent in the United States. It is an effort to describe how, in one community, social segregation evolved into a system of interethnic social apartness.

I extend my sincere gratitude to the Mexican-origin people of Santa Paula who graciously gave their time in helping me to complete this study. I offer special thanks to Victor Salas and Jesus Victoria who helped me locate documents that verified the oral histories I gathered. I am also indebted to Alberta Ward, former librarian of the Ventura County Museum of History and Art, for helping me locate photographs to illustrate events discussed in this study. I am grateful to the National Research Council/Ford Foundation Dissertation and Postdoctoral Fellowship Program for Minorities for the financial support I received to gather my field research and for leave time to write this manuscript. I also extend my appreciation to the Tomás Rivera Center, which served as my host institution during my postdoctoral fellowship period. Subsequent fieldwork was also partially funded by the Wenner-Gren Foundation for Anthropological Research.

Finally, I want to thank my husband, Richard R. Valencia, for his friendship, encouragement, and intellectual support during the lengthy process of making this book a reality.

Introduction

It is my hope in this book to provide an ethnographic history of the prejudice and discrimination experienced by the Mexican-origin people of Santa Paula, California. This work is an attempt to write about their untold local community history and their memories of marginalization and discrimination. It is also my history, as I was raised in this community. Santa Paula is a biracial agrarian community in Ventura County, located sixty miles northeast of Los Angeles. Currently, Santa Paula is an ethnically balanced Anglo American and Mexican-origin community that is politically and socially dominated by Anglo American families who owe their wealth to the citrus industry (Belknap 1968; Menchaca 1989; Triem 1985).[1] The city has a long and unpleasant history of social segregation, which has evolved into an interethnic system that I refer to as "social apartness."

Anthropologists and historians are aware that overt and subtle forms of racial prejudice against racial minorities have been a traditional practice in most Anglo American communities. Nonetheless, in the reconstruction of local histories, such experiences are often treated as unimportant or are altogether ignored (Frisch 1981). Perhaps this omission is due to the common practice of focusing on the local heroes, the power holders, or the founding families of a community. Unfortunately, the result is often unbalanced and univocal documentation of the contributions of the dominant culture—the Anglo Americans—and obscures the contributions of other ethnic groups. Failure to include information about racial minorities results in their depiction as passive community members and not as significant agents of social production and change. This characterization has served to perpetuate the myth that if they are not included within their community's history they must not have merited attention. Racial minorities are essentially robbed of their historical presence and treated as people without a history. Their exclusion also serves to construct a distorted community image because issues of interethnic contact are deleted from the historical discourse. As such, unpleasant events are forgotten or trivialized as past phenomena or, worse, considered to be part of natural processes that develop when two groups of diverse ethnic and racial backgrounds come into contact. Social segregation, police brutality, political disenfranchisement, unfair labor practices, and everyday racist practices against racial minorities become part of the interethnic history that does not merit consideration. Why? Because acknowledgments of such behavior and policies are often thought to be unkind depictions of the dominant ethnic group. This form of historical distortion negates the characterization of racial minorities as agents of social change who have challenged their subordinate social roles and made their communities kinder places to live.

Such historical distortions and omissions aptly describe how the public history of Santa Paula has been written by local historians and subsequently immortalized in the city's museum, library archives, and city government plaques. Anglo Americans, in particular the families who owe their wealth to the citrus industry, are singularly credited for having founded Santa Paula, cultivated the land, established the citrus industry, and institutionalized fair government practices (Blanchard 1961; Cleland 1957; Teague 1944; Thille 1952, 1958). Santa Paula's public history is depicted as uncomplicated because the city is a peaceful one inhabited by Anglo Americans. The problem I see in this characterization is not what has been written but what has been omitted: this omission produces a distorted history. People of Mexican descent and Native Americans are ignored in the historical records, regardless of the fact that Native Americans founded Santa Paula and Mexicans colonized the city, inhabited it since the late 1700s, and planted the first citrus orchards. Indeed, these historical gaps are a problem, as the contributions and accomplishments of Mexican-origin people and Native Americans are attributed to Anglo Americans. Furthermore, by not including within Santa Paula's historical records accounts of the marginalization and discrimination suffered by Mexican-origin people, those who chronicled Santa Paula's past relegated such happenings to insignificance.

This incomplete history has also had consequences in everyday life. People in Santa Paula learn about their heritage and extract a sense of self-worth by hearing about the accomplishments of their ancestors and attending celebrations commemorating the achievements of the city's founding fathers. However, because the local heroes of Santa Paula—according to local history—have been only Anglo Americans, Mexicans are often left with a negative image of their ethnic group. Thus, the question of what Mexicans have to be proud of arises among Santa Paula residents.

Although, as in Santa Paula, many community histories may evade certain facts, the histories of racial minorities are not forgotten by all individuals (Vansina

1985). They continue to live in the oral traditions of the subordinate cultures (Paredes 1973). These unwritten histories, therefore, can be reconstituted by collecting oral histories and verifying these remembrances through a review of primary documents (Burgess 1982). Newspapers, property tax records, speeches, and court cases are among the many primary documents that can verify a peoples' oral histories. Such abundant physical evidence makes possible the historical reconstruction of racial discrimination. Although unpleasant events committed against racial minorities may not be included in the official histories of many communities, these events, nonetheless, can be reconstituted and the traditional histories written by Anglo Americans rectified.

My main goals for reconstructing the social history of Santa Paula's Mexican-origin community were to advance historiographic information about people of Mexican descent in the United States and to examine how past social injustices have influenced the perceptions of self-worth among inhabitants of this community. Thus, this case study examines both historical and contemporary issues. Regarding my first aim, this account illustrates that people of Mexican descent have a long history in California, which contributes to dispelling the myth that all Mexican people are recent immigrants. Although during the Spanish and Mexican periods Santa Paula remained a small village inhabited primarily by Native Americans and a few Mexican families, the presence of Mexicans predates the entrance of the Anglo Americans. Paradoxically, this fact is not acknowledged by local historians and is seldom mentioned in academic histories of California. Historians do acknowledge, however, the presence of people of Mexican descent in the larger, well-known settlements of San Diego, Los Angeles, Ventura, Santa Barbara, San Luis Obispo, Santa Ynez, Santa Cruz, San Jose, and San Francisco— the sites of Spanish missions and the legendary towns where the Dons resided (Camarillo 1979, 1984; Galarza 1964). Indeed, historians do not refute the presence of Spaniards or Mexicans in these California towns, as this history is closely interweaved with the legendary accounts of the Anglo American conquest of the Southwest.

Ironically, the conquest not only marks the beginning of the Anglo American period in the Southwest but also introduces the writing of a history that minimizes the social contributions of the Native Americans and the people of Mexican descent (Paredes 1973, 1978). In the case of Mexicans, for example, there is a vast absence of information about the Mexican communities that surrounded the larger towns and cities. This void has served to perpetuate the myth that besides the large towns and cities founded by the Spanish in California, all other communities were founded by the Anglo American pioneers (Cleland 1930). Seldom is any reference made or historical significance accorded to the *ranchos* (ranches) that were located throughout California (Galarza 1972; Hutchinson 1969; Robinson 1948). For example, the Mexican *ranchos* of Santa Paula, Saticoy,

Carpinteria, Sespe, Oxnard, Camarillo, and El Rio were located near the well-known Mexican settlements of Santa Barbara and Ventura. These were communities composed of small family ranches. In these California *ranchos* Mexicans had built irrigation systems, cleared roads, planted citrus orchards, established sheep herding businesses, and constructed humble adobe homes and chapels. Although the settlements were sparsely settled when California was annexed by the United States in 1848, they were developed to the extent that Anglo American businessmen considered them attractive investment sites. Businessmen subsequently purchased or took possession of these *ranchos* and converted them to Anglo American townships (Gidney, Brooks, and Sheridan 1917; Stuart 1879). Thus, because most historical writings begin their accounts of the Southwest with the entrance of the Anglo Americans, the social and technological contributions of previous populations are obscured and often attributed to Anglo Americans (Cleland 1930; Lamar 1966; Larson 1968; Richardson, Wallace, and Anderson 1970).

This study is an attempt to reconstruct the social history of one of these California communities—Santa Paula. My second aim in this reconstruction is to present the historical background in order to better understand how the past has affected the city's contemporary social relations. Current descriptions of Santa Paula illustrate how, over time, interethnic relations between Anglo Americans and Mexican-origin people improved. These discussions, however, also offer a critical analysis of how past forms of discrimination have evolved into subtle and modern manifestations of dominant group racism. I also examine how prejudice and discrimination have affected perceptions of self-worth in the Mexican-origin community of Santa Paula. That is, although people of Mexican descent are no longer involuntarily segregated in a different part of the city, social segregation has been transformed into a system of interethnic "social apartness." My conception of "social apartness," a construct developed for this analysis, refers to a system of social control in which Mexican-origin people are expected to interact with Anglo Americans only on Anglo American terms. Anglo Americans determine the proper times and places in which both groups can come into contact. Social apartness, therefore, is manifested in a number of ways similar to segregation. Santa Paula's current interethnic relations continue to be characterized by social distance and relationships defined by domination and subordination.

My historical review begins with the Native American period—to demonstrate that Santa Paula was not founded by Anglo Americans and to explain why Mexicans took physical and legal control of the region—and ends in 1991 with a description of how acculturation pressures have influenced the Mexican-origin people of Santa Paula. I have reconstructed the social history of this community using various sources, both ethnographic and historical. My ethnographic research is based on a one-year study conducted in Santa Paula from October 1, 1986, to October 1, 1987, and also on two subsequent visits in 1989 and 1991. The major parts of that research consisted of ninety-four open-ended interviews with community members and institutional representatives, as well as participation in a wide variety of social, civic, church, political, and recreational activities. Of these interviews, seventy-two were conducted with Mexican-origin people and twenty-two with Anglo Americans. The participants' ages ranged from sixteen to seventy-five years, and their occupations varied from farm laborers to citrus growers to attorneys. The participants were asked to respond to questions about Santa Paula's interethnic relations and its history and to describe the city's cultural ambiance. The historical data come from primary sources, including oral histories, church records, genealogies, photographs, newspapers, autobiographies, school records, court cases, and property tax records.

Oral histories provide information on the main features of the history of Santa Paula's Mexican-origin community. Although most of my informants were aware of some phases of Santa Paula's history, five of my Mexican-origin informants were experts on the subject. These individuals consider themselves to be local town historians and guardians of their community's oral traditions. I spent countless days talking to José, Linda, Tony, Isabel, and Roney.[2] Their oral histories dated back to the early 1900s. To verify the accuracy of the oral history accounts and to reconstruct unwritten historical events, I relied on archival records. I reviewed documents that dated back to the late 1800s and early 1900s. Historical records dealing with Santa Paula's Anglo American history were found in the local library, whereas documents about the Mexican-origin community were located in the files of Mexican American civic clubs or Mexican churches. California superior court, state supreme court, and federal supreme court cases provided additional information on the first Mexican settlers. These court records also contained descriptions of the land tenure history of Santa Paula beginning with its Native American period and concluding with the Anglo American homestead claims. Census data, as well as school and property tax records, were used to trace the emergence and disappearance of social segregation practices over time. Genealogies were used to collect information on the kinship systems of the Mexican-origin community. Contemporary information was gathered through interviews, ethnographic observations, the U.S. census, a survey of the Mexican American business sector, and agribusiness and school records.

Because I once lived in Santa Paula myself for twelve years, I also relied on extensive personal knowledge of the community. I arrived in the city as a five-year-old immigrant Mexican child and eventually moved to a nearby city upon entering college. My previous residence in Santa Paula has enabled me to acquire a deep understanding of the city's history, social structure, and economy.

Santa Paula

THE MEXICAN OUTSIDERS

ONE

Political Relations and Land Tenure Cycles in Santa Paula

Chumash Indians, Mexicans, and Anglo Americans

Land tenure cycles best describe the political changes that occurred in Santa Paula, and in other California communities, during the late eighteenth to nineteenth centuries. When control over land changed from one ethnic group to another, political changes followed that did not benefit the former. Our discussion of the Mexican-origin community of Santa Paula will therefore begin with a description of the land tenure history, for this account delineates how Mexicans eventually became a politically subordinate ethnic minority group. Once they lost legal title to the land, they also lost control of their subsistence base, and without land, their only economic recourse was to sell their labor to the Anglo American colonists. The material in this chapter is derived and analyzed from property records, court cases, oral histories, letters, church records, newspaper accounts, and archaeological writings.

THE NATIVE AMERICAN PERIOD

The land tenure history of Santa Paula begins with the Native American period, for this history clarifies why Santa Paula eventually became a Spanish settlement. As Santa Paula was located in a rich ecological zone and already populated by Indians, Spaniards envisioned that it could be converted into a prosperous colony populated by Indians, mestizos (of Spanish and Indian ancestry), and Spaniards (California Land Case No. 550, 1853). Chumash Indians were the original inhabitants of the territories where the California counties of Santa Barbara, Ventura, and Santa Maria now stand. What is now Santa Paula was situated on the original site of two Chumash Indian villages called Mupu and Sis'a (Kroeber 1970). Today, Santa Paula is located in Ventura County.

There were eight subdivisions of the Chumash Indians: Barbareño, Cuyama, Emigdiano, Island Chumash (San Miguel, Santa Rosa, and Santa Cruz Islands), Obispeño, Purisimeño, Santa Ynez, and Ventureño (Swanton 1984). The Chumash from Mupu and Sis'a were part of the Ventureño subdivision. The best-studied group of Chumash Indians are the Island Chumash. Doubts have been raised, however, regarding the relationship of the Island Chumash to the rest of the Chumash Indians (Fagan 1991; Forbes 1982) because the Island Chumash practice a specialized maritime subsistence lifestyle that emphasized fishing and sea mammal hunting, in contrast to the subsistence patterns of the inland Chumash. The Chumash who occupied the inland territories subsisted on animals they hunted and on the seeds and roots they gathered. Archaeologists estimate that before the entrance of the Europeans, the Island Chumash numbered three thousand, while the rest of the Chumash ranged from fifteen to thirty thousand (Aikens 1978; Fagan 1991; Forbes 1982).

Two hypotheses have been advanced to explain where the ancestors of the Chumash came from before they settled in California. Both hypotheses concur that the Chumash Indians descended from Hokan-speakers and were the first inhabitants of the territories they occupied. There is disagreement, however, over where the Hokan-speakers migrated from during prehistoric times and with whom they intermarried. The debate centers on whether the Hokan-speakers share a common origin with Mexican Indian groups. If they do, the prehistory of the counties of Ventura, Santa Barbara, and San Luis Obispo is part of Mexico's ancestral past. And, if there is a Hokan–Mexican Indian ancestral relationship, this prehistory is shared also by Mexican Americans.

One hypothesis proposes that the ancestors of the Chumash, the Hokan-speakers, intermarried with the Yuman Indians (Castetter and Bell 1951; Spicer 1962; Spier 1933; Swanton 1984). The Yuman Indians descended from the Hohokam Indians of northern Mexico (Forbes 1982; Lipe 1978; Swanton 1984). The Hohokam people migrated to the Southwest from northern Mexico in 2300 B.C. (Forbes 1973; Lipe 1978). They first settled in Southern Arizona and later dispersed towards New Mexico and the interior of Arizona by 900 A.D. As they migrated through the Southwest, they introduced agricultural innovations to local Indian groups. The Hohokam had acquired this knowledge from the Indians of central Mexico. In the Southwest, the Hohokam dug irrigation ditches, made pottery, built housing structures, introduced various art forms, and constructed Mexican ball courts. By 1100 A.D., the Hohokam people broke down into several ethnic subdivisions and one group came to be known as the Yuman Indians. About that time, groups of Yuman Indians migrated towards Southern and Central California and intermarried with Hokan-speakers. As a result of this intermixture, the descendants of the Hokan and Yuman Indians began to produce new art forms, pottery styles, and subsistence traditions that distinguished them from their parent stocks (Lipe 1978; Spier 1933), and they came to be known as the Chumash Indians. The hypothesis, therefore, suggests that the Chumash share a common prehistoric ancestry with Indians of northern Mexico. Although there is agreement over the relationship between the Hokan-speakers and the Yuman Indians, very little knowledge has been advanced regarding the Hokan-speakers' origin before they settled in California. In an attempt to account for their origin, Spicer (1962) and Castetter and Bell (1951) propose that the Hokan-speakers and Yuman Indians were most likely ethnic subdivisions of the same ancestral Mexican Indian stock.

An alternate hypothesis proposes that the place of origin of the Chumash Indians' ancestors is uncertain because of insufficient archaeological data supporting any prehistoric migration theory (Aikens 1978). Mexican Indian traits exhibited by Chumash Indians (e.g., chieftain political structure, art forms, and bone and wood artifacts) are attributed to the effects of trade between Yuman Indians and Hokan-speakers rather than to intermarriage. This hypothesis also proposes that because archaeologists have dated artifacts left by the Island Chumash to 1000 B.C., it is likely that either the Chumash descended from Indians who migrated to California prior to the entrance of the Yuman Indians or the eight subdivisions of the Chumash Indians do not share a common ancestral prehistory. The questions of origins and the contrasting hypotheses of the Chumash Indians' prehistory are left up to future scholars to unravel. Still, although this prehistory needs to be explored, we do know that the Chumash Indians erected flourishing villages which eventually came to the attention of the Spanish explorers (Brown 1983). The material culture they produced became a source of interest and wealth for the Spanish.

The exact date when the Chumash Indians migrated to the area of Santa Paula is unknown, as well as when they erected the villages of Mupu and Sis'a (Swanton 1984). Their presence in present-day Ventura County, however, is estimated to date back to between 1000 to 1504 A.D. (Brown 1983; Fagan 1991; Greenwood and Browne 1969). According to eighteenth-century Spanish accounts, by 1769 more than five hundred Chumash Indians resided in Mupu alone (Nathan and Simpson 1962), and more than twenty large grass houses were constructed in Sis'a (Cleland 1957). Both villages were located near a creek and surrounded by oak trees.

THE SPANISH AND MEXICAN PERIODS

The subsequent exploration and colonization of Santa Paula by the Spanish military and Franciscan missionaries follows a sixteenth-century historical pattern that is similar to that experienced by other California communities. In his long journey across California in 1542, the Spanish explorer Juan Rodríguez-Cabrillo came in contact with the Chumash Indians (Nathan and Simpson 1962). Rodríguez-Cabrillo recorded the first European accounts of the architectural village designs and cultural lifestyles of these Native American Indians. He also drafted maps designating the zones where the most densely populated Indian villages stood. Rodríguez-Cabrillo reported that the region, now Ventura County, contained many villages and that the Chumash Indians "dressed in skins and wore their hair very long and tied up with strings interwoven with the hair, their [*sic*] being attached to the strings many geegaws of flint bone and wood" (cited in Triem 1985:12). Although the existence of the Indian villages in what is now Santa Paula was known to the Spanish, Mupu and Sis'a were not extensively explored until Gaspar de Portolá's expedition of 1769. In his journal, Portolá described Mupu to be further advanced in culture than any village he had so far encountered. He reported that "the village contained at least twenty large grass houses, spherical in form" (see Cleland 1957:7). Exactly when the Spanish changed the name of Mupu and Sis'a to Santa Paula is unclear. Nonetheless, both Indian villages came to be known as the territory of Santa Paula by the late 1700s.

During the Spanish colonial period, Santa Paula was selected as a mission site and as a stop along the route of El Camino Real (Cleland 1957). The mountainous coastal valley terrain, however, prevented the implementation of this plan. Thus, the Spanish decided to develop a coastal route and establish their mission and *presidio* (garrison) settlements where the cities of Ventura and Santa Barbara now stand. Santa Barbara became the territorial capital and elite cultural center of California, and Ventura became a major mission and trading center serving the Santa Paula area.

Although a mission was not built in Santa Paula, Franciscan missionaries commenced their colonization plans in 1782. A group of missionaries from Ventura settled in Santa Paula and began to institute technological innovations and to Christianize the local Chumash Indians (*Davidson et al. v. United States Government* 1857; Webster 1967). With the assistance and labor of the Chumash Indians the mission fathers were able to build an irrigation system in Sis'a. Whether the irrigation system was an innovation or an improvement or expansion of the irrigation ditches previously built by the Indians is not known. Nonetheless, the irrigation system was used to bring water from Santa Paula Creek to Sis'a (Webster 1967; Triem 1985). With the irrigation system in place, the missionaries were able to begin planting crops and teach the Chumash new agricultural techniques. In addition, the mission fathers built a chapel near Sis'a and set up an outpost with the help of the Chumash. It appears that at this time relations between the Spanish missionaries and the Chumash were friendly and both groups peacefully coexisted with each other. The missionaries attempted to Christianize the Chumash and in turn the Chumash welcomed the technological changes. Once the Christian settlement was under way, the Spanish Crown selected Santa Paula to be the future site of a land grant which was to be converted into a Spanish township (*Santa Paula Water Works et al. v. Julio Peralta* 1893–1898).[1]

In 1795, the Spanish Crown decided that land in the region, now Ventura County, not designated for mission settlements was to be partitioned into two major land grants, Rancho Simi and Rancho El Conejo (Robinson 1955). Rancho El Conejo, encompassing what is today Santa Paula, was granted to Ignacio Rodríguez and Juan Polanco in 1802 (Almaguer 1979). The Spanish grantees left their sections of Santa Paula virtually undisturbed and under the political domain of the Franciscan missionaries. In the interim, a Spanish township was not erected, and the Chumash Indians were able to continue their daily activities without the presence of Spanish civilians.

In 1821, following the termination of the Mexican War for Independence, the Spanish Crown lost control of Mexico and a new government was formed by Mexican mestizos and *criollos* (Caucasian Spaniards born in Mexico). The transfer of power resulted in immediate political and territorial changes throughout the Southwest. Because the new government considered the mission system of the Southwest to be a paternalistic institution which obstructed the conversion of the Indians into Mexican citizens, the mission fathers were ordered to disband the system (Weber 1982). The mission fathers were given a maximum period of fifteen years to secularize the Indians and to convert them into taxpaying farmers. Each Indian family was to receive a parcel of mission land and was to use it for agricultural purposes. The government envisioned that the Indians would favor becoming commercial farmers, and they would thus become integrated in Mexico's monetary economy. The new government also accorded the Indians full political rights as Mexican citizens and expected them to participate in Mexico's democratic political system (e.g., voting and running for political offices) (Menchaca 1993; Padilla 1979). The government's theory was that by being granted full political rights the Indians would want to acculturate and, when they did so, would become taxpaying Mexican citizens.

To hasten the colonization of the Southwest and to accelerate the acculturation of the Indians the Mexican government passed the Colonization Law of 1833, giving the governor of California the power to distribute vacant land. Under this law, mission lands and some Spanish land grants were to be subdivided into smaller grants (Hutchinson 1969). The land was to be partitioned into small family plots and granted to Native Americans who officially declared Mexican citizenship. If the land was not claimed by Indians, it was to be granted to incoming Mexican settlers or sold to anyone who was willing to establish a *rancho* (León-Portilla 1972; Menchaca 1993; Weber 1982). Acculturated Indians who had already been granted land were given the first opportunity to purchase former mission property. In Santa Paula, a few years after the Mexican War of Independence, titles to the Spanish land grants were reissued and the land transformed into *ranchos*. In 1829, a large tract of land was awarded to Don Carlos Carillo. There he established Rancho Sespe (Sespe Ranch). The *rancho* was located south of present-day Santa Paula. Don Carillo's land grant contained only a small part of Santa Paula. In 1834, most of Santa Paula, however, was partitioned by Governor José Figueroa and granted to settlers (California Land Case No. 550, 1853).[2] Governor Figueroa issued grants to three Mexican citizens, awarding José Joaquín Ortega the largest one, an area that encompassed most of the land in present-day Santa Paula. These Mexican colonists transformed their land into *ranchos* containing farm animals and citrus orchards. Ortega called his *rancho* Potrero de Santa Paula. Governor Figueroa also confirmed the Chumash Indians' legal rights over Mupu and Sis'a and did not distribute this land among the colonists (California Land Case No. 550, 1853:44). According to the Colonization Law of 1833 only land uninhabited or not worked by Indians could be granted or sold to Mexican citizens (Cowman 1977; Ross 1974).

From 1834 to 1840, Mexican colonists and Chumash Indians cultivated their land and lived undisturbed in Santa Paula. During that period, four other Mexican families and several Chumash Indian families migrated to Santa Paula and settled on Ortega's property. Ortega allowed them to become his tenants since a large part of his land remained uncultivated. He was willing to accommodate them because he was in the process of resettling in San Diego on a large land grant that he had recently acquired there. Ortega, therefore, needed settlers to farm his land in Santa Paula; otherwise his uncultivated property could be seized by the Mexican government. In 1839, California's secretary of state, Manuel Jimeno Casarin, became aware of Ortega's land acquisition in San Diego. Jimeno Casarin subsequently filed a petition asking the current governor of California, Governor Alvarado, to dissolve Ortega's title over Potrero de Santa Paula on the basis that the land was abandoned. Rather than asking the governor to award the land to Ortega's tenants, Jimeno Casarin requested that Potrero de Santa Paula be granted to him. At first, Ortega refused to relinquish his property rights. Following two land committee hearings, however, it became obvious to Ortega that his grant would be rescinded. Ortega then requested that two of his tenants, Juan López and the widow Señora Bernardo, be granted the farmland that they cultivated. Governor Alvarado declined Ortega's request and granted Potrero de Santa Paula to Jimeno Casarin. Ortega's former tenants were notified and informed that the new owner had the right to evict them.

Shortly thereafter, Jimeno Casarin renamed the *rancho* Rancho Santa Paula y Saticoy and notified his tenants that they would not be evicted as long as they did not cause injury to him or his family (California Land Case No. 550, 1853; California Land Case No. 328, 1853). He then built new farm buildings, bought cattle and horses, and planted more orchards. Although Jimeno Casarin made improvements on the property, he decided to move to Monterey, California. He hired one of his tenants as the *rancho*'s *mayordomo* (overseer, butler) and left him in charge of the land. Jimeno Casarin departed from Santa Paula in 1842 and thereafter returned only for short visits. His departure was prompted by his occupational duties as California's secretary of state, which required that he travel across California to personally register all California land grants and investigate all land disputes (Ross 1974). These duties forced Jimeno Casarin to maintain several residences throughout the state.

In 1847, Jimeno Casarin returned to Santa Paula to resurvey his property (California Land Case No. 328, 1853). Once again, he sent notices to his tenants reminding them that he was the owner of Rancho Santa Paula y Saticoy. On the day of the survey he was accompanied by a land surveyor, the mayor of Santa Barbara, two neighbors, and four tenants. During the survey, a dispute erupted between Jimeno Casarin and his tenants Pablo Alaya, Antonio Rodríguez, Luis Carillo, and Luis Francisco. Apparently the tenants argued that parts of Rancho Santa Paula y Saticoy should be given to them because they currently occupied several areas. The mayor of Santa Barbara responded that they did not have any legal right to defend their argument. Luis Francisco, a Chumash Indian and representative of several Indian families, continued to challenge the mayor's interpretation of the Mexican property laws. In defense of Jimeno Casarin, the mayor warned Luis Francisco that the Indians had only two options: accept their landlord's charity and remain at the *rancho* or prepare to be evicted. Luis Francisco conceded and peacefully accompanied the surveying group. The survey was completed when Jimeno Casarin's neighbors agreed to the boundary demarcations separating their *ranchos* from Rancho Santa Paula y Saticoy. Thus, in 1847 Santa Paula consisted of one large *rancho* owned by Jimeno Casarin, two small *ranchos* owned by José Moraga and Mr. Olivas, and two Indian *rancherías* (villages inhabited by acculturated American Indians who had adopted many Mexican traditions and practices)—Mupu and Sis'a. Several other *ranchos* were also contained within Rancho Santa Paula y Saticoy but were occupied by tenants that included four Mexican families and several Indian families.

In 1843, the Mexican government completed California's mission secularization program and sold the unclaimed mission property. Any land that had not been granted to Indians was sold (Weber 1982). During that time, Indian *rancherías* inhabited by more than twenty-five families were also notified that they must officially be transformed into Mexican townships or be prepared to lose the uncultivated lands surrounding their villages. The state planned to confiscate this land and sell it at auction (Ross 1974). The head chief of each *ranchería* was responsible for filing township incorporation documents. Unfortunately, only four *rancherías* in California followed this procedure and consequently most Indians lost title to the uncultivated lands surrounding their villages (Robinson 1948). Although the Mexican government took possession of these areas, it protected the Indians' property rights over land they cultivated, inhabited, and used for grazing. However, identification of which land belonged to the Indians was the responsibility of the government and the church. The federal government commissioned state officials and several missionaries to file documents on behalf of the Indians and to register the villages as privately owned corporate property.

In Santa Paula, the Chumash Indians' property rights over Mupu and Sis'a were only partly recognized (California Land Case No. 328, 1853). Like most Indians of California, they were given ownership over only the inhabited and cultivated land, not the vacant land surrounding their villages. To make matters worse, Indians who were not native to Santa Paula but had migrated there during the Mexican period were not awarded land grants. Although many Chumash Indians lost part of their land and other Indian settlers who were not native to Santa Paula became tenants of the Mexican *rancheros,* they continued to reside in Santa Paula. United States land case documents indicate that a large number of Indians were permanent residents of Mupu and Sis'a until at least 1857 (*Davidson et al. v. United States Government* 1857; *Ventura County Historical Society Quarterly* [*VCHSQ*] 1956).

Although we know the Native American land tenure history of Santa Paula, we do not know what happened to the Chumash's cultural or political identity. That is, whether they took advantage of the citizenship reforms of 1821, which gave Indians the right to become Mexican citizens (e.g., vote or run for office), or whether the Mexican government's Indian acculturation program succeeded in Santa Paula (e.g., converting villages to Mexican towns, encouraging Indians to become Catholics and to adopt the Spanish language) is not known. With respect to the majority of Santa Paula's residents, the *rancho* economy was in place by the mid-1800s. Mexican and Indian residents grew crops, planted orchards, and raised sheep and cattle (*Davidson et al. v. United States Government* 1857; *Santa Paula Water Works et al. v. Julio Peralta* 1893–1898; Sanborn [1873–1875] 1959). Indians, however, lost control of most of their ancestral land and many of them were converted into landless tenants.

THE ANGLO AMERICAN PERIOD

Political and social changes once again swept through Santa Paula upon Mexico's defeat in the Mexican American War of 1846-1848. United States troops successfully overpowered Mexican soldiers throughout the

Southwest (Weber 1982). In California, Anglo Americans obtained military control of the Mexican population within one year of the war (Cleland 1930; Weber 1982). The Mexican government's failure to defend its northern colonies was a result of economic problems caused by Spain. In 1821, when the Spanish Crown was overthrown in the Mexican War of Independence, Spanish bureaucrats plundered the treasury and left the country bankrupt (Lafaye 1974). As a consequence, the new Mexican government was economically unable to sustain its military troops in the Southwest (Castañeda 1956; Weber 1982). Most soldiers were asked to return home, and by law, the troops remaining behind had to be supported by the Mexican citizenry. The outposts and garrisons were either abandoned by the federal government or converted to military centers governed by civilians. Mexican citizens were required to take full responsibility for their military defense and were expected to form civilian militia units. Only during time of war did the Mexican government send troops to assist the civilians. In most cases, however, military troops arrived late or not at all. Therefore, during the Mexican American War, the Mexican civilians were unable to defend themselves against the U.S. military.

In Ventura County, a detailed description of a battle that occurred during the Mexican American War was recorded by José E. García, a ranch hand at Rancho Sespe and a member of the local civilian militia (García 1847). It is the only account left of the movement of Anglo American troops through Ventura County. The battle took place at Rancho Sespe. According to García, Ventura County's civilian militia was headed by Don Carlos Carillo. The battle began after Anglo American troops set up camp on the northeast side of the *rancho*. Carillo's men attempted to ambush the Anglo American soldiers, but his men were outnumbered. Nonetheless, the Mexicans attacked the Anglo American soldiers, and a battle ensued between the two opposing forces. García's account describes the reluctance of Anglo Americans and Mexicans to injure each other. Rather than firing guns, the antagonists resorted to ambushing, hiding, and fighting with sticks and stones. As a result of these battle tactics, no casualties occurred on either side. Eventually, the Anglo American troops overpowered Carillo's forces, and the victors left triumphantly, continuing onward to conquer other Southern California towns and cities.

Following the war, an Anglo-Saxon–dominated social order gradually replaced the *rancho* system in California. By 1870, the *rancho* economy and all the Mexican institutions were dismantled. When Anglo Americans took possession of the land, they became the new property owners and transformed the Mexican population into a landless and economically dependent laboring class (Camarillo 1979; Pitt 1966). Mexicans, however, fared better than the Native Americans of California. By 1852, the Indian population was devastated, their numbers reduced from 150,000 to 50,000 (Heizer and Almquist 1971). Most Indians had been eliminated by either disease or homicide. Anglo American settlers preferred clearing the Indians off the land to converting them into United States citizens. Only the former mission Indians survived during the Anglo American period. The majority of them, however, were dispossessed of their land and by 1862 had been made paupers and vagrants. Many of the former mission Indians, who had assimilated within Mexican culture, passed for Mexicans in an attempt to protect themselves from the new colonizers (Forbes 1973; Menchaca 1993; Newcomb 1986; Padilla 1979; *United States v. Vallejo* 1861).

A year after the Mexican American War ended, a mass influx of Anglo Americans entered California, spurred by the discovery of gold. Their dreams of wealth quickly vanished in 1851 when the mines became exhausted and the Gold Rush era ended (Cleland 1930; Heizer and Almquist 1971). Many Anglo American miners returned home, but the majority decided to remain in California and become farmers. Between 1867 and 1880, a flood of Anglo American newcomers settled in the area of Santa Paula expecting to establish land claims under the Land Act of 1851 and the Homestead Act of 1862 (*Santa Paula Water Works et al. v. Julio Peralta* 1893–1898). The act of 1851 legally abolished the Mexican land grant system and the act of 1862 gave settlers the right to claim land if they permanently resided on it and made property improvements. Upon their arrival, however, the settlers found that most of Santa Paula and Rancho Sespe had been recently purchased by several eastern capitalists. Carlos Carillo's family had sold Rancho Sespe and Manuel Jimeno Casarin sold Rancho Santa Paula y Saticoy.[3] The settlers, therefore, were unable to file homestead claims in order to take advantage of the land acts. Only the land owned by the Indians and some Mexicans was left unpurchased by the eastern capitalists (*Santa Paula Water Works et al. v. Julio Peralta* 1893–1898; *Davidson et al. v. United States Government* 1857; *Limoneira Company et al. v. Railroad Commission of California* 1917). The settlers, however, were unwilling to end their westward trek as defeated landless farmers. Ignoring the fact that Santa Paula and the surrounding areas were owned and occupied, they spread themselves throughout Santa Paula and Sespe Ranch (the name had changed by this time). Sis'a and Mupu disappeared within a few years of the mass influx of the Anglo American settlers, as the newcomers usurped the land.

Serious disputes over land also ensued between the homesteaders and the property owners (Triem 1985). The most violent encounter occurred between the homesteaders and the owners of Sespe Ranch, the More family. One night the homesteaders set fire to the Mores' barn, and as Thomas More raced to rescue his animals, he was ambushed and shot to death (Stuart 1879). Although the More family had previously sold a large part of their Ventura County property to the incoming settlers, many others decided to take possession of Sespe Ranch. In response to the violence, the More family sold part of Sespe Ranch and allowed homesteaders to take ownership of the unsold parcels.

Rancho Santa Paula y Saticoy was also partitioned into small parcels and sold mainly to homesteaders by 1867. Before that date, ownership of Rancho Santa Paula y Saticoy had been the basis of legal disputes between the United States government and several land speculators (California Land Case No. 328, 1853; California Land Case No. 550, 1853; *Davidson et al. v. United States Government* 1857). The dispute began in 1853 when six Anglo Americans claimed Manuel Jimeno Casarin sold them the ranch. The claimants also argued that Jimeno Casarin sold them the property inhabited by the Mupu and Sis'a Chumash Indians. They attempted to validate their claims by filing documents with the California Land Commission, but when the commission rejected the claims, they took their case to the judicial courts. In 1857, the United States District Court of Southern California ruled that most of the claims were fraudulent and concluded that only the heirs of John P. Davidson owned some parts of Santa Paula. The district judge ruled that five of the plaintiffs did not have proof that Jimeno Casarin had sold them property. Only part of the land claimed by the heirs of John P. Davidson had a perfect land transaction title. The judge concluded that most of the land in Santa Paula was owned by the heirs of Jimeno Casarin and the United States government. A few years later the heirs of Manuel Jimeno Casarin sold the rest of Rancho Santa Paula y Saticoy to several businessmen, and in 1862 George Briggs bought most of the ranch's acreage from them. Briggs then partitioned his property and sold parcels to Anglo American homesteaders (Belknap 1968; Triem 1985). Initially Briggs' ranch consisted of 17,500 acres. The land was then parceled into tracts averaging 150 acres and sold for approximately ten dollars an acre. The buyers were given ten years to pay for the land. Larger parcels of land were also sold to capitalist investors.

The Anglo American settlers' thirst for land was not satisfied by purchasing the property of the Anglo elite. By using force, the newcomers also took possession of the ranches owned by the Mexican and Indian farmers in Santa Paula. In the early 1860s, with the assistance of the United States government, Anglo American settlers were able to dispossess the Indians of their property. The United States Land Commission rescinded the property rights of the Indians of Santa Paula in 1857 and made the land available to homesteaders (*Davidson et al. v. United States Government* 1857). This policy was based on the rationale that land inhabited by Indians and formerly controlled by Spanish or Mexican missionaries was public land belonging to the United States government. The commission obtained the power to pass this policy based on the United States Supreme Court decision *United States v. Rogers* (1846). Under this ruling Indians did not own the land they inhabited merely because they were the original settlers. In California, Indians owned property only if they or their ancestors had applied for a land grant and proper documentation had been filed during the Spanish or Mexican period.[4] The California Land Commission and the courts also required that Indian claimants verify their land grants by presenting the deeds. Without the deeds they were not considered the legal owners. Indians also could own property if they purchased it and had legal documentation as proof. In essence, the United States government invalidated the former Mexican property laws that granted Indians the land they inhabited, whether or not a claim had been filed. In Santa Paula, since the Indians had not filed a township incorporation application, nor had individual families requested land grants, their property was considered to be public domain by the United States government and therefore eligible for distribution.

Mexicans in Santa Paula also lost possession of their ranches in a similar manner. The California Land Commission apparently confirmed only one Mexican land grant in 1869 and invalidated the property rights of the rest of Santa Paula's inhabitants (*Santa Paula Water Works v. Julio Peralta* 1896:42). In Santa Paula, as in other communities of California, there are few available public records documenting how land was transferred from the small-scale Mexican farmers to the Anglo Americans. Therefore, whether Mexicans sold their land or if they were forcibly evicted is difficult to determine.[5] The only available Mexican land grant records are those that describe the land tenure history of the large Mexican ranches (e.g., ranches consisting of at least one thousand acres), such as the case histories of Rancho Santa Paula y Saticoy and Rancho Peralta. This historical gap in the records can be attributed to two problems. First, Anglo American squatters settled on Mexican property and filed claims that were eventually confirmed by the United States government. Small-scale Mexican farmers did not have the economic resources to challenge the land claims, thus their properties were treated as public domain by the government (Camarillo 1979, 1984; De León 1987). Second, after the Mexican American War, when the Mexican government turned the registry of the Mexican land grants of California over to the United States government, Manuel Jimeno Casarin (the secretary of state charged with the record keeping for the land grants) had only completed the registration of the large California ranches (Ross 1974). A master list had not been completed. Many of the land grant records were left in the possession of the former governors' families or in the archives of the Catholic Church. For obvious reasons the California Land Commission did not retrieve these documents: if there were no available documents indicating which land was privately owned, the unregistered land was automatically owned by the United States government.

Thus, in Santa Paula the land tenure history of only the two largest ranches remains. Those ranches were owned by Manuel Jimeno Casarin and Julio Peralta. As previously mentioned, Jimeno Casarin left a detailed historical account of

Rancho Santa Paula y Saticoy from the Spanish period until 1857, when it was sold to Anglo Americans. In the case of Julio Peralta, the records of his ranch, Rancho Peralta are less detailed. These documents, however, provide a full description of the illegal manner in which Anglo Americans took possession of Mexican property in Santa Paula. Most deal with the American period and were generated during two judicial court disputes between Peralta and several Anglo American homesteaders. Within these legal accounts, a brief history of Rancho Peralta during the Spanish and Mexican periods is also reviewed. We now turn to Rancho Peralta's land tenure history to examine the process by which Mexicans lost their land base.

Similar to Manuel Jimeno Casarin, Julio Peralta was part of Mexico's privileged elite. He was a wealthy landowner who remained economically stable after the Mexican American War of 1846–1848. Thus, when the United States government required Mexicans to file land claims, Peralta had sufficient resources to pay the costs of confirming his grant. Peralta hired four attorneys who were able to defend his claim successfully. They first filed documents with the California Land Commission. Later, when Anglo American homesteaders challenged Peralta's land claim, his attorneys won two cases in the Southern California district court and in the Supreme Court of the State of California. At that time, it was common for a land confirmation case to take over ten years to be resolved.[6] It was an expensive bureaucratic process that small-scale Mexican farmers were unable to afford; consequently only wealthy Mexicans were able to defend their land claims.

In 1864, Peralta purchased property in Santa Paula from the heirs of Juan Rodríguez-Cabrillo and established Rancho Peralta. Rodríguez-Cabrillo had originally obtained the grant during the Spanish period (Almaguer 1979; see *SPDC,* April 30, 1962, 76[6]: section A).[7] Peralta's ranch consisted of part of the uninhabited land adjacent to Sis'a. This tract contained the irrigation system established during the Spanish period by the missionaries and the Chumash Indians (*Santa Paula Water Works et al. v. Julio Peralta* 1893–1898). When Peralta filed his land confirmation application, the California Land Commission accepted it on the basis of two points. First, Peralta held an indisputable and perfect title. Second, under the Homestead Act of 1862 Peralta owned the ranch irrespective of whether or not he had acquired legal title to it during the Mexican period. Based on the act, since Peralta was the first European to inhabit this area and he had complied with the land commission's certification requirements, he was declared legal owner of Rancho Peralta (*Santa Paula Water Works et al. v. Julio Peralta* 1896).

Unfortunately for Peralta, although the United States government declared him to be the owner of Rancho Peralta his victory was short-lived. In 1867, Santa Paula experienced a mass influx of Anglo Americans and several families settled near Peralta's ranch. At first, his neighbors were friendly toward him and accorded him respect for being a prominent citizen of Ventura County (*Signal,* April 29, 1871, p. 3). A few years later, however, Peralta's neighbors became annoyed that a Mexican owned more land than they did. Soon they began terrorizing him and demanding that he leave Santa Paula. They also began to usurp and cultivate part of his land, in spite of his continuous protests (*Santa Paula Water Works et al. v. Julio Peralta* 1893; *Santa Paula Water Works et al. v. Julio Peralta* 1896). To frighten Peralta, his neighbors often shot at him and his hired hands. They also shot at his farm animals and killed several of them. When violence proved ineffective, Peralta's neighbors decided to challenge his land claim and thereby legally evict him. In 1893 the homesteaders filed an overlapping land dispute claim in the Ventura County Superior Court, alleging that Peralta had sold them his ranch and later refused to move. Peralta immediately contested their charges and in turn accused them of squatting on part of his property.

The disputed property was located on the east of town along Santa Paula Creek (*Santa Paula Water Works et al. v. Julio Peralta* 1893). The dispute over Peralta's property centered on two issues: (1) Did Peralta initially agree to sell the land to the homesteaders and then later back out of his agreement? and (2) Was Peralta the legal owner of the property? In court, the homesteaders claimed that they paid Peralta $701 for parcels of land along Santa Paula Creek. They testified that an oral agreement had been transacted with Peralta and to support their allegations they presented as evidence a contract drawn and signed only by them. Peralta denied making any type of agreement with the homesteaders and questioned the legality of the contract because it did not contain his signature. His statement was corroborated, in that the contract submitted to the court by the homesteaders did not have his signature. The homesteaders also argued that Peralta had never held legal title to the land because his grant was situated on mission property and had been identified as public domain by the United States government. Peralta advanced documents proving that he had bought the property from Juan Rodríguez-Cabrillo's heirs. Furthermore, Peralta argued that the homesteaders' allegations were a moot point because under the Homestead Act of 1862 he was the legal owner. The dispute lasted for years as the plaintiffs and defendant kept presenting counterarguments. The court finally ruled on Peralta's behalf. In spite of the ruling, by the turn of the century the homesteaders had chased Peralta out of town and taken possession of his land. They were assisted by one wealthy eastern capitalist who wanted to appropriate Peralta's water rights along Santa Paula Creek. This is an issue I will return to momentarily. In any event, the homesteaders eventually became members of the prominent "founding families" of Santa Paula.

Although Mexicans had become a landless class by the late 1800s, they continued to reside in Santa Paula and were well on their way to becoming a culturally visible population. Nineteenth-century narrative descriptions of the Mexican population appear in the memoirs of three Anglo American residents of Santa Paula. W. J. Sanborn wrote from 1873 to 1875. Olive Mann Isbell provided descriptions of Santa Paula between 1866 and 1893; David W. Mott left an account of the year 1880. The narratives indicate that many Mexicans lived in Santa Paula and that they were considered a culturally diverse people (Sanborn [1873–1875] 1959; *VCHSQ* 1955, 1961). For example, W. J. Sanborn recalled that the Anglo American community observed marked cultural differences between the Mexicans. They classified Mexicans as being either Spanish, Mexican, or Mexican Indian. Although Spanish traditions were generally practiced by all the Mexican groups, some families displayed more Spanish cultural attributes than others did. W. J. Sanborn's memoirs also noted an additional cultural variance among the Mexican population: those Mexicans who were mestizo were derogatorily called "greasers." "Mexican greasers," however, were distinguished from the Mexicans who were of full Indian descent. Sanborn wrote the following:

> *In 1875 . . . in those days our 'other' population was*
> *made up of Californians, some few Spanish, Mexicans*
> *and Mexican Indians, all with a decided Spanish leaning.*
> *. . . Most of our sheep herders were what we called Indians*
> *in distinction from Greasers. We denominated most of*
> *these Indians Sonorians, from Sonora, Mexico—either*
> *directly themselves or their immediate ancestors. (Sanborn*
> *[1873–1875] 1959:4, 10)*

W. J. Sanborn also recalled that when he first arrived in Santa Paula in 1873 the Spanish language was spoken throughout the village, and if the Anglo Americans needed to transact any type of business with the Mexicans, they were forced to use Spanish. What follows is Sanborn's recollection regarding why he learned to speak Spanish.

> *I dare say few there now talk Spanish, but in my day all*
> *who knocked about the country simply had to. I used to*
> *talk it like a native, but now recall but an occasional*
> *expression and a few words—could not carry on any*
> *conversation in that language. I have a sort of glimmering*
> *that when I went into that country the village, and it was*
> *hardly that, was "now called Santa Paula." (Sanborn*
> *[1873–1875] 1959:11)*

He also wrote that when Santa Paula became an Anglo dominated village its Spanish name was not changed. Sanborn stated:

> In my day when Spanish was spoken thereabouts, the
> inclination of those who favored the Spanish pronunciation
> was to call it as I used to pronounce it—Santa
> POWLAH—rather than as the common American
> pronunciation, as in St. Paul. (Sanborn [1873–1875]
> 1959:13)

Thus, despite the inclination to Anglicize the village's name to St. Paul, the name was not changed.

In 1872, title to 2,700 acres of Santa Paula was bought by Nathaniel W. Blanchard and E. B. Higgins, and they transformed this community into an Anglo American township (Heil 1983). Spurred by the investments made primarily by Blanchard, Santa Paula became an Anglo American commercial citrus center by 1875. The establishment of a flour mill and the formation of a citrus industry stimulated its population growth to such an extent that by 1882 it had become a lively town (Sheridan 1926) and by the early 1890s over twelve hundred people were in residence (McFie 1944). By this time, apparently, the Chumash Indians no longer resided in Santa Paula. The residents are referred to as either Mexicans or Anglo Americans in the historical documents (Heil 1983). Whether the Chumash Indians assimilated within Mexican society or migrated someplace else is not known. By 1910, the United States census identified only thirty-eight Chumash Indians residing in Ventura County (Swanton 1984:487).

Santa Paula became an important agricultural town in 1893. In that landmark year, Nathaniel W. Blanchard and other investors established Limoneira Ranch and transformed it into a successful agricultural corporation. Within just a few years, Limoneira Ranch produced the highest yield of citrus in the state of California (Heil 1983; Triem 1985). The growth of Limoneira Ranch also marked the end of the Mexican land grant era in Santa Paula. As previously mentioned, by the turn of the century Julio Peralta, who was the last land grant owner in Santa Paula, lost control of his property. Anglo American homesteaders and the owners of Limoneira Ranch challenged Peralta's legal title to the land along Santa Paula Creek. The homesteaders wanted the land, and the owners of Limoneira Ranch wanted the water rights to the creek. The superior court ruled that Peralta held legal title to the land, but he was obliged to share the creek with other Santa Paula residents. The homesteaders ignored the court's decision and continued to inhabit the disputed property. Nathaniel W. Blanchard was also dissatisfied with the court's ruling because he wanted to limit Peralta's use of the

Mexican and Anglo American lemon pickers in Santa Paula, late 1800s. Courtesy Ventura County Museum of History & Art.

water from the creek. Peralta was using the water to irrigate his orchards and to provide drinking water for his livestock. At that time, there was a shortage of water to irrigate Limoneira Ranch's newly planted orchards (Triem 1985), and when Peralta irrigated his orchards, the available water was reduced. Blanchard and the other owners of Limoneira Ranch, therefore, hoped to stop Peralta from using any water (*Santa Paula Water Works et al. v. Julio Peralta* 1896). To obtain control of Santa Paula Creek, Blanchard and his partners appealed the Ventura County Superior Court decision.

In 1896, Blanchard and his partners' appeal was heard by the California State Supreme Court (*Santa Paula Water Works et al. v. Julio Peralta* 1896). Without question, the court records indicate that the arguments advanced by the plaintiffs in their behalf were undemocratic and racist. W. H. Wilde and Orestes Orr, the attorneys representing Blanchard and his partners, argued that Peralta had no legal right to use the water from Santa Paula Creek because he was a Mexican and a foreigner. They proposed that Peralta had used the water illegally for more than twenty-seven years, since he was not a United States citizen. They also suggested that Peralta was unpatriotic and for that reason alone should not be granted the privilege of irrigating his orchards. To support their allegations, Wilde and Orr argued that Peralta was not a United States citizen because under immigration law he was not eligible to be naturalized or to own property. Therefore, because he did not own the property along Santa Paula Creek, he did not possess any water rights. Wilde and Orr concluded that since Blanchard and his partners were the first Europeans to claim the land along Santa Paula Creek, they, not Peralta, were the legal owners of the land and therefore had the right to use the creek's water.

To contest the arguments advanced by the plaintiffs' attorneys, Peralta hired seven attorneys, Mr. Daly, Mr. Toland, Mr. Shepard, Mr. Eastin, Mr. Gottschalk, R. F. Del Valle, and J. L. Murphy. Peralta's attorneys began their counterarguments by stating that (1) the Ventura County Superior Court had previously ruled that Peralta was the legal owner of the land (*Santa Paula Water Works et al. v. Julio Peralta* 1893) and (2) the State Supreme Court had ruled that Peralta was a United States citizen of Spanish descent (*Santa Paula Water Works v. Peralta* 1895). The latter issue was important because, between 1790 and 1898, naturalization and immigration laws prohibited Mexicans who were not Caucasian from being naturalized and owning property for a prolonged period of time (*Chirac v. Chirac* 1817; *In re Rodriguez* 1897; *People v. De La Guerra* 1870; *United States v. Villato* 1897). Because Peralta was a Mexican of full Spanish descent, however, he was eligible to be naturalized and to enjoy the political rights of an American citizen. Peralta's attorneys also argued that United States water laws allowed people to use the water contained in the property they inhabited, whether or not they held legal title to it. Therefore, whether or not Peralta could use the water from the Santa Paula Creek was a moot issue because for more than twenty-seven years he had lived on the property that contained most of the creek.

After listening to both sides, the State Supreme Court judges upheld the Ventura County Superior Court decision and ruled that Peralta and the owners of Limoneira Ranch must share the water. Judge C. Britt wrote the opinion of the court. The decision was based on two issues: (1) Peralta was the legal owner of the land and therefore had the right to use the water, and (2) Blanchard and his partners did not own the land along Santa Paula Creek but had the right to use the water because they had appropriated part of the land along the creek in 1872.

Britt also admonished the plaintiffs' actions in this entire affair. He stated that no one in Santa Paula had the right to act as an immigration and naturalization agent. That is, no person had the right to dispossess Peralta of his civil rights because they did not believe he was a citizen. Only the United States government had the right to investigate the citizenship status of individuals and determine if they had the right to own land. Furthermore, although Blanchard and his partners had posted notices stating that they were the new owners of Peralta's property, this did not make their claim legal. Only the United States government had the right to litigate land claims. In closing, Judge Britt ordered that Peralta be allowed to resume the use of the water of Santa Paula Creek because several Anglo American citizens had diverted the water and, for months, had prevented Peralta from irrigating his orchards and providing water to his livestock.

Suffice it to say that although Peralta retained legal ownership of his property and the right to use part of the water of Santa Paula Creek, he lost everything. The Ventura County sheriffs did not enforce the court order. Blanchard and his partners ignored the court ruling, and the Anglo American homesteaders took possession of the land. Peralta was chased out of Santa Paula and was forced to move to Los Angeles (*Santa Paula Water Works et al. v. Julio Peralta* 1893–1898).[8] By the turn of the century, only six Mexicans owned property in Santa Paula ("Original Assessment Book, City of Santa Paula 1902–1908"); all of the property consisted of small residential plots. When they purchased their property, however, is unknown.[9] Moreover, at this time all references made about Mexicans in the Santa Paula newspaper, in early biographical accounts (Blanchard 1961; McFie 1944; Teague 1944; Thille 1952, 1958), and in local historical accounts indicate that Mexicans were transformed into landless peasants (Heil 1983; Meany 1941; Triem 1985). An interethnic subordinate–dominant employment structure evolved in Santa Paula in which the Anglo Americans became the owners of the land and the Mexicans became the field hands (Belknap 1968).

THE ROOTING OF RACE RELATIONS OF INEQUALITY IN CALIFORNIA: AN OVERVIEW

The inferior social status of Mexicans in Santa Paula and in other California communities was enforced by the use of laws that directly limited their political rights during the 1800s. In California, after the Mexican American War of 1846–1848, state legislators limited the civil rights of the Mexican population by distinguishing them as being White or non-White. After the war, the United States and Mexico enacted a treaty of peace called the Treaty of Guadalupe Hidalgo, officially ending the war. Under the treaty, Mexicans living in the new United States territory were to be extended the same legal privileges as White citizens. California legislators, however, interpreted the "spirit" of the treaty to mean that only "White Mexican males" were to receive full citizenship rights.[10] State legislators argued that Mexicans of Indian descent should be given the legal rights of American Indians and only White Mexicans should be considered United States citizens (Menchaca 1993; Padilla 1979; see *People v. De La Guerra* 1870). For the Mexican population this interpretation of the treaty was problematic because the American Indians were not considered United States citizens at that time and were not eligible to vote. For example, in the California constitution of 1849, a racial restriction clause stated that only Whites were eligible to vote. In the case of Mexicans, the constitution made it explicitly clear that only *White Mexican males* had the right of suffrage. This meant

Mexican lemon pickers at Limoneira Ranch, 1890s. Courtesy
Ventura County Museum of History & Art.

Mexican Indians and mestizos were ineligible to vote; the implications of this
legislative act left most Mexicans without a political voice. The constitution stated
the following:

> *Every White male citizen of the United States, and every*
> White male citizen of Mexico *[emphasis added], who*
> *shall have elected to become a citizen of the United States,*
> *under the treaty of peace exchanged and ratified at*
> *Queretaro, on the 30th day of May, 1848, of the age of*
> *twenty-one years who shall have been a resident of the*
> *state six months next preceding the election, and the county*
> *or district in which he claims his vote thirty days, shall be*
> *entitled to vote at all elections which are now or hereafter*
> *may be authorized by law. (Constitution of the State of*
> *California 1849, article II, section 1, cited in California)*

The state legislators were aware that this racial restriction infringed upon the
Treaty of Guadalupe Hidalgo and international laws of territorial cession.
However, in order to protect their own interests, legislators were more concerned

Limoneira Ranch, 1890s. Courtesy Ventura County Museum of History & Art.

with preventing Mexicans from obtaining political control of California.

The legislative debates of California's first constitutional convention of 1849 summarized the overriding view that Mexicans were Indians and should not be given the right to vote. Mr. Hoppe, a state legislator, proposed that it was unwise to give the descendants of Mexican Indians the right to vote, regardless of whether or not they were acculturated and paid taxes. He stated in reference to Mexicans:

> There are Indians by descent, as well as full-blooded Indians. . . . Many of the most distinguished officers of the Mexican government are Indians by descent. At the same time, it would be impolitic to permit the full-blooded Indians who held [sic] property the right to vote. Those who held property would, of course, be taxed. (Cited in Heizer and Almquist 1971:102)

The legislators further argued that denying Mexicans the right to vote did not violate the Treaty of Guadalupe Hidalgo because they would be allowed to become United States citizens though at the same time would be denied the right to vote. Mr. Bott, one of the state legislators, proposed:

> *This Treaty . . . is binding in every clause because it does
> not contradict the Constitution of the United States, it does
> not prescribe who shall be our voters. If it had made
> citizens of Mexico directly citizens of the United States, it
> would not have said that they should be voters of the State
> of California. (Cited in Heizer and Almquist 1971:101)*

Mr. Dimmick, another legislator, concurred with Mr. Bott and argued in favor of denying Mexicans the right of suffrage:

> *Are we to admit them to rights superior to those which we
> enjoy ourselves? Does anyone pretend to assert that we are
> under obligation to do this? Does it follow that the right of
> suffrage is one of these rights? . . . It is not necessarily the
> right of a citizen. (Cited in Heizer and Almquist 1971:101)*

The final decision of the convention rested on the premise that the legislators were obliged to give Mexicans the right to vote or else the United States Congress would reject the state's constitution because it violated the Treaty of Guadalupe Hidalgo (Heizer and Almquist 1971:100–102). Nonetheless, the legislators concurred that neither the treaty nor the United States Constitution precluded them from placing racial restriction clauses in the language of California's constitution. They concluded that Mexicans were to be given the right to vote only if they were "White." Ironically, the California state legislators did not clarify what they meant by a "White Mexican" and thus left open to local interpretation what racial criteria constituted a White, mestizo, or Indian Mexican. At the community level, this legal ambiguity allowed Anglo Americans to discriminate against most Mexicans. Each township had the power to determine whether its Mexican residents were White and therefore exempt from or subject to the state's racial laws (Menchaca 1993; Padilla 1979).

Discriminatory actions against Mexicans had no social class boundaries; the Mexican elite also experienced inequalities. In 1870, Pablo De La Guerra, a district judge and a prominent citizen of Santa Barbara, was prosecuted by the State of California for "illegally acting" as a United States citizen. In a California Supreme Court hearing, the attorneys for the State argued that De La Guerra was not a United States citizen since he was of Indian descent and therefore ineligible to be a judge (*People v. De La Guerra* 1870; Menchaca 1993). Although the State supreme court ruled in favor of De La Guerra and concluded that he was White and thus eligible to receive the political privileges enjoyed by Whites, De La Guerra was not reinstated as the district judge.

In addition to prohibiting non-White Mexicans from voting, the state government also passed a number of other laws preventing Mexicans from practicing traditional cultural activities. Bullfights, cockfights, horse races, and other "fiesta activities" were outlawed in 1855 (Heizer and Almquist 1971). The "Greaser Act" was also passed that same year to ensure that Mexicans could not carry firearms in public places. Although most of these discriminatory state laws were abolished by the early 1900s, they were replaced by national legislation that had a far more dramatic impact on the Mexican population. By the end of the nineteenth century, the United States Supreme Court passed racial segregation laws. To pass this legislation, the United States Supreme Court had to overturn the equal rights language of the Civil Rights Act of 1875 and to reinterpret the Civil Rights Act of 1866. Both acts guaranteed all persons born in the United States, excluding Indians, full and equal benefit of the laws. The Civil Rights Act of 1875 also prohibited the social discrimination of people on the basis of race or national origin. At the federal level, the dismantling of the civil rights acts began with the passage of the United States Supreme Court decision *Robinson and Wife v. Memphis and Charleston Railroad Company* (1883). The Court ruled that the first and second sections of the Civil Rights Act of 1875 limited the rights of White citizens and advocated reverse discrimination. The Court concluded that Whites should not be forced to socialize with non-Whites or be forced to provide them services. Basing the arguments on convoluted racist logic, the majority opinion was that allowing non-Whites to be in public places forced Whites to interact with them and thus violated the civil rights of Whites. It also stated that excluding non-Whites from public places was not a violation of the Thirteenth and Fourteenth Amendments because interacting with Whites was a privilege and not a right for racial minorities. The passage of *Robinson and Wife,* therefore, provided the legal basis for exclusion of racial minorities from hotels, inns, restaurants, parks, public conveyances, and public amusement parks. Thirteen years later, the United States Supreme Court passed a more devastating piece of segregative legislation. In 1896, under *Plessy v. Ferguson,* the Court legalized all forms of social segregation for racial minorities. With the passage of this ruling, the federal government unequivocally asserted the states' right to segregate people of color. Citizens could no longer question or challenge the legal basis of racial segregation. Racial segregation was no longer a state issue—it had become a federal law. Ironically, the Court also concluded that the civil rights of non-Whites were not violated by the passage of *Plessy* because they would be provided "separate but equal facilities." In rationalizing *de jure* segregation (i.e., legal—separate but equal), the Court used the same arguments advanced in *Robinson and Wife* to argue that interracial interaction was a privilege and not a right for non-Whites. The ruling also provided more specific language about who could be legally segregated. The Supreme Court justices addressed the problem of racial classifications, ruling that for purposes of segregation every state had the right to determine who was White and who was non-White. The ruling also gave each state the power to decide if any racial minority group should be segregated. That is, although the Court did not mandate that "all racial minorities" be segregated, it supported the states' right to institute segregation if desired by the state legislators.

At the local level, although the federal government did not specifically mention them in the segregationist legislation, there is ample evidence that Mexicans were often classified as non-White and thus were consequently segregated in most social spheres. Although the ratification of the Treaty of Guadalupe Hidalgo guaranteed Mexicans the political privileges enjoyed by Whites, some state legislators in the latter half of the nineteenth century and the early 1900s violated the agreement (Heizer and Almquist 1971; Menchaca 1993; Padilla 1979). The rationale often used to segregate Mexicans and limit their political and social rights was based on the perspective that because most Mexicans were "Indian" they were not White (Menchaca 1993; Menchaca and Valencia 1990; Paredes 1978; Surace 1982). Legislators argued that, because Indians by law were prohibited from voting, residing in White neighborhoods, and attending schools with White children, Mexicans should be prohibited from the same. With the passage of *Plessy,* the state government had the right to determine if Mexicans were White or non-White. Thus, in many communities the segregationist laws were extended to Mexicans on the basis that they were non-White. For example, in West Texas sixty counties practiced local *de jure* segregation laws prohibiting Mexicans from eating in restaurants designated for Whites only (Kibbe 1946). These counties also prohibited Mexican students from attending school with White students. In Colorado and Texas, some Mexicans were not permitted to use swimming pools when the public facilities were restricted to Whites only (*Lueras v. Town of Lafayette* 1937; *Terrel Wells Swimming Pool v. Rodriguez* 1944).

School segregation cases serve to further illustrate how segregationist laws were used against Mexicans. In California, from 1927 to 1935, the attorney generals attempted to classify Mexican students as Indians in order to indisputably place them under the mandate of *de jure* segregation (Donato, Menchaca, and Valencia 1991; Hendrick 1977). Finally, in 1935 the California legislature passed educational legislation officially segregating certain Mexican students on the ground that they were Indians (California School Code of 1935, cited in Hendrick 1977:57). This legislation did not apply to White Mexican students. In Texas, the court case of *Independent School District v. Salvatierra* (1930) also exemplifies how segregationist legislation was applied to some Mexican students. In this case, the judge ruled that only White Mexican students were clearly exempt from the mandates of *de jure* segregation. White Mexicans were those of Spanish descent.

Other Mexicans, however, could be segregated if they were not White or did not speak English. Although the segregationist laws could not legally be applied to all Mexicans because many of them were White, other means were used to segregate them. We now turn to this, and to Santa Paula.

THE USE OF RACIAL DISCRIMINATION IN SANTA PAULA: RESIDENTIAL SEGREGATION

A few decades after the Mexican American War, Anglo Americans were able to enforce discriminatory practices in Santa Paula and in other Southwestern communities because Mexicans had been transformed into landless and politically powerless low-wage earners (Acuña 1972; De León 1987; Gonzalez 1990). In small communities, where the Mexicans' employers were also the political leaders, the Mexicans' dependence on wage work forced them to accept the residential boundaries drawn for them. Using nineteenth-century archival records, historian Alberto Camarillo attributes the first stages of Mexican residential segregation to Anglo racial prejudice. Laws were not needed as Anglo Americans had the sheer power to segregate Mexicans. Camarillo (1979) states: "The old Mexican pueblos were viewed by most Americans as 'foreign,' 'backward,' and undesirable locations in which to live" (p. 224). For example, in California the residential segregation of the Mexicans began as early as 1850, and the process was completed by 1870. In San Francisco, San Jose, Santa Barbara, Los Angeles, San Diego, Santa Cruz, and Monterey, Anglo American settlers restructured the old pueblos by constructing new subdivisions in the towns and prohibiting Mexicans from moving into White neighborhoods. In the 1900s, throughout California the residential segregation of the Mexicans was enforced by racial harassment and violence and, in many cities, by the use of housing covenant restrictions prohibiting Mexicans from residing in the White zones (Donato, Menchaca, and Valencia 1991; Gonzalez 1990; Hendrick 1977; Menchaca 1989; Salinas 1973).

Social historian David Montejano (1987) also reports that a similar process of residential segregation became widespread in Texas. Throughout the state, Mexicans were segregated in separate sections of the cities, and in many Anglo American farm communities local *de jure* laws were used to prevent Mexicans from establishing residence. Residential segregation was planned by the ranchers and town developers and maintained through local laws and real estate policies. For example, in Weslaco, Texas, Mexicans were allowed to buy property only in designated areas near the Missouri Pacific Railroad tracks, and municipal ordinances required that Mexican neighborhoods and businesses be established only in those areas.

In Santa Paula, the growth of residential segregation was strongly linked to Anglo Americans' racial prejudice and their economic and political control over the Mexican population. Santa Paula property tax records indicate that, by 1902, Mexicans were residentially segregated to the East Side, along Santa Paula Creek, regardless of their social class status (see Santa Paula property tax assessment records 1902–1957).[11] They were prohibited from buying property in the new sections of town, where the Anglo Americans resided. Those Mexicans not confined to the Mexican quarters located on the East Side lived in ranch labor camps (Heil 1983). On the other hand, Anglo Americans were allowed to live in any neighborhood in Santa Paula. They, however, preferred to live near the downtown area. Ironically, the Mexicans' residence was confined to the tract of land that at one point had belonged to Julio Peralta and was later converted by the Anglo Americans into a residential area reserved for farmhands. Peralta's usurped property eventually became the residential core of the Mexican community.

Oral histories indicate that Mexican property owners, as well as renters, were confined to living next to the orchards on the East Side. Linda, who was born in 1914, recalled her early childhood when Mexicans were segregated. Most of Linda's remembrances are based on her personal experiences, while the accounts that predate her generation were transmitted orally to her by her grandmother Rosalia. According to Linda, residential segregation dates back to the days of her grandmother's youth. Linda's grandmother migrated to Santa Paula in 1874 and worked as a house maid for a wealthy eastern family. When her grandmother first arrived in Santa Paula, very few Mexicans and Anglo Americans lived in the village. The Mexican population was spread throughout Santa Paula and not confined to the East Side. This oral account is corroborated by W. J. Sanborn's memoirs, which provide a similar description of Santa Paula during the late 1800s (Sanborn [1873–1875] 1959). Linda was told, however, that in the last years of the nineteenth century, when the Anglo Americans became the majority population in Santa Paula, residential patterns changed. During that period, residential norms were instituted, and most of the Mexican families were relocated toward the East Side. Anglo Americans derogatorily began referring to the East Side as "Mexican Town."

Linda also recalled that when she was a child, Twelfth Street was the dividing line between the Anglo American and the Mexican neighborhoods. If Mexicans walked beyond Twelfth Street, they were often harassed by the "rednecks." Linda stated:

> *La calle doce was the main division. The ranchers owned
> the homes in the northeast, and that was for the people
> whose parents worked in agriculture—which would be the
> lemon or the orange. . . . If you worked for them in the
> packing house or picking lemons, that's where you would
> live. . . . Very few owned homes. . . . Now my parents
> happened to buy a house because my grandmother helped
> them. . . . My grandmother worked for the [Smiths]. In
> those days she got paid well. . . . They used to tell us,
> You live in that side and we live in this side. . . . The
> rednecks used to tell us that. (Linda, age seventy-two at
> time of interview)*

Linda's account is corroborated by Santa Paula property tax assessment records which demonstrate that no Mexicans owned property beyond Twelfth Street.

Natalie, a local historian and the granddaughter of 1864 Anglo American pioneers, also corroborated Linda's remembrances. She recalled that her family and other growers sold only cheap, valueless land to Mexicans. According to Natalie, who continues to be a wealthy property owner, local real estate laws were also used to ensure that no neighborhood in Santa Paula be racially integrated. Mexicans were confined to residing in the outskirts of town toward the East Side. Natalie stated:

> *On this side of town land wasn't sold to Mexicans. We
> only sold them cheap worthless rocky land on the East
> Side. . . . Real estate practices restricted selling land to
> Mexicans within the city limits. . . . Most Mexicans were
> agricultural workers, so they weren't able to afford property
> anyway. (Natalie, age forty-five at the time of the
> interview)*

Mexicans were unable to challenge Santa Paula's segregative residential policies, primarily because of their economic dependence on the Anglo American citrus growers, who enacted the policies. For example, early 1900s photographs of Santa Paula's two major employment industries indicate that only low-wage agricultural work was open to Mexicans (Santa Paula Union Oil Museum). Higher-wage employment in the oil industry was exclusively reserved for Anglo Americans (Heil 1983). This information is corroborated by oral history accounts collected by Michael Belknap in his study of the citrus industry's history in Santa

Paula (Belknap 1968). According to Belknap, during the turn of the century, Mexicans were treated as peon workers and were employed only in agriculture. Belknap states:

> *Using these Mexicans, the big citrus growers of Santa Paula set up a sort of semifeudal system. They gave their workers paternalistic care, but at the same time, whether intentionally or not, established them as a low paid fruit-picking caste. (Belknap 1968:127)*

By "fruit-picking caste" Belknap refers to the fact that Anglo Americans considered Mexicans to be an ethnic group suited only for agricultural manual work.

Supporting Belknap's findings of the caste-like employment structure (i.e., a particular type of employment reserved for one ethnic group) are early-twentieth-century public statements made about Mexican labor by Charles Teague, the president of Limoneira Company. At that time he was one of the most powerful citrus growers in Santa Paula. Teague stated that Mexicans "proved to be fairly efficient workmen and it was considered advisable to retain this class of laborers to do certain kinds of work" (cited in Fraysier 1968:160). In his autobiography, Teague also stated his belief that reserving agricultural labor for Mexicans was profitable because

> *Mexicans have always been one of the chief sources of California's labor supply. They are naturally adapted to agricultural work. . . . Many of them have a natural skill in the handling of tools and are resourceful in matters requiring manual ability. . . . The Mexican people are usually good-natured and happy. (Teague 1944:142, 143)*

Teague's comment also indicates that he advised other Santa Paula growers to hire only Mexicans to pick citrus because they were biologically suited for that type of labor.

In the cities adjacent to Santa Paula, similar discriminatory employment practices were implemented by the Anglo Americans. Camarillo (1979) reports that, in Santa Barbara, Mexicans were employed exclusively in farm labor and in other types of undesirable manual work. They were also segregated in "Old Town," the Mexican quarter of Santa Barbara. In his historical account of the citrus industry in Ventura County, Almaguer (1979) also reports that, in the cities of Ventura, Oxnard, and Moorpark, Mexicans were employed exclusively on the farms.

The first Mexican market, 1913.
Courtesy Ventura County Museum of History & Art.

There is evidence indicating that when the Mexican population grew in Santa Paula, in 1913, all forms of segregation became intensified. The growth of the Mexican community was not an isolated incident. National immigration statistics indicate a mass influx of Mexicans to the United States between 1910 and 1924. Social scientists attribute the growth of the Mexican immigrant community in this country to the prolonged civil unrest produced by the Mexican Revolution (Acuña 1972; Galarza 1964; McWilliams 1968). Between 1910 and 1914, 82,588 Mexicans migrated to the United States, and between 1915 and 1924, 340,323 more Mexicans arrived (Samora 1971:36). In Santa Paula, the newcomers were allowed to set up camp only near their compatriots in Mexican Town. Just how much the Mexican population grew during this period is unclear. We do know, however, that in 1913 Mexican migration to Santa Paula peaked. This is suggested by articles in the *Santa Paula Chronicle* describing new tent settlements in Mexican Town. Other tent towns also grew along the outskirts of Santa Paula near Limoneira Ranch and along the East Side (*SPC,* January 10, 1913, 25[42]:1; *SPC,* November 13, 1913, 26[36]:1; *SPC,* November 28, 1913, 26[36]:1; *SPC,* July 17, 1914, 27[17]:1; *SPC,* December 11, 1914, 26[38]:5).

With the influx of Mexican immigrants to Santa Paula, citrus growers allotted more land for residential purposes, yet confined the growth of the Mexican neighborhoods to the East Side. As a result of the new land allotments, Mexican

Town doubled in size by 1916 and came to encompass the entire east side of present-day Santa Paula (Santa Paula property tax assessment records 1902–1915). The *Santa Paula Chronicle* also indicates that when the Mexican community experienced a population boom, new buildings were constructed and new roads were built (*SPC*, January 10, 1913, 25[42]:1; *SPC*, December 11, 1914, 26[38]:5). A modest Mexican business district, which contained a market, two bars, and a cafe, also appeared in Mexican Town (*SPC*, November 22, 1912, 25[35]:1; oral histories, Linda, José, and Natalie). Photographs found in the Ventura County Museum of History and Art corroborate the descriptions found in the *Santa Paula Chronicle*.

In summary, by the first two decades of the twentieth century Mexicans were socially incorporated as a low-wage agricultural laboring class in Santa Paula, and fewer than a handful of them were property owners. All the Spanish and Mexican institutions were dismantled, and the Anglo Americans gained total control of the community's social, political, and economic institutions. When Mexicans lost control of the land, their social system apparently disintegrated, to be replaced by an Anglo-dominated social structure. Without their *ranchos,* Mexicans were unable to subsist on their own means, and thereby they became dependent on wage work and financially reliant on their Anglo American employers. Unfortunately, one of the worst consequences of this turn of events for Mexicans was the loss of political power; Anglo Americans could treat Mexicans as they chose. Mexicans could be discriminated against and deprived of basic civil rights, such as selecting their place of residence.

We now turn to the unfolding of social segregation within the Mexican community of Santa Paula. This racist practice was one of the earliest forms of discrimination experienced by Mexicans. It began with residential segregation and immediately expanded into other social domains.

TWO

White Racism, Religious Segregation, and Violence against Mexicans, 1913 to 1930

The Anglo American community of Santa Paula was not satisfied with merely segregating Mexicans on the East Side. When the size of the Mexican population rapidly increased during 1913, Anglo Americans responded by segregating them in separate churches, rationalizing that God did not want Mexicans and Anglo Americans to socialize (Menchaca 1989; Menchaca and Valencia 1990). The basis of this logic was that Mexicans were inferior and immoral, whereas Anglo Americans were "God's Chosen People." Once Anglo Americans were able to justify such a blatantly un–Christian act, it became morally correct to dehumanize Mexicans and to institutionalize all forms of social segregation in Santa Paula.

The perspective that Mexicans were one of the biologically and culturally inferior races was not particular to Santa Paula. White supremacist ideologies surfaced at the national level and became widespread throughout the nineteenth century and into the early 1930s (Gossett 1953, 1977; Surace 1982; Weber 1975). Spearheading the national racial movement were the Social Darwinists, who alleged that racial minorities were physically inferior to Whites (Blum 1978; Feagin 1989). To maintain the racial purity of the Anglo Americans, Social Darwinists promoted a philosophy of social segregation. They also advocated sterilization programs in order to regulate the size of the non–White population. This practice was believed advisable if Whites were to maintain political control of racial minorities. By the mid–1920s, the pseudo-scientific theories of the Social Darwinists came under overwhelming attack by anti-hereditarian research that underscored the influence of environment on behavior. Leading the attack, Franz Boas convincingly argued that there was no scientific base to the belief that Whites were superior (Caffrey 1989). As evidence, Boas presented several studies indicating that intelligence and other social characteristics, such as poverty or wealth, were not genetically transmitted. Following Boas' devastating critique, the influence of Social Darwinism as a scientific explanation for White superiority lost support within academic circles. However, the debate generated the need for a new rationale for racist cultural hypotheses. Although Boas' research was influential in destroying the scientific basis for Social Darwinism, the belief continued that Anglo Americans were superior. Biological theories were gradually replaced by cultural hypotheses. These new claims argued that racial minorities were culturally inferior and, therefore, should be segregated from Anglo Americans. Segregationist views persisted as the new racist logic promoted the position that interracial interaction caused White cultures to degenerate. To avoid such problems it was necessary to segregate non-Whites. In particular, IQ testing provided the new scientific rationale justifying segregation (Hendrick 1977; Wollenberg 1974, 1976). In California and in other areas of the Southwest, Mexicans were victimized in the maelstrom of racially discriminatory intelligence-testing practices (Valencia and Aburto 1991).

At the national level the religious sector was not excluded from promoting racist ideologies. The popular belief that Anglo-Saxons were God's Chosen People provided the religious rationale for racist practices (Feagin 1989). Though in the United States the doctrine of the Chosen People was first claimed as a religious tenet by the Anglo-Saxons, it eventually was adopted by other White ethnic Protestant groups (Gossett 1953, 1977). A major manifestation of this belief was the separation of Whites and racial minorities in different churches or in separate sections of a church. In the early to mid-1900s, Protestant pastors often prohibited racial minorities—including Mexicans—from attending services in the Anglo American churches (Cadena 1987; Glazer and Moynihan 1963; Menchaca 1989; Menchaca and Valencia 1990).

In Santa Paula, the belief that Anglo Americans were racially and culturally superior and therefore should live apart from Mexicans came to be legitimized by the use of religion. By the early 1900s, White supremacist views influenced Anglo Americans to extend social segregation into all social domains. These racist views were infused with religious tenets and used to justify segregation, including segregating Mexicans into separate churches. In 1913, an account of a meeting held in an Anglo American Presbyterian church illustrates why socially segregating Mexicans was considered the best mechanism to prevent the intermingling of the White and non-White races in Santa Paula. The purpose of the meeting was to discuss the racial problems occurring in town. Apparently, at that time the Mexican community was at odds with the Anglo Americans, and a series of violent confrontations had erupted between them, which had alarmed Anglo American civic leaders. Given the racial tension, coupled with the dramatic growth of the

Mexican population that year, local leaders called a meeting to discuss the "Mexican problem."

The anger of the Mexican community had been aroused when Juan Ortega was accused of murdering the town's marshal. Mexicans considered this an unfair accusation and protested what they believed to be an overtly racist act. In an attempt to defend Juan Ortega, they closed Mexican Town to all Anglo Americans, including the Anglo American policemen who tried to enter Mexican Town to arrest Ortega. The racial battle continued for several days and alarmed the citrus growers and the Anglo American community because they could not control the Mexican population. D. Webster, the editor of the *Santa Paula Chronicle,* described the racial confrontation in a blatantly biased report. According to Webster the trouble was caused by a group of ruthless and uncivilized Mexicans who were riling the Mexican community and encouraging people to commit violent acts. Webster gave the following account in the *Santa Paula Chronicle* and compared the Mexicans' uproar to the Mexican Revolution. His intent, it appears, was to dehumanize the Mexicans and make their civil protest appear unjustified and savage.

> *One would think that the scene of the Mexican revolution had shifted from the neighbor republic to our own little Glen City [Santa Paula]. While the trouble has not assumed proportions that are overwhelming or beyond control, there is reason for careful consideration and wise counsel in handling it. . . . Few people realize the gravity of the conditions now existing in Santa Paula. Not only has a citizen—an officer in the discharge of his duty been murdered, but there is a feeling of exultation over the fact in some quarters. Threats are made open against other officers and citizens . . . the Mexicans who are causing the trouble in Santa Paula are American born and have lived here many years. Take some ten or a dozen unruly spirits from the local Mexican colony and peace would reign. The same men are arrested time after time. They are fined ten dollars which is paid by some one [sic] else if they themselves happen to be broke and they go away laughing at the "fun" they are having at so small a price. One man now in jail has said that he will "kill the whole bunch when he gets out" [sic]. (SPC, November 28, 1913, 26[36]:2)*

Webster, after vehemently dehumanizing the Mexican community and blaming them for the racial conflict, moderates his tone when he refers to the Anglo Americans. His words are no longer acrimonious when he describes the "defensive" actions of the Anglo American community. According to Webster, Juan Ortega, a gang member from the Mexican quarter, brutally and viciously murdered Henry N. Norman, who was a brave and faithful officer of the law.

> *Henry N. Norman is dead. A kindhearted noble man and*
> *affectionate father and husband, and a brave and faithful*
> *officer was stricken down by a murderous bullet last*
> *Sunday night about ten o'clock. For several weeks there*
> *have been especially on Saturday and Sunday nights, shots*
> *fired by disorderly Mexicans. . . . Suspicion pointed*
> *strongly to Juan Ortega as one of the members of the gang*
> *and it was reported that Ortega had returned to his room*
> *in the Mexican quarter and hastily packed his suit case*
> *[sic] and left after the officers had searched the district.*
> (SPC, *November 28, 1913, 26[36]:1*)

After this account, the *Santa Paula Chronicle* does not provide any further information about Henry N. Norman's murder investigation. We do know, however, that Juan Ortega was arrested. The *Chronicle* did report that the Anglo American community held a church meeting to discuss interethnic conflicts and concluded that this conflict began because Mexicans did not practice any religion and thus needed to be Christianized. Those present at the meeting unanimously decided that, in order to pacify the Mexicans and avoid future interethnic conflicts, a separate church must be built for them.

Convoluted White supremacist views and religious tenets were offered to rationalize the religious segregation of the Mexican community. What follows is the Thanksgiving Day sermon given by Reverend [George] B. Cliff to five hundred Presbyterians. In this sermon he explains why it is necessary to segregate Mexicans in Santa Paula. Reverend Cliff begins by stirring the emotions of the Anglo Americans and reminding them that they are the most superior culture in the entire world because they are God's Chosen People. In his opening statement, Reverend Cliff proclaims:

> *God has had a great purpose in the establishment of every*
> *great nation that has ever existed upon the face of the*
> *earth. The Jewish people were established for the develop-*
> *ment of religion; the Greek for the development of art and*

> *philosophy; the Roman for the development of civil law;
> the Anglo-Saxon for the birth of a new civilization
> dominated by Christianity. To the American people God
> is entrusting the most stupendous task that he has ever
> given to any nation since the world began . . . the
> diversified temperate climate which is ours and the
> institutions which we have developed is a race of people
> unsurpassed in the world for, general intelligence,
> shrewdness, and initiative [sic]. (SPC, November 28,
> 1913, 26[36]:1)*

Continuing with the sermon, Reverend Cliff reminds the congregation that Anglo Americans were made a superior race as part of God's "divine destiny" and that God expects Anglo Americans to govern the "foreigners." Thus, by using theology, Reverend Cliff justifies the power of the Anglo Americans over the Mexicans. He states:

> *God has not showered these blessings upon us for naught.
> He has a right to expect great things of a nation which he
> has so signally [sic] blessed and fitted to fulfill a large
> destiny. The task God has for us is to care for and
> Christianize the millions of foreigners who are crowding
> our shores. . . . The immigrant will soon be crowding us in
> California. We must be ready, not to proselyte among
> them, but to Christianize them in the fullest sense. First
> of all we ought to banish the saloon in 1914. (SPC,
> November 28, 1913, 26[36]:1)*

Changing the tone of his sermon, Reverend Cliff shifts from ideology to practice. At that point he tells the congregation that they should be compassionate toward the ignorant Mexicans because God expects the Anglo American community to be kind and generous to foreigners and animals. Comparing Mexicans to dogs, Reverend Cliffs tells the congregation that, although Mexicans harbor low moral ideals and have no respect for human life, the Anglo Americans' duty is to Christianize them. Using a form of parallel logic, he asserts that because dogs respond to caring masters, the Mexicans will respond in kind to the Anglo Americans. As Reverend Cliff states metaphorically:

> *If you hand a dog a bone he will look up into your face
> and wag his tail in thanks. He who is unthankful for the*

> *ordinary blessings of life is lower than the dog. But I shall*
> *call your attention to a practical method of expressing your*
> *thanks. . . . Now as to the Mexican situation in our city.*
> *We are all shocked by the awful calamity which has just*
> *befallen us. The easiest thing to do about it is curse the*
> *Mexicans. Personally, I do not feel that my hands are*
> *clean. I am humiliated when I think that while* these
> people with their low ideals and ignorance *[emphasis*
> *added]* have been living by my side for the last year, I have
> *done not one thing to uplift them and help to avert just*
> *such a calamity as has befallen our good city marshal.*
> *(SPC, November 28, 1913, 26[36]:1)*

Reverend Cliff then suggests that the best way to prevent the Mexicans from committing inhuman actions is either to deport them to Mexico or to uplift their low ideals and Christianize them. He, however, believes that God prefers Mexicans to be Christianized and taught civil behavior. Reverend Cliff sympathetically states:

> *We have talked about this matter a great deal but have*
> *utterly failed to make an adequate attempt to bring the*
> *power of the Gospel of the Son of God to bear upon the*
> *needs of this people. . . . The easiest thing to do with them*
> *is to send them back to Mexico. But we would be utterly*
> *failing in the mission for which God has built and*
> *prospered us as a people. We ought to call in the Home*
> *Missionary Superintendent of one of our churches and put*
> *the situation before him and offer to pay the expenses of a*
> *missionary whom he shall send to work with us in the*
> *uplift of these people. (SPC, November 28, 1913,*
> *26[36]:1)*

This sermon spurred liberal Anglo Americans to upgrade the Mexican lot. Instead of sending the Mexicans back to their homeland, they would attempt to instill Anglo-Saxon Protestant virtues in these "ignorant people." Immediately after the sermon, Nathaniel W. Blanchard, founding father of the city—and largest employer of Mexican labor—arose and asked Reverend Cliff, "What can we do about it?" The reverend replied, "We ought to establish religious services and leadership for them" (Zambrano 1982:5). A committee, composed of the local pastors, the city father, businessmen, and the citrus growers, was formed to uplift the low ideals of the Mexicans. Ironically, their Christian tolerance went only so far, as the intermingling of the races was not permitted. The committee was organized to finance the construction of a "Mexican church." Mexicans were to be Christianized on their own side of town and were not permitted to attend services in the Anglo American churches. The religious instruction of the Mexicans was allocated to the Methodists, and Pastor Enrique Narro from Southern California was recruited to begin the pastoral work.

Late in 1914, the building committee purchased a lot and began planning for a chapel in Mexican Town, near Twelfth Street ("Assessment Roll 1909 to 1915, City of Santa Paula"). Finally, on July 30, 1915, the Anglo American pastors of Santa Paula gathered in Mexican Town and, in an ambiance of Christianity, built a wooden structure and called it the Spanish Union Mission. The current pastor of the Spanish Union Mission reconstructed this historic account, based on church records, in an unpublished report on the religious segregation of the Mexican community of Santa Paula. Reverend Zambrano wrote that the Spanish Union Mission was the first Protestant church established for Mexicans in California:

> *Most of the work on the chapel was voluntary and amateur. The pastors of the different churches in the city laid the floor and did the shingling. The pews were donated by the First Methodist Church of Santa Paula. Attorney [M. L. Crawford] donated his services in preparing the Articles of Incorporation of the Spanish Union Mission, which was accomplished on July 30, 1915, making it the first Protestant Spanish mission incorporated in the State of California.* (Zambrano 1982:6)

The institutionalization of the Spanish Union Mission commenced an era in which the social distancing of Mexicans from Anglo Americans was considered the natural process between an "inferior" and "superior" race. Between 1915 and 1929 all the churches constructed in Santa Paula were segregated (Santa Paula property tax assessment records 1915, 1931; Menchaca 1989; Menchaca and Valencia 1990). Mexicans were allowed to attend only churches located in the Mexican zone. Paradoxically, the religious segregation of the Mexicans served to sanction other forms of racial segregation and to promote their treatment as an inferior ethnic group.

THE GROWTH OF
RELIGIOUS SEGREGATION:
THE MEXICAN CATHOLICS

In the early 1920s, the Anglo American civic leaders of Santa Paula praised the pastor from the Spanish Union Mission for his efforts in improving the moral character of the Mexican Protestants. Because the Anglo American leadership viewed the mission activities as having fostered interethnic peace among the Protestants, they envisioned that providing religious instruction to Mexicans from other denominations was advisable. A letter found in the archives of the Spanish Union Mission exemplifies how some Anglo Americans perceived religious instruction to be an efficient approach to subordinating Mexicans and to teaching them to be productive workers. F. A. Shipley, a local realtor and citrus grower, wrote a letter to the pastor from the Spanish Union Mission informing him that the mission activities were very useful in converting Mexicans into productive farm workers and domestic servants: "The securing of jobs and farm help has been greatly simplified by the help of the Mission. The domestic help in the homes has also been greatly improved" (Shipley 1922).

Shipley added that the baser and bad elements of the Mexican community were disappearing as a result of the mission activities. Mexicans were no longer challenging the Anglo Americans' authority because the Protestant Mexicans were now partly civilized, and they in turn were teaching the "bad Mexicans" proper social comportment. Shipley concluded that most Mexicans were no longer a menace to the White civilization:

> *There was a time in Santa Paula, when the Mexican*
> *situation was a serious problem. There was a very decided*
> *race line if not to say color-line drawn between the*
> *Americans and Mexicans. It was believed that the*
> *Mexican would be a growing menace to our white*
> *civilization . . . the Mexican is racially clanish and*
> *naturally interested in each other; the good and the bad*
> *alike. When the Mission came and interest was being*
> *manifested in the welfare of their race by the Americans,*
> *and the Sunday School began to get interested in the*
> *children, there was a visible division among themselves; the*
> *baser element began to disappear and as time went on the*
> *better element grew stronger and the atmosphere cleaner and*
> *cleaner. (Shipley 1922)*

In other words, Shipley suggested that Mexicans were finally beginning to accept their subordinate position in Santa Paula. Shipley also advised that the mission activities should be extended to other Mexicans. This would help to uplift the Mexican race and to promote interethnic peace. According to Shipley,

> *The outlook for good and better citizenship as well as aliens of the Mexican race is very hopeful . . . where continued interest is taken in the welfare of the foreign race, [religious instruction] must have a very vital influence upon relationship. (Shipley 1922)*

Other letters written by prominent Anglo American citizens to the pastor of the Spanish Union Mission provide similar opinions about the Mexican community. They concur with Shipley that the mission activities were helping the Mexicans become industrious workers and be less unruly and more thrifty. The president of the Santa Paula Retail Merchant Association wrote:

> *In reply to your inquiry regarding business conditions existing between the Merchants of Santa Paula and the Mexican People, at the present time, as compared with conditions of say five years ago, I am pleased to report that there is a noticable [sic] difference. The writer has made a personal canvass among the merchants and without exception all say that conditions are much improved. Many of them say that they personally feel that the Spanish Mission here is responsible to a large degree for the changed condition. We find that the Mexican is not seeking credit as formerly, but instead are becoming good shopkeepers and are preferring to pay cash. (G. W. Caldwell 1922)[1]*

In a second letter, written to the administrative committee of the Spanish Union Mission, Shipley also stated:

> *The Spanish Mission, established in Santa Paula, has, in my opinion, contributed more to the efficiency and general well being of our Spanish and Mexican population. . . . I find my Spanish labor more industrious, sober, and thrifty. . . . Glad to say that our Saving Bank records disclose the fact of an increasing number of Mexican depositors during the past six months. (Shipley 1922)*

To improve the Mexican lot, Americanization programs were also sponsored by the Anglo American civic leaders. The *Santa Paula Chronicle* reported the success of the programs and the enthusiasm expressed by the Mexicans. Limoneira Ranch, the largest agricultural corporation in Santa Paula and biggest recruiter of Mexican family labor, spearheaded the gratuitous Americanization programs (*SPC,* June 10, 1920, 32[12]:10).[2] For middle-class Mexicans, Santa Paula High School offered literacy and Americanization classes at a cost of $240.15 annually per student in average daily attendance (Belknap 1968).

Providing religious services to the Mexican Catholics at first appeared to be a Christian act and an attempt to Americanize them. The Anglo Americans' underlying motives, however, became apparent when it was proposed that religious services be offered in a segregated form. José, who was born in Santa Paula in 1913, recalled the hypocritical manner in which Mexicans were segregated. Apparently, Mexican Catholics were segregated in a tactful manner in order not to appear un-Christian. Separate religious services were provided because Mexicans allegedly preferred to attend mass where the Spanish language was spoken (Los Angeles Archdiocese 1967). According to José, this was a rather comical excuse advanced by the Anglo Americans, in that there was no church structure available for the Mexicans. Looking back at that period, he wonders how any person believed Mexicans preferred to attend services in the open fields, particularly when it rained. José also recalled that the segregation of the Mexican Catholics followed two phases and began when he was a child. The first phase was informal as they were ordered, but not forced, to attend separate religious services. The second phase soon followed with the construction of a Mexican Catholic church in 1929. At that point they were asked to attend their own church.

The first phase began a few years after Mexican Protestants were segregated in the Spanish Union Mission. The head pastor of Saint Peter's Church initiated the process when he requested that the Los Angeles Catholic Archdiocese send a Mexican priest to Santa Paula. The priest was to officiate Spanish-language masses for the Mexicans. Mass, however, was to be held in the Mexican neighborhoods, rather than in Saint Peter's Church. José recalls that the Mexican community was upset about the new policy but felt obliged to accept the priest's orders, for fear of being completely ostracized. José also noted that although the Mexican Catholics were segregated, the Mexican Methodists were worse off. Mexican Catholics were at least allowed to attend religious services with the Anglo Americans during special holidays. They were also allowed to use church facilities for weddings and baptisms.

When a Hispanic priest was sent to Santa Paula, two services were offered on Sundays. One was held at Limoneira Ranch and the other in Mexican Town. José attended the services at Limoneira Ranch and recalls that Mexicans from various

*El Brillante market and the car. Courtesy Ventura County
Museum of History & Art.*

Santa Paula labor camps and from other surrounding farm communities gathered
at the ranch. Though the Sunday ritual was a joyous occasion and often more than
three hundred Mexicans would congregate at Limoneira Ranch, José resented
that they were forced to attend mass apart from the Anglo American parishioners.
Most of all he was displeased with the problems caused by the segregated religious
system. Many Mexicans who attended mass at Limoneira resided in labor camps
located closer to Saint Peter's Church than to the ranch. These individuals had to
travel several miles to get to the ranch, and because they did not own cars, such
a journey was a major hardship. Most Mexicans walked, rode horses, or rode in
wooden carts pulled by horses. Moreover, since the roads connecting the labor
camps to Limoneira were unpaved in those days, by the time people arrived at
Limoneira, they would be covered with soil. Only during major events, such as
weddings or funerals, were some Mexicans transported by car. On these
occasions, the grocer or one of the other middle-class Mexicans who owned a car
gave them rides.

   As a child José and other Mexicans attended mass in the orchards. When he was
twelve, however, the management of Limoneira Ranch built an adobe hut
adjacent to the citrus packing house and permitted them to use it as a chapel. José
sadly recalled:

> *Catholic Anglos went to [Saint Peter's]. . . . Masses were*
> *said at the camp. There was a priest who went to the*
> *camps. A priest used to go to the Limoneira Ranch—there*
> *by the packing house there used to be an old adobe hut,*
> *that's where they used to say mass on Sunday [his*
> *emphasis—told in an angry tone]! People from all the*
> *outlying camps would come from there. We used to walk*
> *from the different camps to that area. . . . We had a*
> *Mexican priest.*

Roney, who is José's cohort, has ambivalent feelings of those days. She also recalls that Mexicans were segregated in separate churches but feels that it was not a result of racism. She believes that since most Mexicans had to walk to church obviously they would have arrived covered in mud. Consequently, the Anglo parishioners discouraged them from attending Sunday services in order to avoid soiling the church. In Limoneira this obviously was not a problem, for there was no church to soil. Although Roney is uncertain that Anglo Americans intentionally segregated them, she bitterly recalled that because she and her grandmother did not own a horse and carriage they had to walk on the dirt roads. Most of the time attending Sunday services was not a problem for them, but when they got caught in the rain, she and her grandmother would arrive at Limoneira drenched and splashed with mud. Roney stated:

> *I don't think they [the Anglo Americans] were all racist.*
> *If we went to church there, we would get them dirty, and*
> *get mud in the church. . . . I wished they had built us a*
> *church in Limoneira. . . . I lived with my grandmother.*
> *. . . We didn't have any men to buy us things. . . . We*
> *always had to walk. . . . My grandmother stopped going*
> *to church on Sundays when it rained and then she stopped*
> *going. . . . I remember that she didn't want to go after this*
> *Sunday that we got wet. I was wearing my new dress. . . .*
> *She also looked pretty. . . . The rain started and we got*
> *full of mud. . . . Everyone looked like wet chickens when*
> *we got to church.*

According to Roney, the conditions people had to endure discouraged her grandmother and many Mexicans from attending Sunday services. In the case of the Mexicans from the downtown area, attending church was not as problematic because they lived within the city limits, and most of them only had to walk a few blocks to attend mass. Furthermore, when it rained, mass was held in a vacant lot under a makeshift tent (Los Angeles Archdiocese 1967).[3]

A few years after the construction of the Spanish Union Mission, the citrus growers selected a vacant lot on the East Side where Catholic services could be held. It was not until 1929, however, that the growers constructed a church for the Mexican Catholics. That year, the Thilles, one of the wealthiest families in Ventura County, together with the head priest of Saint Peter's Church, initiated a plan to construct a Mexican Catholic church. The church was to be located in Mexican Town—four blocks from the Spanish Union Mission. The Thille family donated $8,000 for the construction of Our Lady of Guadalupe Church, and Father Nava was selected to be the priest of the parish. What follows highlights this historical event when, during the height of the Great Depression, Catholic Mexicans were officially segregated in their own ethnic church. Allegedly, Mexican Catholics were segregated because they, like Mexican Protestants, preferred to attend church where Spanish was spoken. Records from the Los Angeles Archdiocese describe this ironic and clearly immoral Anglo American–imposed religious segregation. An official representing the Los Angeles Catholic Archdiocese wrote:

> *In 1927, Rev. Father J. J. Cox, pastor of the Catholic Church of [Saint Peter's], invited Father Buenaventura Nava, a Franciscan Missionary, to preach to the Spanish-speaking people. The zealous Missionary quickly understood that the Mexicans had to be instructed and guided in their own language and that the best way would be to construct a church under the patronage and help of Our Lady of Guadalupe. . . . The generosity of Mrs. Thille . . . who donated $8,000, together with all the patient efforts of our people to raise money for payment of the finishing touches, made the construction of Our Temple of Guadalupe a reality. . . . And on December 1, 1929, he was happy to behold the fruits of his labor. . . . It was necessary to make it an independent parish provided with a pastor totally dedicated to its good and simple people. (Los Angeles Archdiocese 1967:10–13)*

With the completion of the mission, the Spanish-speaking people officially became the parishioners of Our Lady of Guadalupe Church on December 1, 1929. This event was marked by religious festivities that began in Saint Peter's Church. That evening, the Mexican congregation was allowed to attend mass in Saint

Peter's Parish in order to thank God for the construction of the Mexican parish. Immediately following the mass, the Mexican congregation continued to celebrate and took the jubilant affair to the streets, initiating a one-mile procession that ended at Our Lady of Guadalupe Parish, Mexican Town. Father Nava, who had been selected to serve as the pastor of the Mexican congregation, led the procession. Walking behind Father Nava, who held the American flag, Mexicans left the Anglo American zone, crossed the Mexican–Anglo American border zone, and ended the procession on Oak Street in the heart of the *barrio*. The *Santa Paula Chronicle* also describes this historic day, when Mexican Catholics were officially segregated in Our Lady of Guadalupe Church.

> *Mexican Catholic People Parade to Church Edifice . . .*
> *Led by Fr. Bonaventura Nava, Mexican missionary*
> *priest, who is to be their pastor at the new Church of Our*
> *Lady of Guadalupe on North Oak Street. Mexican*
> *Catholic people paraded yesterday from the [Saint Peter's]*
> *Church on Ninth Street to the new church edifice that is*
> *now nearly complete. . . . There were more than six*
> *hundred in the procession. Fr. Bonaventura Nava carrying*
> *the American flag at the head of the line with various*
> *societies of the church carried by leaders of their respective*
> *groups [sic]. SPC, December 2, 1929, 7[52]:1)*

Thus, by 1929 the not-so-subliminal message given to Mexican Catholics was: "We are all God's children, but some races are superior to others, so stay on your side of town." Following the construction of Our Lady of Guadalupe Church it became quite obvious that racial prejudice was the motivating force behind the building of a Mexican church. That same year, Anglo American Pentecostals segregated their Mexican congregation into a separate church, located two blocks from Our Lady of Guadalupe. With the completion of the Pentecostal church, all Mexican churchgoers in Santa Paula were officially segregated in ethnic churches located in Mexican Town (see Map 2).

In retrospect, oral histories and early 1900s documents unequivocally demonstrate that the religious segregation of the Mexican community was planned by the town's leaders and such forced separation was fueled by racist Anglo American ideologies and a belief in the need to separate the races. In the 1990s, one may ask in disbelief, How could these events have occurred? Why did Mexicans tolerate their religious segregation? Why didn't they fight back? As previously explained, it was very difficult for them to challenge segregation because (1) Mexicans were employed by the Anglo Americans and were economically dependent on them

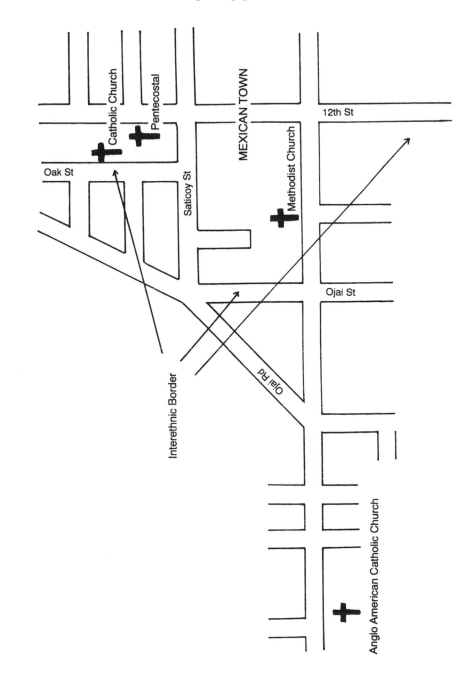

Segregated Mexican Churches

and (2) national ideologies and practices allowed Mexicans to be discriminated against in various social sectors. At that time, segregation was legal in the United States and considered to be a proper practice. Also, Mexicans were unable to fight back because they lived in fear of the violence that would be launched against them if they challenged segregation. We will now turn to this issue and examine early 1900s accounts of unequal race relations maintained by the use of Anglo American violence against Mexicans, thereby illustrating why Mexicans were reluctant to rebel against their oppressors.

MAINTAINING RACIAL INEQUALITY: ANGLO AMERICAN VIOLENCE AGAINST MEXICANS

Physical violence was often used by Anglo Americans to intimidate the Mexican community and to maintain it in a subordinate position. Violent actions committed against Mexicans ranged from police brutality to Ku Klux Klan intimidation. Although police brutality was the most common form of violence, Mexicans on occasion were suspiciously and accidentally maimed by "law-abiding" Anglo American citizens. Between 1912 to 1930, many articles appeared in the *Santa Paula Chronicle* reporting crimes experienced by the Mexican community. Mexicans were described as cowardly heathens who provoked their own attacks, while the Anglo Americans were described as innocent victims who were forced to retaliate against Mexicans. An account reported by the *Santa Paula Chronicle* illustrates this point.

On March 1, 1912, the *Santa Paula Chronicle* described the violence committed against Juan Morales by Constable John Trotter. The report stated that Juan Morales sued Constable Trotter for the loss of his left eye, after a brutal assault committed by Trotter. Apparently Trotter and the bondsmen attacked Morales while he was in jail and then assaulted him with a heavy whip, causing Morales to lose his left eye. With the assistance of attorney W. E. Shepard, Morales filed a claim against the constable and the bondsmen, asking for $10,000 in damages. Ironically, although the description of the assault was provided, the reporter reinterpreted the details and suggested that the incident was provoked by the drunken Mexican.

> *Trotter's Victim Sues for Ten Thousand Dollars. Man*
> *Injured by Constable Sues Officer and Bondsmen. Juan*
> *Morales by his attorney, W. E. Shepard has filed suit*
> *against John P. Trotter. . . . The damages sought amount*

> *to $10,000 against the constable and $500 against the*
> *bondsmen. . . . The suit arises over an encounter between*
> *Constable Trotter and Morales on the date named.*
> *Morales it is claimed, was drunk and intoxicated and*
> *resisted arrest. . . . The complaint alleges that said*
> *defendant, John E. Trotter did violently and intentionally*
> *assault and beat the plaintiff on his head with a heavy*
> *whip, causing him great pain, loss of blood and the sight of*
> *his left eye.* (SPC, March 1, 1912, 25[49]:3)

The outcome of the case is unknown, as the *Santa Paula Chronicle* failed to report the final adjudication of the court trial. Whether Morales lost the case or was awarded damages is uncertain. It is certain, however, that similar experiences served to generate distrust between the Mexicans and the police.

Newspaper accounts also illustrate that in Santa Paula the police sided with the Anglo Americans even when Mexicans were innocent. An account of a labor strike at Limoneira Ranch illustrates how the citrus growers used the police to intimidate Mexicans. On March 29, 1917, the *Santa Paula Chronicle* described the adroit manner in which the growers prevented the outbreak of a citrus strike in Limoneira. A reporter described Mexican strikers to be hotheaded and demanding unreasonable wage increases. The Anglo American growers, on the other hand, were described as honest businessmen who had recently given Mexicans a twenty-five-cents-per-day raise. Allegedly, during the strike, the growers were forced to ask for police assistance in efforts to end the irrational demands of the Mexicans. A reporter wrote the following:

> *Incipient Strike at Limoneira Ranch Is Quickly Ended.*
> *. . . An incipient strike among the Mexicans employed on*
> *the Limoneira ranch was under way Monday morning, but*
> *prompt measures on the part of the Limoneira managers,*
> *aided by the sheriff of the county with a force of five*
> *deputies, and the peace officers of Santa Paula, quickly put*
> *an end to it. The Limoneira people, two weeks ago, gave*
> *all this class of labor employed on the ranch an increase of*
> *25c per day, and this was done without solicitation. This,*
> *evidently, led some of the more hotheaded of the employees*
> *to believe that they had only to demand a further increase*
> *and shorter hours to have their demand granted. . . . At*
> *this writing no further trouble has resulted and none is*
> *looked for.* (SPC, March 29, 1917, 23[2]:1)

It is not surprising that in the presence of the county sheriff, his deputies, and Santa Paula police officers, the Mexican strikers promptly ended the strike. In other cases, Mexicans were made criminal suspects for the slightest reason. Such an event occurred in February 22, 1917, when two Mexicans were arrested by the town marshal. This case also illustrates why Mexicans were afraid of the police. While Marshal Millard oversaw labor work on a storm drain under a bridge, he saw two Mexicans pass by in an automobile. The marshal immediately suspected something wrong was taking place. To the marshal, that two Mexicans were driving a car and not working in the fields was reasonable cause to suspect that they were criminals. The marshal assumed these Mexicans to be thieves from Los Angeles, and therefore he decided to follow them. The *Santa Paula Chronicle,* once again, praised the wit of the Anglo Americans and their clever arrest of the alleged Mexican thieves. A reporter described the chase scene:

> *About 10 o'clock Sunday the marshal was in charge of some men at the storm drain bridge across River street [sic] in the outskirts of the city. While here he noticed an automobile passing toward Saticoy having, as passengers, two Mexicans. One of these he at once spotted as a man who has been pursued by the Los Angeles peace officers for several weeks past. Knowing that he was powerless to overtake the men without an auto, Millard made known the fact to Roger Edwards who happened to come along in a fast car, and Edwards, like the good citizen he is, speeded up in pursuit.* (SPC, February 22, 1917, 28[44]:1)

The reporter also left an unintentionally amusing account of the two Mexicans being arrested. He was quite amazed that the Mexicans had the audacity to resist arrest and blamed them for causing the scuffle that ensued between the marshal and one of the suspects, called Garcia. Apparently, the marshal attempted to arrest the two Mexicans when they stopped their car to board some passengers. When they resisted arrest, a fight immediately broke out between the marshal and Garcia. As they fought, the marshal's gun went off, and the bullet inflicted a wound on his own wrist. Paradoxically, Garcia was subsequently blamed for the gunshot, even though he was unarmed and had not provoked the scuffle. The encounter ended when both Mexicans were arrested and placed in jail. The reporter wrote:

> *The men were soon overtaken, where they had slowed up their auto to permit some pedestrians getting on board.*

> *This gave the marshal a chance to get his man and this he*
> *proceeded forthwith to do. Having made the arrest the*
> *return trip was entered upon. Mr. Edwards still acting as*
> *chauffeur. . . . A stop was made to permit of the officer*
> *getting his coat [sic]. . . . Millard raised his arm and*
> *turned, for an instant only. . . . But that instant was*
> *enough for Garcia to attempt to make his escape, even*
> *though he had to shoot a man in order to do so. Like a*
> *flash he grabbed for the officer's gun and a struggle ensued*
> *. . . the bullet from which inflicted a slight wound in the*
> *Marshal's wrist.* (SPC, *February 22, 1917, 28[44]:1)*

Following the arrest, the *Santa Paula Chronicle* reported only one version of the incident and failed to include the two Mexicans' statements. The newspaper also did not include comments from the passengers who had boarded the suspects' car. No further information was reported regarding the details of the arrest or whether the case was dismissed. It is unlikely that the two Mexicans were eventually identified as Los Angeles thieves, for that type of information would have been newsworthy.

Although police brutality was the most common form of physical discrimination experienced by Mexicans in Santa Paula, on occasion more severe violent acts were committed against them. The murder of fifty-year-old Marcio Tapia on September 4, 1917, is a case in point. It also demonstrates that, when a Mexican was murdered by an Anglo American, the case could easily be dismissed as an accident, regardless of the mounting evidence indicating premeditated murder. One evening the ten-year-old son of an Anglo American citrus grower shot Marcio Tapia in the back and fatally wounded him. Tapia was the servant of the boy's parents and lived in a tent located a quarter of a mile from his employers' home. While Tapia washed the dinner dishes adjacent to his tent, the young boy approached Tapia from the rear and shot him with a .22-caliber gun. The bullet entered Tapia's back and tore upwards. Tapia's death was deemed an accident because the boy alleged that he had shot the Mexican unintentionally. The case was closed and the evidence suggesting premeditated murder dismissed. The fact that Tapia was shot in the back and at close range did not change the course of the investigation. The *Santa Paula Daily Chronicle*[4] described the event as an unfortunate accident.

> *Boy Shoots Mexican. Tuesday evening Howard, the ten-year-*
> *old son of Mr. and Mrs. Erving Hunt, east of town, accidently*
> *[sic] shot and fatally wounded Marcio Tapia, a Mexican.*

> *Tapia, who is about fifty years old, had been employed*
> *by Mr. Hunt on the ranch for some time. He lived in a tent*
> *about a quarter of a mile from Hunt's place and was busy at*
> *his evening work of washing up the dishes when shot.*
> *Howard . . . is in the habit of taking his gun along. Only*
> *the night before he had shot and killed a rabbit. . . .*
> *Tuesday evening, however, he had had no luck and had*
> *failed to secure any game when he reached the tent.*
> *Thinking he might do better going back, he sat down, when*
> *about fifty feet from Tapia, to reload. It was then that the*
> *accident occurred. The ball, which was of 22 calibre, entered*
> *the left lower chest in the back and tore upwards.*
>
> *Dr. Merril was called and he took Tapia to the Bard*
> *Hospital in Ventura, where he succumbed at 9 P.M.*
> *Wednesday. (SPDC, September 4, 1914, 27[24]:1)*

Tapia died within a few hours of the gunshot.

Similar suspicious incidents occurred in 1930 when a string of unsolved deaths puzzled the residents of Ventura County. Within ten days, three men had met similar and suspicious deaths. Hilario Salinas, one of the victims, was from Santa Paula, and the other two men were from adjacent farm communities. On June 5, 1930, Salinas mysteriously drowned while measuring the water level of his employer's pool. The other victims had also drowned. Allegedly, Salinas met his death when he fell into a deep pool at the Hardison Ranch. In this case, premeditated murder was not dismissed as the cause, because the incident paralleled the string of deaths previously identified in the county. An inquest was arranged to investigate the murder. A *Santa Paula Chronicle* reporter wrote:

> *H. Salinas Victim of Accident. Hardison Ranch Employee*
> *Falls Into Deep Pool While Measuring Water Depth.*
> *Inquest Set For Tonight. Hilario Salinas, 20 years of age,*
> *was drowned this morning in the Hardison Ranch. . . .*
> *Dr. H. B. Osborn . . . was summoned by fellow*
> *workmen at the ranch and worked frantically for two hours*
> *in an attempt to revive the man. The rescue squad from*
> *Santa Paula sent the resuscitator to the scene but this also*
> *proved futile after two hours' work. . . . An inquest will be*
> *held tonight by Coroner Oliver Reardon. The tragedy is*
> *the third of its kind in Ventura county within ten days.*
> *(SPC, June 5, 1930, 38[9]:1)*

Although Salinas' death cannot be attributed to anti-Mexican clandestine activity, Santa Paula did have a chapter of the Knights of the Ku Klux Klan (KKK, Chapter No. 55 of California).[5] The KKK effectively terrorized Mexicans and displayed their racial hatred toward them. KKK activities began to appear in Santa Paula in the early 1920s and heightened during the Great Depression.

Although in the early 1920s Ku Klux Klan activity was criticized by liberal Anglo Americans, there was strong public acceptance of the Klan in Ventura County.[6] In Santa Paula, disapproval of the Klan was occasionally voiced by liberal Anglo Americans. Critical commentaries appeared in the *Santa Paula Chronicle,* for example, voicing personal opinions of the Klan: "But the 'Klan' with its 'Keagles,' 'Grand Goblins, ' 'Imperial Wizards' and that sort of thing, should have no place in Ventura County or any other law abiding American community" (*SPC,* June 1, 1922, 34[12]:1). Ku Klux Klan activity was also viewed as a sign of ignorance and bigotry by a minority of Anglo Americans. Personal advertisements appeared in the *Santa Paula Chronicle:* "Whenever the Ku Klux Klan is discussed it is well to remember that it began and still continues as a most profitable exploitation of ignorance and bigotry. It was started, in other words, to fool people out of their money, and everything else it stands for is secondary" (*SPC,* January 4, 1923, 34[44]:5). Although KKK activity was criticized by some individuals, however, there is overwhelming evidence indicating that the majority of the Anglo Americans in Santa Paula approved of the Klan.

Photographs, newspaper accounts, and oral histories suggest that the Ku Klux Klan was a very large organization in Santa Paula and in the surrounding cities. Oral history accounts collected by Ventura County historian Judith Triem indicate that joining the Klan was considered a prestigious activity and attracted people from various professions. In her book, *Ventura County: Land of Good Fortune,* Triem found that during the early 1920s "joining the Klan was considered the 'thing to do' by many white Anglo-Saxon Protestants, including those who held prominent positions in the community, such as ranchers, police chiefs, judges, and ministers" (Triem 1985:126). Two photographs of Klan gatherings held in Santa Paula during 1923 and 1924 indicate that Klan meetings were popular and often attracted over two hundred members.

In the city of Santa Barbara, located approximately forty miles from Santa Paula, KKK meetings were much larger and often attracted several thousand people. Santa Barbara was apparently the main headquarters of the Ku Klux Klan, as this was the city where the grandest Klan gatherings were held, as well as the publishing home of the magazine *Ku Klux Klarion.* The magazine, which advertised regional Klan news, was distributed around the counties of Santa Barbara and Ventura. For example, an article appearing in the *Ku Klux Klarion* describes one meeting held in the hills of Santa Barbara. The gathering was a grand

Ku Klux Klan burning a cross in Santa Paula.
Courtesy Ventura County Museum of History & Art.

affair attracting thousands of spectators from the counties of Santa Barbara and
Ventura (Knights of the Ku Klux Klan 1923a). The crowd gathered in a natural
amphitheater that placed them above a klavern, situated in a large gully near the
summit of the hill, where the Klansmen performed their White supremacist ritual.
The ceremony began with the traditional cross burning and the donning of the
white hooded masks. Once the cross was fully ablaze and could be seen from any
part of the city, the hooded Klan officers began the ritual. Inside the klavern the
officers placed a small burning cross next to the American flag and commenced
the speeches. A reporter for the *Ku Klux Klarion* described this memorable
ceremony:

> *A large number of people were in Santa Barbara last
> Saturday evening to witness the open air ceremonial of the
> Knights of the Ku Klux Klan which was held on the mesa
> west of the city. The affair was witnessed by several
> thousand people and the work was put on in full view of
> the spectators. . . . The Klavern was situated in a large
> gully near the summit of the hill, the spectators enjoying
> the natural amphitheatre which placed them above the
> Klansmen and made the affair more enjoyable. On the
> summit of the hill was a large fiery cross which could be*

> *seen from any part of the city. Inside the Klavern and near*
> *the head officer's station, was a large American flag, while*
> *at the altar was another smaller flag and a small fiery cross.*
> *The Klansmen were in full regalia and were unmasked*
> *except during the ceremonial. (Knights of the Ku Klux*
> *Klan September 1923a, 1[1]:1)*

In Santa Paula, Ku Klux Klan meetings were also often held at the summit of a hill. Tony, a Mexican American businessman and self-appointed town historian, recalled that the meetings were sometimes held on the hill that overlooked Mexican Town. He proposed that when the citrus growers wanted to intimidate Mexicans, KKK meetings were held there. Although Tony never experienced Klan activity, he recalls childhood stories about the Klansmen. His father, Daniel, told Tony that on occasion the Klansmen burned the cross to frighten Mexicans and to "put them in their place." To his knowledge the Klan never physically abused anyone in Santa Paula, as its purpose was to intimidate and frighten Jews and Mexicans. According to Tony, in Ventura the Klan persecuted Jews and in Santa Paula it harassed Mexicans. Tony recalls an account of an evening when the Klan burned a cross on the hill that overlooked Mexican Town.

> *The only thing I remember is what people used to tell me.*
> *. . . The Ku Klux Klan used to harass them [Mexicans]*
> *just like the Blacks. . . . There was a lot of KKK activity*
> *in Ventura and Saticoy. . . . In Ventura they were after*
> *the Jews. . . . There are particular histories. . . . Some*
> *people used to say that on top of the hospital [located*
> *within the city limits, on top of Santa Paula's only hill]*
> *there used to be a cross. There was a mystery why the cross*
> *was there. . . . In the early days there were rumors that it*
> *was a KKK cross. They used to burn the cross up there, so*
> *that people could see that they were up there—and around.*
> *They [KKK] didn't do things as in the South. They used*
> *it as a scare tactic. . . . I heard rumors that some of our*
> *famous citizens from Santa Paula were members.*

Four other townspeople corroborated Tony's remembrances; José, Linda, Isabel, and Roney remembered their pre-teenage days, when the Klan attempted to intimidate the Mexican community. As pre-teenagers, they never heard stories about the Klan lynching Mexicans. They did remember, however, that the Klan was a secret organization that once in a while tried to shock Mexicans by appearing

Ku Klux Klan meeting in Santa Paula.
Courtesy Ventura County Museum of History & Art.

dressed in white robes. Their attitudes toward the Klan also differed. Isabel considered the Klansmen to be "a bunch of racist fools who on occasion got together and got drunk and afterwards did stupid things." José also agreed that the Klansmen were racist fools. His analysis, however, differed somewhat. José believed that in Santa Paula there had always been two rival clans—the Mexicans and the Anglos. During certain periods, tensions heightened between the groups, and as a consequence they feuded. According to José, when the Ku Klux Klan appeared in public, they did so merely as the Anglo American way of demonstrating group solidarity and not necessarily to frighten Mexicans. Roney and Linda disagreed. They believed that the purpose of the Klan was to scare Mexicans. For example, they remembered that when Klan gatherings were held, their parents were very nervous and forbade family members from leaving the house. Linda was the only one of this group who actually saw the Klansmen in action. She recalled that one evening she saw a few hooded Klansmen pass by her home. That evening she was awakened by her grandmother's loud call, asking her to come to the window and watch a group of Klansmen parade along Twelfth Street. Linda recalled her grandmother nervously saying, "Look at that bunch of bigoted Arkies."

Today, other remembrances of the KKK appear to be somewhat comical, but in those earlier times encounters with the Klan were certainly nerve-racking experiences. Tony recalled that the KKK used several tactics to intimidate Mexicans, for example, writing threatening letters or appearing in the fields dressed in their full Klan regalia. Apparently, mailing threatening letters to Mexicans was a common form of harassment. A letter published in the *Ku Klux Klarion* corroborates Tony's analysis. On September 13, 1923, one such letter was mailed to John J. Cordero, a resident of Santa Barbara, and later published in the Klan's newsletter. The Klansmen accused Cordero of adultery and demanded prompt response to their notice. Their underlying motive, however, was not to uphold the moral virtues of the community. Their intention was to collect the house rent allegedly owed by Cordero's mistress. The KKK threatened Cordero with "action" if he did not pay the past-due rent. The Knights of the Ku Klux Klan addressed the letter:

> *Mr . John J. Cordero:*
>
> *Dear Sir.*
>   *There lives in the rear of 1117 De La Vina Street, in a home established by you, a woman and three children without a legally established name. . . . The house rent for months past is unpaid. . . .*
>   *Mr. John J. Cordero, you have an income sufficient to care for this little home and you are living at another address. The Santa Barbara Knights of the Ku Klux Klan have employed a counsel and they have full details of this matter and are ready for action. We mean to see this through. . . .*
>   *This letter was at your address September 13, 1923. On Friday September 14, 1923, we will make this letter Public by publishing same. . . . Our address is P.O. Box 500, Santa Barbara, California. Our attorneys in this matter are Balaam, Balaam & Learned, 1119 State Street.*
>
> *Santa Barbara*
> *Knights of the Ku Klux Klan*
> *(Knights of the Ku Klux Klan, September 1923b, 1[1]:1)*

Tony's account that the Klan attracted a large number of males from Santa Paula is corroborated by Triem's findings. Triem, using oral history accounts to create a composite of KKK gatherings, found that in Santa Paula, KKK meetings were well attended and often held in the hills. Triem describes one such event in

1924 when a Klan initiation meeting was held in Santa Paula. Four hundred new members were initiated and asked to endorse the Klan's philosophy: White supremacy, protecting the purity of White women, preventing labor strikes, and limiting immigration. Triem states:

> *In 1923 the Klan organized a membership drive in Ventura and Santa Barbara Counties, where over 400 new members were initiated. Klan activity took place throughout Ventura County with membership ceremonies held in the Ojai hills in 1923 and in the Santa Paula hills in 1924. . . . The Ku Klux Klan held an initiation meeting in the hills behind Santa Paula on the night of June 10, 1924. . . . The* Ventura Daily Press *for July 31, 1923, reported, . . . "the Klan is an organization for all native-born white Americans. It believes in the tenets of the Christian religion, white supremacy, protection of our white womanhood, preventing unwarranted strikes by foreign agitators, limitation on immigration, and that much needed local reform, law and order." . . . The Klan gradually fell out of favor in Ventura County, but discrimination, especially against the Mexicans, remained, particularly in those communities throughout Southern California with large concentrations of Hispanic farmworkers. (Triem 1985:126, 127)*

Triem also concurred with Tony's analysis that in Santa Paula and in other Southern California communities, Mexicans were the prime target of the KKK. A brief description of the Klan's creed illustrates the rationale behind the persecution of non–Anglo-Saxon groups. Their main principles were to uphold "White supremacy" and to promote racism. The *Ku Klux Klarion* outlined the main tenets of the Klan's creed:

> *We avow the distinction between the races of mankind as same has been decreed by the Creator, and shall ever be true in the faithful maintenance of White Supremacy and will strenuously oppose any compromise thereof in any and all things. . . . That the Ku Klux Klan has announced a set of principles that are much needed today is undoubted. She stands for American idealism. . . . Her espousal of Protestant Christianity, her interest in the word of the*

> *living God, her defense of the American home, her*
> *stubborn loyalty to virtue of womanhood and honor among*
> *men, her battle for public school education and freedom*
> *from Roman control within that institution, her position in*
> *favor of white supremacy in this nation and a store of other*
> *most worthy and patriotic principles.(Knights of the Ku*
> *Klux Klan, September 1923c, 1[1]:2, 3)*

Although the Klan fell out of favor in Ventura County by the late 1920s, Anglo Americans in Santa Paula continued using the KKK to subordinate Mexicans. It appears that Klan activity heightened when the Mexican population grew dramatically from 913 in 1920 to 3,250 by 1930, a 256 percent increase (United States Census Bureau 1922:122; 1932:57). With the growth of the local Mexican population and the hard times brought by the Great Depression, Anglo American public repression of Mexican culture increased. KKK meetings were no longer kept secret and were used as oppressive means to subordinate the Mexican community. Klan meetings were held in public places such as at the bus terminal and under the clock tower by the Woolworth store. Advertisements announcing KKK meetings, such as the following, appeared in the local newspaper: "Come see and hear the Ku Klux Klan in action, at Santa Paula, next Saturday night 8:00 P.M., follow the white robes" (*SPC,* September 21, 1929, 6[299]:4).

Not until the mid-1930s did Santa Paula's Klan activity disappear from public view. Triem proposed that throughout Ventura County, Klan membership began to dwindle when the American Legion launched an attack against it. Tony also recalled that in Santa Paula the American Legion broke apart the KKK. Apparently, the Klan fell out of favor in Santa Paula when the citrus growers realized that it was frightening the farm workers and consequently their workers' productivity was declining. That is, a pattern had begun to emerge among the farm workers: in the evenings when a KKK meeting was scheduled, Mexicans left the fields early and returned home. After a few incidents of this type, the large-scale growers who were also members of the American Legion, concluded that the Klan was not profitable for business. Tony recalled:

> *Ku Klux Klan came to Santa Paula in the 1920s. To my*
> *knowledge the Anglos wanted to keep the Mejicanos in*
> *their place. . . . My father told me what happened. . . .*
> *The Mejicanos got scared so they started staying at home.*
> *The successful agricultural farmers didn't like this because*
> *the Mejicano wasn't doing his work so the American*
> *Legion told the KKK to get out.*

Although the end of the KKK in Santa Paula alleviated interethnic racial tensions, it did not end dominant group racism. When the American Legion pressured the KKK to disband, it did so to increase worker productivity, not to end racial discrimination. Throughout the 1930s, White supremacist ideologies continued to influence Santa Paula's interethnic relations. Mexicans were treated unequally by the Anglo Americans and continued to be segregated in the churches, theaters, restaurants, stores, and neighborhoods. There is also ample evidence indicating that when KKK activity ended, the school segregation of Mexican students became the main means for preserving unequal race relations in Santa Paula. We now turn to a discussion of the school segregation of Mexican students and describe how relations of inequality were reproduced over time.

THREE   *School Segregation*

*The Social Reproduction of
Inequality, 1870 to 1934*

By the early 1900s, most school boards in the United States practiced some form of institutionalized school segregation, and that functioned as the primary vehicle to maintain a segregated society (Feagin 1989). The targeted populations were Blacks, Asians, American Indians, and Mexicans. The rationales used by the school boards differed, but in general they were racial in origin. One of the main reasons school segregation was institutionalized was to ensure that racial minority groups would not come into contact with Anglo Americans (Hendrick 1977; Konvitz 1946; Menchaca and Valencia 1990). Scholars of school segregation propose that this racist practice was motivated by several factors. Its main impetus, however, was the belief that, if the children of the White and non-White races were not allowed to socialize in school, the groups would not intermarry, and thus the purity of the White race would be retained (Donato, Menchaca, and Valencia 1991; Gonzalez 1990; Weinberg 1977). In Santa Paula, the school administrators' intentions for segregating Mexican students are obscured because written accounts of their personal motives are not available. School board minutes containing this information have been discarded by the Santa Paula School District Office. Although the definitive rationales are not available, records do exist that delineate the history of school segregation in Santa Paula. These documents indicate that school segregation adversely affected Mexican students and this inequitable educational system was used to discriminate against them. The consequences of this schooling practice resulted in the provisioning of inferior education to Mexican students.

The purpose of this chapter will be to examine the foundation and institutionalization of the school segregation of Mexican students in Santa Paula and the consequences of this discriminatory practice. Although in Santa Paula the school segregation of Mexican students began in the late 1800s, and to this date has not been dismantled, this chapter will focus on the period from the late 1800s to 1934. The contemporary school segregation of Mexican students will be examined in later chapters.

INTEGRATED ANGLO AMERICAN SCHOOLS BEFORE THE MEXICAN AMERICAN WAR

In Santa Paula, as in other California communities, when the first Anglo American pioneers settled in the Southwest, school segregation was not practiced. It was not until a few years after the Mexican American War, in 1855, that we find evidence indicating that in California the government required Whites and non-Whites to attend separate schools (Hendrick 1977). During the Mexican period, when the first Anglo American pioneers settled in California, it was an accepted practice for Mexican students to attend the Anglo American schools. Evidence of this is provided, for example, by the life history and memoirs left by Mrs. Olive Mann Isbell, who was the first schoolteacher of California and a resident of Santa Paula (Santa Paula School District Board of Trustees 1963; Webster 1967). A brief review of Mrs. Isbell's career as a schoolteacher will illustrate that the first school in California was racially integrated. Her life history will also be used to set the contextual background for the appearance of school segregation in Santa Paula.

The first Anglo American school in California was established in 1846, and Mrs. Isbell was hired to teach Anglo American, Mexican, and American Indian students (*VCHSQ* 1955). She arrived in California at the request of Colonel John C. Fremont and immediately established her school in the Santa Clara Mission de Assisi, near present-day San José. In her memoirs she wrote an account of the founding of her school, describing the school as follows:

> *My first teaching in California was commenced in the month of December 1846, in a room about 15 feet square, with neither light nor heat, other than that which came through a hole in the tile roof. The room was in the Santa Clara Mission, near San Jose. There most of the families that crossed the plains that year were housed by Colonel John C. Fremont. . . . We had only such books as we chanced to bring with us across the plains, and as superfluous baggage was not to be thought of, our stock of books was limited. I had about 20 scholars. (VCHSQ 1955:1)*

Mrs. Isbell did not remain long in the Santa Clara Mission; within a few months she moved to Monterey, California. Her departure was prompted by the outbreak of the Bear Flag Rebellion that started at the mission and forced the Anglo Americans to leave. Following the rebellion, the Mexican American War of 1846 to 1848 broke out, and Anglo American settlers were forced to gather themselves in Monterey, where the United States government had set a military outpost. Hundreds of Anglo American settlers migrated to Monterey seeking refuge from the civil unrest caused by the war. While in Monterey, Mrs. Isbell was asked by the first American consul, Thomas O. Larkin, to reopen her school (Santa Paula School District Board of Trustees 1963; *VCHSQ* 1955; Webster 1967), so she opened a school house located on top of the city jail. Anglo American and Mexican students attended the school, with two-thirds of the students being of Mexican descent (Santa Paula School District Board of Trustees 1963; Webster 1967). Mrs. Isbell provides a written account of her remembrances of the schoolhouse in Monterey:

> *When our soldiers were disbanded, some five or six*
> *families moved to Monterey, California, where the first*
> *American consul, Thomas O. Larkin, engaged me to teach*
> *a three months term. They specially fitted up a room for*
> *me over the jail. I had 56 names enrolled, at $6 each for*
> *the term. Part of the scholars were Spanish and the other*
> *part the children of emigrants. (VCHSQ 1955: 2)*

Two years after the Mexican American War ended, Mrs. Isbell and her husband, Dr. Issac Isbell moved to Texas, where she opened another school (Webster 1967). And in March 1872 they moved to Santa Paula, where they established permanent residence.[1] Upon her arrival at Santa Paula the residents asked Mrs. Isbell to be a teacher in one of their recently established schools. However, unlike the previous integrated schools that she had established, Santa Paula's schools were racially segregated.

EDUCATIONAL EXCLUSION OF MEXICAN STUDENTS: THE EARLY YEARS

When Mrs. Isbell arrived in Santa Paula in 1872, a private and a public school had already been founded. Neither school enrolled Mexican students, regardless of the fact that approximately half of the population in town was Mexican (*VCHSQ* 1959; Santa Paula School District Board of Trustees 1963; Webster 1967). The location and the name of Santa Paula's first private school is unknown because classes were initially held in private residences and no schoolhouse was built. We do know, however, that lessons were first offered in 1870 and a permanent schoolhouse was established within a few years after classes began. The building was erected near present day Glen City School (Santa Paula School District Board of Trustees 1963; *VCHSQ* 1959). Eight Anglo American students were in attendance, and Mexicans were not enrolled. In 1872 or 1873 the first public school was established toward the West Side of Santa Paula, near the Anglo American settlements (Heil 1983). The school was named Briggs and was located in the northwest corner of Cummings and West Telegraph roads, far from where the Mexicans were residentially segregated. Approximately twenty Anglo American students were enrolled.

Why Santa Paula's Mexican students did not attend the Anglo American schools during the mid- to late 1800s is unclear. There is strong evidence, however, suggesting that state policies made it difficult for them to attend public school. In 1855, the California state legislature passed an educational law prohibiting school boards from using funds to educate non-White students (California Assembly Journal, 6th session, 1855, section 18:97–98, cited in Hendrick 1977). If any public school district was found enrolling non-Whites, the legislators could legally withhold state school funds. Public education was finally extended to non-White students in 1864, on the condition that they be instructed in separate schools apart from Whites (Hendrick 1977). This privilege, however, was not guaranteed. Parents of racial minorities first had to petition the state government of their intent, and then the local school board could initiate the process. If the petition was approved by the state, the school board was authorized to fund the school on the basis of the property taxes collected from non-White residents. Public revenues could not be collected from White citizens to fund the racial minority schools.

At that time the majority of the Mexican population of California was considered non-White and therefore subject to discriminatory school codes. In 1849, the first state congress discussed the racial status of the Mexican population and overwhelmingly agreed that Mexicans practiced a European culture but were genetically Indian. That same year, the state legislators passed a citizenship law differentiating Mexicans by racial ancestry and ascribing full citizenship rights only to White Mexicans (Donato, Menchaca, and Valencia 1991; Heizer and Almquist 1971; Menchaca 1993; Padilla 1979). Based on this legislation, Mexican mestizos and Mexican Indians were not entitled to be treated as White citizens and therefore were ineligible to receive full citizenship rights.

In the case of Santa Paula, exactly how state educational policies were implemented at the local level is unclear, but that they did contribute to the schooling exclusion of Mexican students is apparent. Three methods can be documented. First, based on state law, if Mexicans did not own property they were unable to establish a public school for their children because they were not qualified to receive government aid. Only if Mexicans could prove that their property base was sufficient to sustain the cost of funding a school would the state approve the construction of a public school for Mexicans. In Santa Paula, by 1902, only seven Mexicans owned property in town ("Original Assessment Book, City of Santa Paula, 1902–1908"). Obviously, their property taxes were insufficient to obtain state approval to fund a school. Second, in that the Mexican community of Santa Paula was ineligible to receive government funds to construct its own school, the only recourse the residents had was to send their children to private school. This was not a realistic option because most parents did not have the money to do so. As previously discussed in chapters 1 and 2, the Mexican population lost their land base in the late nineteenth century and became economically dependent on Anglo Americans for employment. The farm labor wages they received were very low, sufficient only for subsistence needs. Third, because state law prohibited non-White children from attending public school with Anglo American students, it is unlikely that Santa Paula residents broke the law by allowing Mexican students to go to school.

THE SCHOOLING OF MEXICAN STUDENTS IN SEPARATE CLASSROOMS IN THE LATE 1800S

Ventura Street School was established in 1882 and South Grammar School in 1898 (Menchaca and Valencia 1990). Both schools were constructed near Anglo American neighborhoods (*VCHSQ* 1959). Linda and José recalled being told by their parents that in the late 1800s and early 1900s a few Mexicans were allowed to attend the Ventura Street and South Grammar Schools. Although there are no available records to verify their remembrances and provide documentary evidence that Mexicans were provided schooling facilities before 1913, there is evidence indicating that some Mexicans were eventually allowed to attend school in certain agricultural towns of Ventura County. The following account is presented to illustrate and corroborate this idea.

During the late 1800s, the agricultural industry of Ventura County boomed, and large-scale farmers were forced to attract workers to their farms (Heil 1983).

One way to recruit farm labor was to provide educational facilities for the children of Mexican farm workers (Gonzalez 1990). The growers took this approach in Sespe, a town adjacent to Santa Paula (*VCHSQ* 1958). At that time, part of the land in Santa Paula and Sespe was owned by the same grower (Teague 1944). Clara Smith, a retired school teacher from the Sespe School District, wrote a short history of the founding of the first schools in Ventura County. Interestingly, she offered a frank discussion of the earliest accounts of school segregation in Ventura County. Smith wrote that records from the Sespe School District indicate that only Anglo American students were permitted to attend school. Finally, in the 1880s, when the agricultural industry prospered, the growers decided that providing some type of schooling for the children of the Mexican farm workers was in their own best interest. Mexican children, however, were required to be schooled apart from Anglo American students. In approximately 1887 a special school was constructed for Mexican students and named San Cayetano. Smith wrote:

> *The region consisted of a Mexican land grant, and around the edge of this grant the white settlers established their homes. A school for the white settlers' children naturally followed. In 1874 or '75 a schoolhouse was built on the north side of the Santa Clara River. . . . There are no names of children born of foreign parents. Nor do the census reports show that there are any foreign born children in the school. The railroad was built in 1887, and soon afterwards a water company developed and distributed water from Sespe Creek. The growing of citrus fruit began. The population increased. Mexicans came to work in the orange and lemon groves. . . . Three districts were formed out of West Sespe and three schools were built; one further up the canyon was on what is now Grand Avenue, the second was the present San Cayetano and the third was Fillmore. San Cayetano became the school for the Mexican children. (VCHSQ 1958:12, 13)*

Although we are unsure if this schooling process was replicated in Santa Paula, Smith's account reveals that in Ventura County communities schools were built for Mexican students after the growers recruited a large number of farm workers to the area. Santa Paula seems to have experienced a similar development a little later, not until 1913.

SEPARATE MEXICAN SCHOOLS:
INFERIOR SCHOOLING

In Santa Paula the first Mexican school was built for the specific purpose of educating Mexicans apart from Anglo Americans (*VCHSQ* 1959). The school, called Olivelands, was founded in 1913. It appears to have been established as an incentive for the growers to recruit Mexican farm labor to the area. The owners of Limoneira Ranch, who were the wealthiest citrus growers in Santa Paula, donated land for the school and provided the financial support for its construction. The school was built on the outskirts of Limoneira Ranch and situated adjacent to the Mexican farm labor camps. Only Mexican students were allowed to attend Olivelands School. A brief description of the school's founding is provided in an article in the *Ventura County Historical Society Quarterly* (1959). Mexican students were sent to Olivelands, and Anglo American students who lived near Limoneira Ranch were placed in Briggs School. The *VCHSQ* offers the following description:

> *Olivelands School, which is part of the Briggs School District, was built in 1913 on the present site of one and one-half acres. The land was purchased from the Limoneira Company for $10. . . . The school at Olivelands was solely for Mexican children.* (VCHSQ 1959:16)

The construction of Olivelands School coincides with a dramatic increase in the Mexican farm labor force in Santa Paula. In 1913 and 1914 the *Santa Paula Chronicle* reported that a large number of Mexicans were settling in town (*SPC*, November 14, 1913, 26[36]:1; *SPC*, January 10, 1913, 25[42]:1; *SPC*, November 28, 1913, 26[36]:1; *SPC*, December 11, 1914, 26[38]:5; *SPC*, July 17, 1914, 27[17]:1). Although the local newspaper does not provide specific demographic statistics, it offers visual descriptions of the sudden growth of Mexican neighborhoods. Agricultural labor statistics also suggest that Santa Paula's farm labor community increased as a result of the success of the agricultural industry. By 1905, Santa Paula had become one of the largest citrus production centers in California. That year, Santa Paula farm workers harvested 38 percent of California's lemons (Blanchard 1961). By 1925 this percentage had grown to 85 percent (Fraysier 1968). Such an enormous growth in the citrus industry in Santa Paula suggests that the growers were successful in recruiting farm labor; otherwise, harvesting the increasing yield of citrus would have been impossible.

Ventura County historian Judith Triem provides further evidence that the school segregation of Mexican students was closely related to the needs of the agricultural industry in Santa Paula. According to Triem, around 1910, when Santa Paula experienced a substantial growth of its Mexican population, the school segregation of Mexican students began. She then suggests that the growth of the Mexican community was associated with the increasing production of agriculture in Santa Paula. Triem states:

> *Segregated elementary school classrooms began as early as 1910 when Mexican children in Santa Paula were placed in separate classrooms. . . . Civil War in Mexico and increased agricultural production brought a huge influx of Mexicans. . . . It became necessary to build more schools, and segregation was underway on a large scale. Entire schools in Ventura County's agricultural communities were Hispanic, and classrooms sometimes held as many as sixty pupils of all ages. (1985:127)*

Historian Gilbert Gonzalez corroborates this analysis. Gonzalez found that in the early 1900s when California's agricultural industry experienced a boom, it became necessary to increase the size of the labor force. In Ventura County, the growers established schools as a means of competing for the state's scarce labor force. The curriculum designed for the Mexican students, however, prepared them for manual work and familiarized them with Anglo American culture. Although the students were taught reading and math, the curriculum centered around the topics of hygiene, home economics, and work-related English. The students attended school from 7:00 A.M. to 12:00 P.M. Afterward, they would join their parents in the fields and work for five to six hours (State of California Superintendent of Public Instruction Report 1924 [cited in Gonzalez 1990:95]).

In 1914, the inferior schooling for Mexican students in Ventura County, including Santa Paula, came to the attention of the Mexican government, and the Mexican Consulate of California filed an official complaint against the Ventura County school system. The Mexican Consulate charged that Mexican students were being intentionally segregated in separate schools, where they received inferior schooling (*SPC,* September 4, 1914, 21[24]:1). The school boards denied the charge. Mrs. Reynolds, the superintendent of the Ventura County public schools, responded by alleging that Mexican students were separated from Whites because they needed special attention. According to Mrs. Reynolds, this practice did not constitute segregation. It was merely the school district's attempt to prevent Mexican students from adversely influencing Anglo American students, the argument being that the former students would slow the academic development of the latter. She alleged that the separation was for the common good of all students. What follows is a description of the complaint filed by the Mexican government and the response offered by Mrs. Reynolds. The *Santa Paula Chronicle* reported:

> *School Segregation Here Being Investigated. The Mexican children in the schools of Santa Paula constitute a problem to solve [on] which local school authorities expend much time and thought. . . . Mr. Wood [state superintendent of schools] brought word that the Mexican government had entered complaint with the governor of California that Mexican children were being discriminated against in the matter of school attendance. . . . They [Mexican students] were placed in separate schools and thus segregated from other school children. It was complained that Southern California is using this method of treatment of Mexican children, and this is what brought the state superintendent to Ventura County. . . . Mrs. Reynolds [county superintendent] explained that there is no general segregation here and no discrimination shown, but explained that foreign children of all races, when they cannot speak the English language . . . are separated from other children, this being mainly in the lower grades. This action is necessary absolutely, not only for the benefit of the English speaking, but for the benefit as well of the non-English speaking pupils. (SPC, September 4, 1914, 21[24]:1)*

The charges filed by the Mexican Consulate had no impact in Santa Paula. On the contrary, within a few years Santa Paula's school board initiated new segregative practices. In 1919, when the size of the Mexican community again increased, the school board was forced to admit many Mexican students to the Ventura Street and South Grammar schools (Webster 1967:54). Although allowed to enroll in the Anglo American schools, Mexican students were subjected to other forms of racial discrimination, such as being segregated in separate classrooms and forced to bathe in showers constructed especially for them. The school board of Santa Paula justified their discriminatory actions by using three smoke screens: (1) Mexican students had language problems, (2) Mexican students were unhygienic, and (3) Mexican students had learning problems and therefore needed to be taught proper behavior in special Americanization classes.

The main pedagogical rationale used to justify the alleged language problem was that the limited- or non-English-speaking children impeded the academic progress of Anglo American children (Belknap 1968; Webster 1967; *SPC,* June 26, 1919, 29[14]:1; Santa Paula School District Board of Trustees 1963). The racial overtones in this practice were blatantly visible when Mexican students who did not speak Spanish were also forced to attend separate classrooms. Oral histories collected from three Mexican residents in Santa Paula illustrate the unfounded basis of the language rationale. José, Linda, and Isabel recall that when they attended Ventura Street and South Grammar schools all the Mexican students were segregated in separate classrooms because of their race and not because of any language problem. For example, although they themselves were English speakers, they were placed in segregated classrooms. José and Linda agree that they were segregated because the Anglo Americans were "rednecks" and did not like Mexicans. Isabel has a somewhat different explanation. Though she agrees with José and Linda that the language problem was an invention, Isabel believes that perhaps Mexicans were segregated because they were slow learners. She also believes that the English-speaking Mexicans were segregated because some of the Mexican immigrants came to school improperly bathed. According to Isabel, Mexican students who recently arrived in Santa Paula did not have a place to bathe; therefore, their unkempt appearance bothered the Anglo American teachers. In essence, Isabel blames the Mexican immigrant children for having caused the school segregation of all Mexican-origin students. Isabel commented:

> *I don't think we were segregated because we didn't speak English. I spoke English and so did my sisters, but we were kept with the Mejicanitos. They segregated us because we didn't learn as fast. The Anglo kids were smarter. . . . When I was a kid, I was the smartest kid in the classroom so they put me in a room with the Anglo kids. . . . I used to play a lot, so they put me back with the Mejicanitos. . . . I think they also separated us because the Mejicanitos came to school dirty and smelly.*

José and Linda disagree with Isabel, recalling that most of the Mexican-origin students were clean when they went to school.

Nonetheless, whether or not hygiene was a problem, for Mexican students to be characterized as dirty, dull, and lacking social etiquette was common. Before attending class, Mexican students were required to bathe in showers constructed especially for them (Menchaca and Valencia 1990; Webster 1967). The Parents and Teachers Association (PTA) of Santa Paula recommended that Mexican students be required to follow strict hygiene rules before they could enter the classroom. Irrespective of the fact that they took showers, however, Mexican students were placed in classrooms apart from the Anglo Americans. In the South Grammar and Ventura Street schools they had to attend classes in a bungalow located adjacent to the main school. José, who was one of the youths who attended Ventura Street School, recalls that his classroom was very small. He alleges that because the size of his classroom was intolerably confining many of his peers dropped out of school. Today, he compares the size of his grade school classroom to that of an oversized closet. Isabel, who also attended Ventura Street School, recalls that her peers were practically ignored in class. She remembers that the Mexican students were not required to study. On the contrary, they were improperly supervised in the Americanization classes and allowed to play most of the time.

The issue of the Mexican students' hygiene was perhaps the most effective rationale used to justify segregating students without the school board's or the PTA's appearing racist. In other words, the language and Americanization rationales were blatant lies, as a large number of Mexican students were English speakers and their parents were third- or fourth-generation California residents. These children did not need to attend special classrooms. However, by using the "hygiene rationale," the school board's actions were protected by law: since the late 1800s California's state government permitted school administrators to prohibit children from attending school or to segregate them if they were filthy or identified as unhealthy (California School Code 1.12, 1929, cited in California State Department of Education 1929).

THE GROWTH OF THE MEXICAN COMMUNITY AND THE CONSTRUCTION OF A SECOND MEXICAN SCHOOL: THE CASE OF CANYON SCHOOL

The attendance of Mexican students in the Anglo American schools was tolerated for only a few years. Plans to resegregate the schools were initiated when the Mexican population increased in number, more than doubling in size between 1920 and 1930 (United States Census Bureau 1922; 1932). The school board determined that Mexicans were no longer to be admitted to the Anglo American schools; instead, a separate school must be built for them. Santa Paula's Mexican population had more than doubled in size between 1920 to 1930.

In 1925–1926, the Anglo American community of Santa Paula fully implemented its policy of "separate but equal education." That year, the school board decided to build two new schools, Canyon and Isbell, which separated Mexican and Anglo American students. Mexicans went to Canyon School, which was constructed on the East Side. Anglo American students were sent to Isbell School, which was located on the West Side, near the Anglo American neighborhoods (see Map 3).

The school board justified its actions by purporting that two new schools were needed because South Grammar School was overcrowded (Webster 1967). Without a doubt, the elementary student body of Santa Paula needed two new schools, since South Grammar School had increased to over 1,600 students. Why increasing enrollments necessitated racially segregated schools, however, is unclear. The school board merely stated that the Mexican students needed their own school because of language and health problems. The *Santa Paula School District Development Report* (Santa Paula School District Board of Trustees 1963) explicitly describes the official rationale used to justify the construction of Canyon School. According to the report, in 1925 Canyon School was built to accommodate about 1,000 Mexican students. Many of these students were the children of Mexican farm workers who had recently moved to Santa Paula. The report states that a special school was needed for these children because of their language and health problems. What was meant by "health problems" (e.g., infectious diseases or inadequate hygiene) is unclear; neither does the report explain why English-speaking Mexican students were also sent to the Mexican school. The report states:

> *In 1925, the Canyon School, 345 North 11th Street, later renamed Barbara Webster was built. . . . The agricultural interests of the area—citrus, walnuts, etc., required the services of many workers. In the early 20s many Mexican families moved to Santa Paula from Mexico to do this work. Since they spoke no English and had many health problems, the Canyon School was built with their specific needs in mind. . . . At the time of the peak enrollment, there were 950 students in grades Kindergarten through eight. (Santa Paula School District Board of Trustees 1963:7)*

The report also demonstrates that the school board, besides practicing segregation, consciously decided to provide Mexican students with inferior schooling. For example, 950 Mexican students attended a school that had eight classrooms, two bathrooms, and an office (Santa Paula School District Board of Trustees 1963:7),

Location of Canyon and Isbell Schools

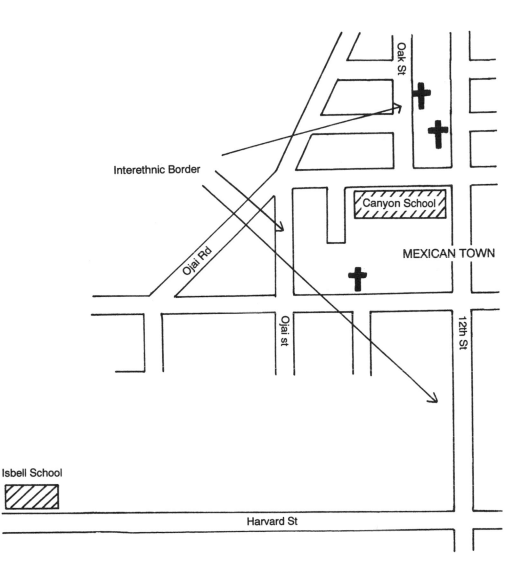

Interethnic Border

Oak St

Canyon School

MEXICAN TOWN

Ojai Rd

Ojai st

12th St

Isbell School

Harvard St

Inequitable educational facilities: Canyon School.
Courtesy Ventura County Museum of History & Art.

while 667 Anglo American students attended Isbell School, with twenty-one classrooms, a cafeteria, a training shop, and administrative offices (Webster 1967:34). The school board moved the Mexican students to a small wooden house located next to the citrus orchards in Mexican Town and transferred the Anglo American students to a spacious and modern concrete building.[2] Webster describes this event:

> *In 1925 . . . Canyon School was built . . . in the*
> *Mexican section of the city, with their needs in mind.*
> *Classes were developed especially for the Spanish-speaking*
> *children. . . . There were eight classrooms, two restrooms*
> *and an office. A few years later a bungalow was moved*
> *onto the grounds and used for the cafeteria. . . . Isbell*
> *School was constructed in the years of 1925 and 1926, at*
> *the corner of Fourth and Harvard Streets. It boasted of*
> *twenty-one classrooms, an auditorium, a cafeteria and*
> *administrative facilities. (Webster 1967:28, 29, 32)*

Inequitable educational facilities: Isbell School.

A description of both schools clearly indicates that Mexican students were both segregated and subjected to unequal school facilities.

The perspective that Mexican students should be segregated in separate schools was shared by many Anglo Americans throughout California and was not particular to Santa Paula. In 1927, California government officials attempted to classify Mexicans as Indians in order to assign them a non-White racial status (Donato, Menchaca, and Valencia 1991). Thus, based on United States Supreme Court ruling *Plessy v. Ferguson* (1896), Mexicans would come under the mandate of *de jure* segregation.[3] On January 23, 1927, General U. S. Webb, the attorney general of California, offered the opinion that Mexicans could be treated as Indians and, therefore, should be placed under *de jure* segregation (Hendrick 1977:56). At this time, however, a state law allowing Mexicans to be segregated on the basis of race was not passed because *Plessy v. Ferguson* could not be applied to Mexicans of full European descent. Nonetheless, in 1930, the attorney general again issued a similar opinion (Gonzalez 1990). According to Webb, Mexicans were Indians and therefore should not be treated as White: "It is well known that the greater portion of the population of Mexico are Indians and when such Indians migrate to the United States they are subject to the laws applicable generally to other Indians" (cited in Weinberg 1977:166). The opinion of the attorney general, however, once again failed to convince state legislators that most Mexicans were Indian.

Although the attempt to pass a segregationist law was defeated because the racial status of the Mexican population was ambiguous, school boards continued to segregate Mexican students. In 1931, the California state government reported that 85 percent of California schools segregated Mexican students in some form (Hendrick 1977:90). School boards justified their actions by stating that Mexican students had language, hygiene, and learning problems. These were all hollow justifications, obscuring the actual racist motives of school board members.

In Santa Paula, during the Great Depression, similar anti-Mexican attitudes were expressed against Mexican students. The views in Santa Paula, however, were more racist than those held by government officials. Many Anglo American parents wanted to strip Mexican students of any right to obtain an education. They felt that providing education to Mexicans was a violation of their own civil rights. In several meetings, Anglo American parents complained that their tax money was unjustly being used to educate Mexican children, and they demanded an end to this practice (*SPC*, October 7, 1932, 10[5]:1; *SPC*, October 27, 1932, 10[22]:1). The school board had recently allowed a few Mexican students to attend the Anglo American schools because Canyon School was overcrowded. By 1932, the Mexican elementary student population was 52 percent of the total student body and far exceeded the accommodations available at Canyon School (*SPC*, October 7, 1932, 10[5]:1). Anglo American parents reacted angrily to this temporary racial intermixture. In response to the angry protests, the school board added a new classroom to Canyon School and the Mexican students were asked to return there (*SPC*, March 14, 1934, 9[135]:1; *SPC*, April 18, 1934, 9[165]:1). When the school improvements were completed, Canyon School was renamed Barbara Webster.

SCHOOL SEGREGATION IN THE CITIES NEAR SANTA PAULA

At the state level, the school segregation of Mexican students intensified during the Great Depression, as it did in Santa Paula. By the late 1920s school segregation became widespread throughout California and sharply increased in the early 1930s. In 1931, most California schools segregated Mexican students (Hendrick 1977:90). There is evidence that in the towns near Santa Paula school segregation was also practiced. For example, Carpinteria, a coastal town located approximately forty miles from Santa Paula, segregated

Mexican students and other racial minorities. However, the school board of Carpinteria, unlike that of Santa Paula, was not politically astute in advancing a "safe" rationale to justify school segregation. In 1927, after California's attorney general was unsuccessful in lobbying the government to pass legislation that would segregate Mexican students on the basis that they were part Indian, Carpinteria school authorities ignored the state government's decision. The school board announced that Mexican students would be segregated in Carpinteria because they were Indian. The action caused political turmoil. In 1929, the *Santa Paula Chronicle* commented on Carpinteria's school segregation practices. A newspaper reporter offered the opinion that the school board should find more subtle methods of justifying school segregation, without using race as the main rationale. The methods used by the Santa Paula school board were cited as excellent and tactful examples.

> *School authorities of Carpinteria have caused considerable interest in all parts of the state with their decision in declining to accept the ruling of Attorney General U.S. Webb that they cannot segregate Mexican[s]. . . . The Carpinteria school board takes the ground that children of Mexican born parents are Indians. . . . In Santa Paula the Mexican situation is handled in a tactful manner, school authorities believe. Many of the Mexicans are going to school in the Canyon and Ventura schools situated in their own sections of this city. . . . The schools situated in their own districts take care of the majority of the Mexican children, and special courses of study have been arranged for them. They are said to be happy in their own schools.* (SPC, October 5, 1929, 7[5]:6)

The reporter suggested that the Santa Paula school board (unlike Carpinteria's, which segregated Mexicans by classifying them as Indians) was careful in selecting a rationale. That is, in order for school authorities to legally segregate light-skinned Mexicans, who did not come under the mandate of *de jure* segregation, they had to be cautious in presenting their criteria for segregation and justify their actions by citing language or hygiene problems (see *Independent School District v. Salvatierra* 1930).

Unlike the Chinese, Japanese, and American Indians who had been classified as non-White—and therefore subject to school segregation—not all Mexicans could be segregated. Some legislators argued that Mexicans were of Latin American descent and, because there was no federal law mandating that Latins be segregated, Mexicans should not be segregated on the basis of their Latinized appearance (Wollenberg 1974). On the other hand, other legislators argued that Mexicans were Indian and therefore could be segregated because they were "colored" (Hendrick 1977). This debate continued until 1935, when the California legislature offered a convoluted decision regarding Mexican students. The new educational legislation officially segregated some Mexican students on the basis that they were Indian while it exempted "White Mexicans." Without explicitly mentioning Mexicans, the 1935 school code prescribed that schools segregate Mexicans of Indian descent who were not American Indians. The California school code of 1935 stated:

> *The governing board of the school districts shall have power to establish separate schools for Indian children, excepting children of Indians who are the wards of the United States government and children of all other Indians who are the descendants of the original American Indians of the United States, and for children of Chinese, Japanese, or Mongolian parentage. (Cited in Hendrick 1977:57)*

The ambiguous school code made some Mexican students the principal target of discrimination and released American Indians from mandated school segregation (Donato, Menchaca, and Valencia 1991). Dark-complexioned Mexican students could be classified as Indian and the segregationist educational code applied to them.

California school boards now had the legal right to use race as a rationale to segregate Mexicans. Most school boards, however, continued to use alternate methods to justify segregation, since still not all Mexicans could be legally segregated under California's educational codes. For example, in the coastal city of Oxnard, only fifteen miles from Santa Paula, Mexican students were segregated by creative means. A *Los Angeles Times* article (January 19, 1975, 94, Part II:1, 3) reported that in the early 1930s the Oxnard school board pursued deliberate yet subtle racial segregation policies in the elementary schools by (1) building of a "Mexican school" in the Colonia (the largest Mexican neighborhood in Oxnard), (2) manipulating attendance zones, and (3) staggering playground periods and end-of-school-day release times so as not to allow the Mexican and Anglo students to mix in the one school attended by both. By 1970, when a desegregation law suit was filed, three of Oxnard's elementary schools were 95 percent or more minority in enrollment and three were 75 percent or more Anglo American. Judge Harry Pregerson, who heard the court case, ruled that the 1970 conditions of segregation in Oxnard were inextricably tied to a historical process—that is, the well-planned scheme of forced segregation pursued in the 1930s.

Other California case studies show that the segregation of Mexican students was common in the 1920s and 1930s—for example, in Los Angeles County (Gonzalez 1974), Orange County (Gonzalez 1985), and San Diego County (Alvarez 1986, 1988). In each county, language, hygiene, and the "special needs" of Mexican students were cited as the main reasons why segregation was practiced. Interestingly, in several ways Gonzalez' case study in Santa Ana (Orange County) (1985) demonstrates a process parallel to that by which Mexican students were segregated in Santa Paula. First, in both cities the discussion of segregation arose in 1913, a time, as Gonzalez notes, that coincides with the incipient phase of Mexican migration to the Southwest. Second, in both Santa Ana and Santa Paula the school boards demonstrated a willingness to organize their schools and school programs to accommodate the labor needs of the growers. Third, both communities employed a common strategy to develop their dual school systems—the building of separate school facilities for Mexicans because they allegedly needed special instruction.

In sum, in California the school segregation of Mexican students was widespread during the 1920s and 1930s. Each school district used its own rationale to validate school segregation. For now, we will leave the topic of school segregation and examine the type of resistance that the Santa Paula Mexican community exerted against segregation and other racist practices.

FOUR

Mexican Resistance to the Peonage System

Movements to Unionize Farm Labor

One may ask why the Mexican community of Santa Paula failed to launch a campaign to desegregate the schools and the neighborhoods. The answer is simple: they did not have any economic or political power, as the Mexican community was controlled by and economically dependent upon the Anglo American citrus growers. If the Mexicans challenged the Anglo American–written rules, the citrus growers could retaliate by evicting them from company housing and terminating their employment. As we shall examine in this chapter these were common practices used by citrus growers to harass Mexicans.

Thus, school segregation and its continuous expansion were merely one way in which Anglo Americans discriminated against Mexicans and kept them in a peonage position. For example, in spite of the fact that California courts ruled in 1947, in *Mendez v. Westminster School District* (1946, 1947), that the school segregation of Mexican students was illegal, Santa Paula's school board ignored the decision. Life in Santa Paula continued as if the *Mendez* ruling had never passed. Olivelands and Barbara Webster schools were not desegregated. On the contrary, in 1952, two new segregated schools were constructed to accommodate the growing elementary school population. Grace S. Thille School was constructed for the Mexican students and Glen City School for the Anglo American students (Menchaca and Valencia 1990). Although the segregation policies angered the Mexican population, they were unable to intervene because they lacked political voice within the school board. Each time Mexican candidates ran for school board positions, they were defeated at the polls (Ornelas 1984). Even the more affluent Mexicans were unable to stop school segregation or change the racial order in Santa Paula. The few privileged Mexicans who were self-employed and financially stable were unable to influence city government politics.

Mexicans should not be deemed apathetic simply because they were unable to desegregate the schools. On the contrary, the Mexican community of Santa Paula has a long history of resistance against discrimination. From 1912 to 1918, the *Santa Paula Chronicle* reports numerous accounts of Mexicans' organizing resistance movements against Anglo Americans (*SPC,* December 6, 1912, 25[37]:1; also, see chapter 2). Included among these movements was the 1915 citywide protest against police brutality and the unfair accusation that Juan Ortega killed the town's marshal. Moreover, between 1919 and 1931 the Mexican community organized mutual aid societies to defend its citizens' political rights and to provide financial assistance to compatriots in economic distress (e.g., Mutualista Mexicana Society and Fraternidad Mexicana).[1] In 1932, the Mexican community also established its own newspaper, *La Voz* (The Voice). The paper's aim was to disseminate local news about the Mexican community and to instill ethnic pride in its readership. Another example of Mexican resistance occurred in 1941 when numerous Mexicans ran for public office, basing their campaign platforms on civil rights reform (see chapter 5).

Perhaps the most confrontational examples of resistance were a series of labor strikes organized by the Mexican farm laborers. The strikes were launched in an attempt to challenge unfair labor practices and to obtain union representation. The first labor strikes included only a few workers. Over time, the strikes became better organized, and the farm workers formed coalitions with other agricultural workers around the county. Forming unions became the workers' main vehicle for obtaining decent working conditions. Unfortunately, national labor unions were uninterested in helping Mexican farm workers, and the farmers were strongly determined to destroy any union movement in Santa Paula.

What follows is a description of several farm labor movements in Santa Paula. These case studies document the agricultural workers' efforts to challenge unfair labor practices. They also illustrate how people of Mexican descent were discriminated against within the labor market and were prevented from obtaining union representation.

SMALL-SCALE INCIPIENT FARM LABOR STRIKES, 1915 TO 1937

The first documented account of strike activity in Santa Paula occurred in 1915. On New Year's Day, thirteen Mexican farm workers went out on strike at the Corbett Ranch. Unlike Limoneira Ranch, which was the largest citrus employer in Santa Paula, Corbett Ranch was of moderate size and employed only a few workers. The strike activity began when the farm workers demanded higher wages and a reduction in the work day (*SPC,* January 1, 1915, 26[1]:1). Interestingly, the strike was perceived by the owners of Corbett Ranch as another example of the Mexicans' lazy nature. They were perplexed that Mexicans refused to work on New Year's Day. But, most of all, the citrus growers were bewildered by the strikers' demands. In retaliation, the owners of Corbett Ranch fired the strikers and threatened their families. To punish the workers, the owners immediately asked the city government not to give the families of the strikers charity relief. This harsh act was intended to teach other employees that strikes would not be tolerated at the ranch. When interviewed by a *Santa Paula Chronicle* reporter, the owners of Corbett Ranch stated that the strikers were "so lazy they refuse to work, preferring to allow their women and children to go hungry" (*SPC,* January 1, 1915, 26[1]:1).

For the Mexican workers, the first strike in Santa Paula ended in disaster. The outcome of this labor protest, most likely, would have been different if the strikers had received some type of assistance from one of the national labor unions. At the time, however, Mexican farm workers were excluded from joining the American Federation of Labor (AFL) or any other national labor union (Reisler 1976; Sosnick 1978; Weber 1973). Union leaders shared popular Anglo American stereotypes of Mexicans and were antagonistic toward them. They believed that Mexican immigrants competed for scarce jobs and that their presence adversely affected American labor. National labor unions were more interested in lobbying against Mexican immigration to the United States than in helping Mexicans organize local unions. For example, the AFL was actively involved in increasing restrictive immigration policies in order to limit the size of the Mexican population in the United States. Its purpose was to protect the American labor market from Mexican immigrants who allegedly depressed wages and lowered employment standards. According to the AFL, Mexican immigration had to be stopped because employers preferred to hire cheap Mexican labor rather than American workers. In this view, Mexicans were the preferred labor force because they worked for the lowest wages. The AFL based its exclusionist anti-Mexican policies on several government labor studies, including the report of the Dillingham Commission, which found, in 1911, that Mexicans, in comparison to other ethnic groups, were paid the lowest wages in the country for farm labor. The Dillingham Commission was created by the Immigration Act of 1907 to investigate the status of immigrants in the United States. The commission concluded that, on the average, a Mexican farm worker was paid $1.42 per day, while members of other ethnic groups were paid at minimum fifty cents more (Dillingham Commission 1911:36–37, cited in Reisler 1976:19). The commission also found that in the railroad industry it was a common practice to pay Mexicans lower wages. For example, since 1908, Southern Pacific Railroad paid Greek labor $1.60 per day, Japanese $1.45, and Mexicans $1.25 (Dillingham Commission 1911:13–19, cited in Reisler 1976:4).

Santa Paula's second labor strike was launched on March 25, 1917, against Limoneira Ranch (*SPC*, March 29, 1917, 23[2]:1). Once again the workers did not receive support from any national labor union. However, unlike the strike at Corbett Ranch in which only a few people joined the work stoppage, at Limoneira the strike leaders convinced a hundred workers to participate. Their main demand was higher wages. During the first day of the strike, it appeared that the Mexicans would undoubtedly win because they successfully crippled the ranch's citrus production. On the second day, however, Limoneira management threatened to put the protesters in jail if they did not return to work. Within a few hours of the announcement, the police arrived at the ranch to warn the strikers to return to work or suffer the consequences. To intimidate the strikers, the police arrested their leaders and placed them in jail. The next day, Limoneira management warned the remaining strikers to return to work or else they would be fired. One hundred strikers conceded and the work stoppage ended. Although the labor crisis was over, thirty-six employees refused to return to work and continued the protest.

Twenty years later, on May 7, 1937, a third labor strike was launched by the Santa Paula Agricultural Workers' Union (SPAWU) (*SPC*, May 17, 1937, 14[183]:1). Earlier that year, field hands and packing-house workers formed Santa Paula's first labor union. The strike was led by Rodolfo Marquez, the president of SPAWU. The union had been formed in order to unify the different labor sectors within the agricultural industry and thereby increase their chances of winning a strike, as together the harvesters and packers could cause a total work stoppage. The workers went on strike against the Santa Paula Orange and Mupu Citrus associations. In total, 147 Mexican farm workers walked out on strike. Union leaders demanded a wage increase from twenty-three cents to forty cents an hour. They also demanded that the citrus associations allow collective bargaining and permit Rodolfo Marquez to be their arbitrator. This meant that the growers would ratify the union and allow the elected president to represent the workers. The growers would also be obliged to negotiate a contract that was acceptable to both groups.

The formation of Santa Paula's first labor union coincided with the emergence of farm labor unions throughout California (Weber 1973). During the mid-1930s, because national labor unions were reluctant to organize farm workers, Mexicans and other minority groups established their own unions. In 1935, Paul Scharrenberg, secretary of the California Federation of Labor, expressed in a *New York Times* interview an attitude that had long been held by the AFL toward farm workers (cited in Reisler 1976). He publicly stated that only communists and fanatics were willing to live with farm workers and have their heads broken in the interest of migratory labor. Only on occasion did a few union organizers take it upon themselves to help farm workers (Craig 1971; Galarza 1964). This type of assistance was informal. Among the Mexican unions were Confederación de Uniones Campesinas y Obreros Mexicanos (CUCOM), Mexican Mutual Aid Society, and Confederation of Mexican Labor Unions (CMLU). Interracial farm labor unions were also organized, such as the San Joaquin Valley Agricultural Workers' Industrial League (AWIL) (Taylor 1975), with Mexican, Japanese, Filipino, Hindu, and Chinese members.

In the case of Santa Paula, throughout the duration of the Santa Paula Orange and Mupu Citrus Strike, national labor unions did not provide monetary or legal assistance to the strikers. The only type of aid offered was unofficial—informal advice from a few AFL members. For example, on the fifth day of the strike, three AFL organizers met with the Santa Paula strikers. The AFL visitors advised the strikers to hold the line and to continue with their demands. The advice came too late, though, since the strike leaders had recently withdrawn their original demand for a forty-cents-an-hour wage. They were willing to accept thirty cents an hour, which was less than an eight-cent increase. AFL organizers recommended that the original demands be reinstated, lest the growers view this indecision as a sign of weakness.

When the growers heard that AFL organizers were in town, they decided to "play hard ball" and scare the farm workers. Rather than negotiating, the growers began to replace a few of the strikers with Anglo American "dust bowl" refugees. The threat did not achieve its goal. The strike continued for five more days until the growers "lost their patience" and decided to end the strike by violently intimidating the strikers. They once again sought the assistance of the Santa Paula police. On May 17, the strike was broken when the police threatened to arrest the protesters and deport the undocumented workers. In full view of the protesters, the police arrested Rodolfo Marquez and took him to jail (*SPC,* May 17, 1937, 14[183]:1). Marquez was immediately deported to Mexico. The outcome of the strike, however, cannot be attributed only to police intimidation: the growers also voiced public threats against the workers. The strikers were warned that if they failed to return to work, dust bowl refugees would permanently replace them and no employee would be rehired. This threat was significant because dust bowl refugees were gradually replacing Mexican farm workers throughout California.

From 1935 to 1940, as a result of depressed farm conditions and devastating dust storms in Texas, Arkansas, and Oklahoma, a mass emigration of rural Anglo Americans to California occurred. More than 350,000 adults entered California in need of manual employment. By 1937, 80 to 90 percent of farm workers were

Anglo Americans (Reisler 1976). The impact of the dust bowl refugees on the Mexican population was devastating. In many California farms an oversupply of labor allowed growers to reduce wages by half and consequently many Mexicans were forced to seek employment elsewhere. This displacement pushed many toward urban centers, and thousands of Mexicans found themselves unemployed or underemployed in service occupations that often paid less than their former agricultural jobs. Moreover, with the arrival of the dust bowl refugees, Mexican labor unions were forced to disband or rely on an ad hoc structure. Unions had no power as the oversupply of labor gave the growers the capacity to set and determine work conditions as they pleased (Reisler 1976). As the result of these events, Mexican farm labor unions were weakened and set back for many years.

In the case of the Santa Paula farm workers, the threat of losing their jobs convinced many Santa Paula Orange and Mupu Citrus strikers to return to work and to abandon the union movement. They had no other recourse because the federal government did not give farm workers the right to form unions or to bargain collectively with their employers. Lack of legal recourse was a common problem among California farm workers, since in the 1930s the federal government took a position of non-intervention with regard to farm labor strikes (Sosnick 1978). The government's laissez faire stance was evident in the Wagner Act of 1935, which exempted farm workers from a minimum wage and from the right to collective bargaining. These were rights reserved for industrial workers. The federal government's actions were rationalized under the guise that farmers provided an important national service that had to be protected by law (Sosnick 1978). Because farmers required and had the right to an inexpensive and adequate supply of farm labor, any law that encouraged trade union organization among the farm workers threatened the basic rights and stability of the agricultural industry in the United States. For that reason farm workers could not be given the right to collective bargaining or to be included under the protection of the Wagner Act.[2] At that time, then, for farm workers in Santa Paula and other communities, to resist the unjust practices was almost senseless, as the U.S. government legally sanctioned the farmers' discriminatory practices. Nonetheless, regardless of the lack of support extended by the government, farm workers in Santa Paula continued their labor struggles.

CHALLENGING A SACRED COW: THE STRIKE OF 1941

After the Santa Paula Orange and Mupu Citrus Strike ended in defeat the Santa Paula Agricultural Workers' Union (SPAWU) disbanded. The union was not revived until 1941, when Santa Paula farm workers joined six thousand Ventura County lemon pickers and packers to launch another agricultural workers' strike. SPAWU members formed a coalition with other Mexican and Filipino workers who were part of the Ventura County Agricultural Workers' Industrial Union. The massive work stoppage finally came to the attention of the American Federation of Labor. By law, AFL could not officially assist the farm workers because they were exempt from obtaining labor arbitration advice or assistance. However, because a large number of the strikers were industrial workers (e.g., canners and packers), the AFL argued that these workers were protected by the Wagner Act. After a period of negotiation talks, the government finally allowed the AFL to intervene, as long as the union represented only the packers and cannery workers. This unprecedented breakthrough permitted the AFL to take a leadership role on behalf of the strikers.

On January 31, 1941, with the assistance of the AFL, a coalition of Ventura County agricultural unions called for a county-wide strike, the first agricultural strike in which the AFL was officially involved. The strike was eventually called the "Ventura County Six Month Strike." The coalition of unions immediately crippled the county's lemon industry because the walkout prevented the harvesting, packing, and distribution of all citrus. In essence, there was a complete work stoppage because the harvesters, packers, and canners were all on strike. The growers were unable to resume their daily production quotas. Local labor leaders were optimistic because in a matter of weeks thousands of pounds of lemons and vegetables would decompose if they remained improperly processed and packed. Assured of their success, the strikers presented four primary demands: (1) the right to collective bargaining, (2) official recognition of their unions, (3) an hourly wage increase from thirty to forty cents, and (4) payment for "wet-time" (i.e., time spent in the fields while waiting for the weather to improve before starting to harvest) (Triem 1985). In addition, other demands were presented addressing improved housing and working conditions.[3]

On the other side of the picket line were the Ventura County citrus growers. Charles C. Teague, the president and co-owner of Santa Paula's Limoneira Ranch, was the representative of the growers. When the workers confronted Teague, they demanded that the AFL be allowed into the negotiation talks. Teague immediately denied them the right to be represented by the AFL and refused to meet with leaders of the strike coalition or with AFL organizers. Teague also refused to speak to any person not on the Limoneira strike committee. Teague's tactics were obvious. If he negotiated only with his employees, he and the other growers would hold the upper hand. It would be easy for Teague to intimidate his employees because he had the power to fire them and evict them from company housing.

For six months, Teague refused to meet with the AFL and the leaders of the local unions. Throughout the duration of the strike he argued that most growers could not afford to pay the wage increase, therefore they would not enter negotiation talks. On the other hand, the workers refused to concede their demands. Thus, the opposing groups reached a stalemate, and the situation worsened for both sides. The growers lost thousands of dollars in citrus, and the workers' poverty increased (Meany 1941). My informant, Roney, who was in her late twenties at the time of the strike, recalls that the growers and the agricultural workers were playing "hardball politics." Both groups refused to compromise on any issue. Roney recalls that the agricultural workers were able to "hold the strike line" because they were receiving financial support from various sources that included local sympathizers, the AFL, and the Mexican community of Los Angeles. In particular, the Los Angeles Mexican mutual aid societies provided the greatest amount of financial and spiritual support. Each week Los Angeles mutual aid societies would bring food, clothing, and money. Ventura County sympathizers also provided financial support by donating money and food and organizing door-to-door fund-raising campaigns. Roney remembered that when her family joined the strike, they were immediately put to work either on the picket lines or in some type of fund-raising activity. Because Roney was a high school graduate, she was asked to be a liaison between the Limoneira employees and a few of the Los Angeles mutual aid societies. As part of her assignment she was asked to travel to Los Angeles for part of the week and to help coordinate the collection drives. While in Los Angeles, she stayed with a Mexican physician whose home served as a donation collection center. Roney accepted the assignment thinking that she would primarily serve as an interpreter and work as a typist. However, to her amazement not only was she expected to perform secretarial duties but she was also asked to participate in the door-to-door collection drives. After several months of working as a liaison, Roney decided to return to Santa Paula and work on the picket lines. Roney amusingly recalls that, although picketing was dangerous, it was an easier task than the activities in Los Angeles. She remembers gratefully that if it had not been for the hard work of the Los Angeles Mexican community the strikers would have gone hungry. She also recalls the faces and compassionate words offered by the Mexican families whom she met when she collected donations. Many of these urban Mexican families were poor, yet they were willing to help the farm workers by offering food, money, or clothing.

Throughout the duration of the strike, Teague asserted that it was an illegitimate assembly and that the AFL did not have the right to represent the farm workers. Teague and other citrus growers launched a media attack against the AFL (Meany 1941; Mines and Anzaldúa 1982), accusing the AFL of forcing farm workers to go out on strike. According to the growers, if a farm worker refused to join the strike, he would be intimidated and brutalized by an AFL organizer. In his memoirs, Teague summarized the position taken by the growers (Teague 1944), describing in a condescending tone the growers' disbelief that their good-natured Mexicans willingly engaged in strike activity. The growers could not understand why the workers refused to return to their jobs when plenty of tasks suited their unintellectual "nature." Teague stated:

> *Mexicans have always been one of the chief sources of*
> *California's labor supply. They are naturally adapted to*
> *agricultural work. . . . Many of them have a natural skill*
> *in the handling of tools and are resourceful in matters*
> *requiring manual ability. . . . The Mexican people are*
> *usually good-natured and happy. . . . In 1941 about*
> *6,000 Mexican citrus workers in Ventura County were*
> *persuaded by professional organizers . . . to strike for*
> *higher wages. . . . When I say "persuaded" I should*
> *perhaps say "intimidated" because it was quite apparent*
> *throughout the entire strike that the great majority of the*
> *Mexican workers were not in favor of the walkout. (Teague*
> *1944:142, 143, 148)*

Rather than accepting the reality that Mexicans wanted to be part of organized American labor, Teague preferred to believe that outside agitators coerced the six thousand Mexicans to join the strike.

Toward the end of the fourth month the workers refused to concede their demands (Meany 1941). They continued to ask for a 30 to 35 percent wage increase, as well as for the growers to recognize the AFL as their bargaining agent. The growers, on the other hand, refused to compromise. They were determined to hold wages at thirty cents an hour, or three cents per box, and to avoid recognizing the AFL as the official bargaining agent (Fraysier 1968). In a press release, Teague summarized the sentiments of Ventura County growers: they preferred to lose their crop, rather than accept unionized farm labor in the county. To the growers, allowing farm workers the right to collective bargaining meant the end of cheap labor and a total restructuring of the agricultural industry—an idea with which they would never agree. If the Mexican farm workers were unwilling to accept present work conditions, then recruitment of a new labor force was necessary.

> *If these organizers can demonstrate to these easy going*
> *kindly Mexican people that all they have to do regardless*

*of the condition of the industry, is to make a demand for
more pay and get it by striking, the control of our business
is gone. We must fight to the finish. It would be better for
us to let the fruit now on the trees drop to the ground than
grant this demand. (Cited in Fraysier 1968:130)*

Conceding to labor demands threatened the growers' source of cheap labor and challenged their paternalistic peonage system. The growers felt that, at all costs, they had to retain their workers in a subordinate position, to ensure high profits and low operating expenses. Therefore, in efforts to end the labor unrest, the growers followed through with their threats. In the fourth month of the strike, they recruited a large number of Anglo American laborers to replace the strikers. At that time, the growers also threatened to evict the strikers from company housing if they did not return to work by early May. Since the strike was not called off on May 5, 1941, the growers carried out their second threat and evicted the farm workers. This was a devastating experience for the workers especially since many of them had resided on the ranches for two or three generations (Triem 1985).

Though the strike pushed the workers and their families into the streets, they continued their struggle. They peacefully vacated the labor camps and then proceeded to establish three strike campgrounds in the county parks. This act of defiance became a major embarrassment for the growers as the campgrounds were named after the most influential ranching families. The formation of the camps also helped the agricultural workers to obtain public support for their cause.

With over six thousand Ventura County workers and their families now on the streets, the state government was forced to become involved (Triem 1985). The state allowed the strikers to set up temporary shelters in three county parks, and the State Relief Agency was required to provide food for the families. In Santa Paula, the Mexican farm workers set their campsite in Steckel Park and called it "Teagueville," after the president of Limoneira Ranch.

José, one of my informants, who was twenty-five years old at the time of the strike, recalls that the families stayed in the camp for approximately two months. During the first month at Teagueville, the evicted residents appeared to be in good spirits. It was common to see children playing in the camp and to see their parents visiting one another in the provisional tents. José also remembers that in the evenings, after the adults returned from the picket lines and after families had eaten their dinner, people would gather around a *guitarrero* (guitar player). The families would also entertain themselves by singing songs and exchanging jokes and stories.

After the first month and a half of living in Teagueville, José recalls, several of the families who owned cars left the camp. Their departure demoralized the

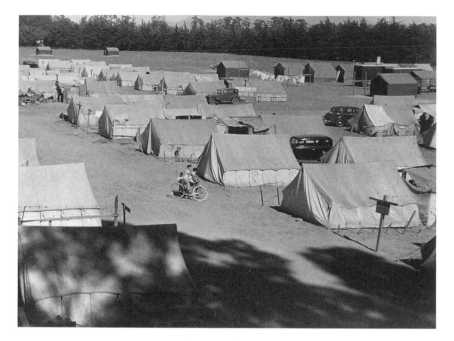

Evicted Mexican families at Teagueville, 1941.
Courtesy Ventura County Museum of History & Art.

strikers, and many other families soon followed. Overall, the community's spirits were extremely low. Exacerbating matters was the growers' continuous refusal to recognize the AFL as the strikers' representative. The strikers were further distressed by the government's lack of interest in the labor negotiations. The National Labor Relations Board (NLRB), which represented the government, refused to intervene on the grounds that the majority of the strikers were field hands and not industrial workers. In other words, the NLRB sided with the growers' view that the agricultural workers did not have the right to collective bargaining (*SPC*, July 14, 1941, 55[51]:1).

By the end of the sixth month of the strike, many of the families living in the parks had left to seek employment elsewhere. To them, it was obvious that the strike was unsuccessful. On July 7, 1941, however, the NLRB decided to enter the negotiation talks (*SPC*, July 14, 1941, 55[51]:1). The spirits of the remaining strikers were temporarily uplifted, as they expected the NLRB to protect their right to collective bargaining. To their amazement, on July 14, 1941, the NLRB offered its analysis of the strike: the strikers should return to work because the growers had the right to replace them with "scab labor" (strike breakers). The NLRB assured the strikers that the growers would allow them to return to their homes and jobs and that no one would be discriminated against. There was, however, a condition. Workers would be reemployed based only on the availability of jobs. The NLRB also sided with the growers on the issue of union representation. Although employees of over thirteen packing houses were on strike and were considered industrial workers eligible to be represented by the AFL, the NLRB concluded that union representation was unnecessary. The cannery and packing house workers were disqualified from union representation because most of the strikers were farm workers. At that point, the AFL advised the strikers to return to work because the government was on the side of the growers and would not grant the industrial workers the right to collective bargaining (Meany 1941).

On the last day of the strike the growers issued a repressive public statement to their workers. A spokesman for the growers announced that "there will no longer be a preferred class, as there was for so many years, when we were hiring Mexican workers" (*SPC,* July 14, 1941, 55[51]:1). Mexican workers were thus warned that they would not be given any special privileges. Farm workers were also informed that if they wanted their jobs back they would have to wait five months. My informants, José and Roney, remember that the latter point was an empty threat because most strikers were rehired within a few days after the strike ended. The growers were desperate to regain their employees and resume normal relations. Only those strikers who had held leadership roles were black-listed. Interestingly, despite the fact that most workers were rehired, a large number of the families left Santa Paula and migrated north toward San José, California, where farm labor was being actively recruited. Roney and José were among the families who decided to remain in Santa Paula. Both stated that they were second-generation Santa Paula residents and they did not have any relatives in other cities. Santa Paula was their home. They were both rehired within a few days after the strike ended and so were able to remain in town. Unfortunately, once again the Mexicans' attempt to resist discrimination ended in defeat, and the growers' unfair practices were sanctioned by the government.

THE AFTERMATH OF THE STRIKE: THE BRACERO PROGRAM

In response to the farm labor unrest in Ventura County, the growers organized the Ventura County Citrus Growers Committee (VCCGC), for the purposes of prohibiting farm labor organization in the county and averting labor strikes. The VCCGC launched a lobbying campaign to pressure the government to pass laws that would prohibit such activities. VCCGC eventually joined forces with other farm associations that had similar concerns, and the agricultural associations became powerful lobbying blocs pressuring Congress to legislate for (1) a Mexican guest workers program, (2) laws prohibiting strike activity, and (3) military deferments for pickers (*SPC*, March 3, 1943, 56[235]:1; *SPC*, January 3, 1945, 58[200]:1). All these proposals could potentially affect the farm workers adversely.

The farming associations' lobbying efforts were successful, as their demands converged with the outbreak of World War II. With the nation at war, the growers developed an influential platform from which to pressure the government to meet their demands. Because the government required farmers to increase their food production, the government in turn was pressured to comply with the agricultural associations (Craig 1971). If the government failed to cooperate, the agricultural associations argued, they would not be able to fulfill their production quotas. The guest worker program, in particular, was of major importance to the agricultural associations, since their male labor force was going to be drafted, which would create a labor shortage and make the farmers vulnerable to strike activity. With the American Farm Bureau Federation at the forefront of the lobbying, on August 4, 1942, Agricultural Labor Law No. 45, establishing a temporary workers' program, was signed by President Roosevelt (Craig 1971:24). The purpose of the act was to ensure that the growers would not experience labor shortages. The American Farm Bureau Federation, in league with other agricultural agencies, was also successful in excluding American farm labor from the National Labor Relations Act, the Fair Labor Standards Act, and several unemployment compensation laws. In other words, farm workers were not allowed to unionize and were excluded from minimum wage laws, and child labor was virtually ignored. With the emergence of a strong coalition among the American farmers, union organization became more difficult. In Santa Paula, all union activity ceased for over thirty years (Mines and Anzaldúa 1982).

The impact of Agricultural Labor Law No. 45 was felt throughout the United States as it formally established the "bracero program" and permitted the importation of Mexican workers. These laborers were called "braceros," meaning "imported arms." The braceros were recruited by government agents and were offered employment on American farms for a period of six months (Galarza 1964). Upon the termination of their contracts, the braceros were shipped back to Mexico. However, if they received satisfactory work evaluations, they were allowed to apply for new contracts.

While in the United States, the braceros were either placed at one farm for the duration of their contracts or routed to several farms. Scholars argue that most braceros were placed only at large-scale agribusiness farms and rarely sent to work on the small farms (Galarza 1964; Gonzalez 1985; Hull 1974; Mason 1969). During

World War II, the government rationalized its labor placement policy by contending that braceros had to be located on large farms where massive quantities of crops were being produced for the war effort. Allegedly, it was necessary to place the braceros where they would best benefit the country.

When World War II ended, the routing of braceros to large-scale farms persisted, regardless of the fact that massive quantities of crops were no longer needed for the war effort (Galarza 1964; Gonzalez 1985; Hull 1974; Mason 1969). After the war, the braceros were used for the benefit of the large-scale growers and not for the nation's interest. On the contrary, large-scale growers had switched from producing low-cost vegetables, such as potatoes, sugar beets, citrus, and string beans, to high-profit, labor-intensive crops such as mushrooms, strawberries, and tomatoes. Agricultural lobbyists also demanded that the government continue the bracero program. In response to the lobbying pressures, the government passed Public Law No. 78 in 1951, and the bracero program was extended for an indefinite period.

To this date, the impact of the bracero program on the United States economy and on American labor is debatable. On the one hand, scholars concur that the bracero program benefited the economies of both the United States and Mexico (Craig 1971; Hull 1974; Mines and Anzaldúa 1982). In the United States the bracero program (1) lowered labor costs, which in turn increased the growers' profits, (2) enabled the United States to harvest massive quantities of crops, and (3) lowered the cost of food, thus benefiting consumers. In Mexico, the bracero program reduced unemployment and stimulated local economies through the braceros' wages that they sent home. On the other hand, some scholars argue that the bracero program was devastating to American farm labor. It brought to an almost complete halt farm labor union organization, and it depressed the wages of domestic farm workers (Galarza 1964; Hull 1974; Mason 1969). Because large-scale growers were able to recruit farm labor as needed, domestic farm workers could no longer threaten growers with labor strikes. Without the ability to launch successful strikes, farm workers had no negotiating power and therefore were rarely able to organize labor unions. Farm labor wages were also affected by the bracero program because the government set very low prevailing wages in accordance with the recommendation of agribusiness associations. Government surveys indicate that between 1942 and 1964, when the bracero program was in operation, farm labor wages remained the lowest in the country. In the 1940s, the minimum hourly wage was set at thirty cents an hour, in the 1950s at fifty cents, and in the 1960s at eighty cents (Galarza 1964:152). For example, in the 1950s, a farm worker could earn an annual salary as low as $456 (Galarza 1964:103). On the average most farm workers received a salary of $500 dollars a year. And, in 1967—when the wages of the farm workers increased—the federal government set their minimum wage forty cents below the federal minimum wage (Sosnick 1978:38). It was not until 1984 that the Fair Labor Standards Act of 1938 was applied to farm workers, making most of them eligible to receive the federal minimum wage (Shulman 1986:55).

For the growers the bracero program was profitable, but for the domestic farm workers it served to perpetuate their powerlessness. In the case of Santa Paula, the bracero program had the same effect on domestic labor as it did on the rest of the farm workers in the country. For example, the Santa Paula Agricultural Workers' Union was once again disbanded in 1942, and for thirty subsequent years no other labor union was organized. The union was disbanded because domestic workers could easily be replaced by braceros. Moreover, strikes did not take place during this period. If the farm workers were dissatisfied with their wages or work conditions, their only option was to leave Santa Paula because there were many braceros prepared to fill their jobs.

The Santa Paula bracero program began on November 23, 1943 (*SPC,* November 23, 1943, 57[178]:1, 2), as part of the Ventura County program. An office was established in Santa Paula to manage the program. One of my informants, Jack, who was the manager of the Ventura County Agricultural Association during the bracero program, recalls that most of the braceros sent to Ventura County were placed in Santa Paula. The *Santa Paula Chronicle* corroborates his remembrances. In the last days of November seventeen hundred braceros were brought to Ventura County with the majority of them being sent to Santa Paula (*SPC,* November 23, 1943, 5[178]:1, 2). Most braceros in Santa Paula were employed by Limoneira Ranch, and a few were distributed among the small-scale ranches. The braceros hired by Limoneira Ranch were lodged in small, two-bedroom houses located at the ranch. Braceros hired by other farmers were placed in a provisional labor camp set up on the Mexican East Side. This labor camp eventually was called El Campito (the Little Camp). After World War II ended, the importation of braceros to Santa Paula continued on a regular basis. Jack recalls that during the entire period of the bracero program there were at least a thousand braceros in Santa Paula at all times. His remembrances are confirmed by the *Santa Paula Chronicle.* Newspaper articles indicate that, on the average, two thousand to seventeen hundred braceros were imported to Ventura County, and approximately half of them were located in Santa Paula (*SPC,* June 13, 1946, 60[37]:1, 2; *SPC,* September 6, 1947, 61[109]:1; *SPC,* May 2, 1949, 62[303]:1; *SPC,* May 11, 1951, 65[11]:1; *SPDC,* May 21, 1957, 71[21]:1; *SPDC,* May 31, 1963, 77[28]:1). Moreover, in the aftermath of World War II, Santa Paula growers also began to recruit the braceros' families (Mines and Anzaldúa 1982; Menchaca 1989). For example, in 1946, over one hundred new labor-camp houses were built on Limoneira Ranch to accommodate the expected influx of Mexican families (*SPC,* June 13, 1946, 60[37]:1, 2). Several small-scale citrus growers in Santa Paula also constructed new housing for the families of the braceros in order to keep them at the farms. A *Santa Paula Chronicle* news article illustrates the growers' participation in the recruitment of Mexican families to Ventura County, including Santa Paula. The article provides a summary of a media announcement presented by the Ventura County Citrus Growers Committee. The growers stressed that it was critical for them to recruit the families of the braceros in order to harvest the county's crops. A representative of the VCCGC stated:

> *Unless more housing is provided to care for the needs of agricultural labor in Ventura County, citrus and tomato growers will be facing the coming harvesting season with a critical labor shortage. . . . Every effort is now being sent to provide housing for the needs of imported laboring families. (Cited in SPC, June 13, 1946, 60[37]:1, 2)*

Nationwide, throughout the duration of the bracero program, over five million contract laborers were imported and approximately 20 percent were placed in Ventura County (Galarza 1964:53–54, 80, 89). There are no records, however, as to the number of families who settled in Santa Paula or in other parts of the county. Based on United States census records, however, we can estimate the size of the Mexican national population residing in Santa Paula during the bracero program. Census figures do not include the braceros and refer only to Mexican immigrants and undocumented residents,[4] but the records indicate that in 1940, before the bracero program, there were only 824 Mexican nationals in Santa Paula, and in 1960, toward the end of the program, there were 3,095 Mexican nationals (United States Census Bureau 1942:91, 1963:6–384) (see Table 1 for United States Census Bureau statistics on the number of Santa Paula's residents born in Mexico). Thus, the census data indicate that in Santa Paula the Mexican national population increased dramatically during the bracero program, and newspaper articles suggest that a large number of these people were the families of the braceros.

CITRUS GROWER POLITICS AND THE CLOSURE OF THE BRACERO PROGRAM

By the late 1950s, opposition to the bracero program had grown throughout the United States. Unions, churches, and Mexican American political activists cautioned the United States government about the adverse effects the program had on American labor standards. These pressure

TABLE I   *Mexican-Origin Residents in Santa Paula by Nativity,*
                            1930 to 1980

Decade	Total Residents of Santa Paula	Mexican American Residents Born in the United States	Mexican Residents Born in Mexico
1930s	7,452	3,250	732
1940s	8,986	NA	824
1950s	11,049	NA	1,078
1960s	13,279	NA	3,095
1970s	18,001	5,588	1,740
1980s	20,552	6,753	3,623

NA = not available

Sources: United States Census Bureau 1932:57; United States Census Bureau 1942:83, 91; United States Census Bureau 1952:107; United States Census Bureau 1963:6-384; United States Census Bureau 1973:6-779, 6-836, 6-931; United States Census Bureau 1983a: 6-733, 6-796.

groups argued that it (1) depressed the wages of the American farm worker, (2) obstructed the formation of farm worker unions, and (3) encouraged American businessmen to lobby for the extension of the bracero program to industry as well (Craig 1971; Galarza 1964). On December 31, 1964, the lobbying efforts of groups opposing the bracero program succeeded, and the United States government terminated the program.

In Santa Paula, the growers reluctantly followed the instructions of the government and deported the braceros (*SPC*, January 26, 1965, 78[195]:1). In response to losing their cheapest labor, Santa Paula agricultural associations began to actively recruit their former braceros (Menchaca 1989; Mines and Anzaldúa 1982). In a study of the agricultural industry of Ventura County, scholars Mines and Anzaldúa reported that in several interviews they conducted with Limoneira Ranch management they were informed that many growers in Santa Paula sent representatives to the Mexican villages where their former employees resided in order to offer former braceros and their families employment. Mines and Anzaldúa's same informants also stated that, although recruitment efforts were successful, the labor shortage was not immediately resolved. As a consequence, many Santa Paula growers began to compete for the local farm labor force by improving working conditions in the fields and raising wages. For example, in 1965, Limoneira Ranch practically doubled its wages and offered domestic farm workers $2.15 to $2.45 an hour (Mines and Anzaldúa 1982:33). This was an ambitious effort on the part of the growers to hire local workers after the braceros left. The company also offered housing, expanded benefits to include vacation pay, pension benefits, and health insurance, and provided free picking equipment and transportation to the fields (Mines and Anzaldúa 1982:40).

With the closure of the bracero program in Santa Paula, farmers were no longer protected against strike activity because they would once again need to depend on domestic labor. This potential threat became an incentive to upgrade working conditions in order to avert farm labor union activity. In three interviews that I conducted with Peter, the manager of Limoneira Ranch (1985), he reported that upgrading the working conditions at the ranch was one of the company's main strategies to prevent union activity. Limoneira management reasoned that, if they offered optimal working conditions, their farm workers would not be interested in forming a union. The growers were wrong. Within a few years after the closure of the bracero program, the Mexican labor community of Santa Paula once again began to organize.

Ironically, although in Santa Paula the bracero program obstructed union activity for three decades, the departure of the braceros generated the conditions by which growers could no longer maintain the peonage system. The growers had not prepared themselves to adequately deal with the labor market changes of the braceros' departure. During the bracero program there had been an oversupply of farm labor in Ventura County, and many domestic farm workers had entered other occupations; consequently, when the growers once again needed to hire local labor, the labor pool had dwindled, and they had to compete aggressively for workers (Mines and Anzaldúa 1982). This meant domestic labor had the opportunity to demand better working and housing conditions.

Before discussing the growers' response to changing labor market conditions, we need to examine what transpired in the Mexican community of Santa Paula during the bracero program. This will further describe the Mexican community's efforts to dismantle their subordinate status. Although their attempts to improve employment conditions in the fields came to a halt during this period, other forms of resistance succeeded.

FIVE

*Movements to
Desegregate the
Mexican Community,
the 1940s and 1950s*

At the end of World War II, the soldiers returned home
and were embraced by loved ones and the nation as a whole. Unfortunately, this
endearing welcome was not felt, in many instances, by soldiers of color (Morin
1963; Kibbe 1946).[1] In Santa Paula and in other cities of the Southwest, Mexican-
origin veterans frequently came home to townships where they were treated by
the Anglo Americans as foreigners in their native land. Although they had fought
against the global enforcement of a Nazi philosophy of Aryan superiority and for
the protection of democracy at home, in Santa Paula they continued to be treated
as inferiors and as unworthy to socialize with the Anglo Americans. Mexican
veterans also returned to a community where segregation was the norm. Their
people continued to be residentially segregated on the East Side, and they were
not permitted to rent or buy homes outside the Mexican *barrios*. In the recreational
sphere, such as the movie theater, Mexicans were forced to sit apart from the
Anglo American clientele. In the educational domain, Mexican students continued to be segregated in separate Mexican schools. For the returning World War
II soldiers, little regarding ethnic relations had changed.

Within the labor force, Mexicans also continued to be discriminated against
and were offered only work in farm labor.[2] This overall social atmosphere, full of
inequities, was disconcerting to the Mexican veterans. They were expected to
accept the same jobs and social conditions as before, and they were not given any
social rewards for having fought for U.S. democracy. My informant José recalls
that, when he returned from the war, Limoneira management offered him his old
job, yet he was not given a wage increase. While he and other Mexican soldiers
were gone, domestic workers did not receive any raises (Belknap 1968). The
growers had no reason to increase wages, for the federal government had set the

prevailing farm labor wage at thirty cents an hour (Galarza 1964:152; Teague 1944) and there were many braceros prepared to accept the existing wage.

Not surprisingly, after having fought in the war and proved they were loyal Americans, the Mexican soldiers became intolerant of the peonage system they had left behind. These young men clearly saw the contradictions of serving their country and then coming home to a society that did not treat them as equals. Thus, upon their return to Santa Paula they began to form cultural and civil rights organizations. To the benefit of the larger Mexican community, this resistance movement converged with a significant economic change occurring within the Mexican business sector. As a result of the bracero program, a few Mexicans became economically independent of the citrus growers, and the Mexican business sector was strengthened. This process was triggered by a dynamic tension: the braceros had recreational needs, and the growers were uninterested in providing their workers with leisure activities. Frankly put, the economic base generated by the braceros' consumer needs allowed the Mexican business sector to grow. A ramification of this economic change was the growth of the Mexican middle class and the emergence of an upper class. These privileged Mexicans became intolerant of the segregated society in which they were living and, similar to the Mexican veterans, began to defy their limited social roles. Together, the Mexican businessmen and veterans joined forces and formed organizations to dismantle social segregation in Santa Paula.

This chapter will examine the actions taken by the Mexican community to transform Santa Paula into a less racially segregated society. In particular, it will examine the pivotal roles played by Mexican businessmen and veterans. The focus of this discussion will be on the economic diversification of the Mexican community and the political mobilization that occurred from the 1940s to 1960s. This period coincided with the bracero program.

OPENING OF OPPORTUNITY STRUCTURES: ECONOMIC DIVERSIFICATION WITHIN THE MEXICAN COMMUNITY, THE 1940S AND 1950S

The economic diversification of the Mexican community of Santa Paula was strongly influenced by governmental policies instituted after World War II and during the bracero program. In the case of Mexican veterans, the GI Bill of Rights generated radical changes in 1944 (Morin 1963). For the first time in American history, Mexican veterans became eligible to rights under the GI Bill, thereby qualifying to obtain government loans to start businesses, attend college, or buy homes (Morin 1963). The GI Bill opened economic opportunities that previously had never been available to Mexicans. A concurrent event taking place was the establishment of the bracero program that stimulated the growth of the Mexican consumer market. To serve the braceros' consumer needs Mexicans opened *cantinas* (bars), grocery stores, boardinghouses, barbershops, and cafes. In particular, grand-scale nightclub activity in the *cantinas* became a lucrative source of income for some Mexican businesspeople. The *cantinas* included El Jalisco, La Marimba, Carmelitas, El Chiguagua, El Patio, and El Gato Negro.

Six of my informants, José, Isabel, Linda, Tony, Roney, and Raymundo, recall that World War II and the bracero program generated many events that permanently changed the Mexican community in Santa Paula. Among the most important changes, the Mexican middle-class increased in size, many males left the fields and began working in non-farm occupations, and a small group of Mexican businessmen became very wealthy. Overall, my informants agreed that these changes benefited the Mexican community because people became more outspoken against racial discrimination. They also recall that some Mexicans began changing their ethnic label to "Mexican American" during this period, attributing this change to the Mexican veterans who preferred to call themselves Mexican Americans upon their return. José, who was a World War II veteran, explained that he began to use the label "Mexican American" because his national identity was American and his ancestral culture Mexican. At this time most Mexicans, however, still preferred to call themselves "Mexicans" or "Mejicanos."

According to my informants, the Mexican business strip boomed in Santa Paula and its atmosphere radically changed within a year after the bracero program started. Before the appearance of the braceros, the weekends were quiet and very few people visited the Mexican business zone. There was little reason to visit this area because it had only one cafe, two grocery stores, and a cantina. Once the braceros settled in Santa Paula, Mexican entrepreneurs began opening more businesses. By the mid-1940s, there were at least six *cantinas,* three grocery stores, one bakery, two cafes, and three boardinghouses. The town's newspaper corroborates my informants' remembrances, as an article in the *Santa Paula Chronicle* describes how the Mexican business sector became an entertainment center during the bracero period. In particular, one article vividly describes how on Saturdays and Sundays over two thousand braceros "partied" in the local *cantinas.* A reporter of the *Santa Paula Chronicle* wrote:

> *Supervised recreational facilities are badly needed for the*
> *2,000 Mexican nationals brought here to pick citrus each*

> *season, the City Council was told last night during a*
> *discussion of the proposed $500 dancing fee for night spots*
> *serving liquor in Santa Paula. . . . "They're only*
> *human," the council was told by Albert [Hap] Sonora.*
> *. . . "They have good housing, good food and jobs which*
> *keep them busy five days a week. But what about*
> *Saturday and Sunday? They're turned loose on the town,*
> *just like GI's from a near-by Army camp. . . . They head*
> *for Santa Paula's night spots." (SPDC, May 21, 1957,*
> *71[21]:1)*

Although the Mexican business sector grew, its shops were confined to the East Side. Mexican businessmen were allowed to open shops on Main Street where the Anglo American businesses were also located, but Main Street was divided into the Mexican and Anglo American sections. Tenth Street intersected Main Street and served as the dividing business ethnic border, and Mexicans were permitted to buy or rent property only on the east side of Tenth Street. Santa Paula property tax assessment records (from 1928 to 1957) corroborate my informants' memories. These records indicate that in the 1940s and 1950s all the Mexican businesses were confined to the east side of Tenth.

Throughout the 1940s and 1950s, the continuous flow of braceros to Santa Paula stimulated the local Mexican consumer market and sales boomed. At first, during the 1940s, the main types of businesses that opened were drinking, food, and boarding establishments. By the early 1950s, however, Mexican businessmen were able to open large grocery stores where the braceros purchased food, clothes, and household goods. Luxury items, such as radios, bicycles, and toys were also sold. Before then the grocery stores had stocked only essential items. Tony also recalled that the more successful Mexicans, including himself, were able to open small department stores. They did so by obtaining loans from wealthy Mexican businessmen. His father, Daniel Guzman,[3] who was a millionaire by the mid-1940s, was one of the men who extended loans to several Mexicans. According to Tony, Daniel knew that lending money was a risky investment, but he wanted to help his community prosper. For example, Daniel gave Tony a loan to open a radio and television shop during a time when very few Mexicans were able to afford these luxuries. Tony's father felt, however, that it was important for a Mexican to sell luxury items. Although at first Tony was able to sell only a few televisions, later he made a small fortune selling radios and bicycles to braceros and other townspeople. To Tony and other businessmen, the profits from the stores allowed them to save money, buy homes, and live comfortably. Tony recalls how successful his business was during the bracero program. He stated:

Overall, the bracero program was good for Santa Paula.
The growers got their cheap labor and Mexican business-
men profited. Sales were booming. Several Chicanos
[Mexican Americans] made fortunes during this period.
My father was a millionaire by the early 40s, and I made
a fortune selling radios and televisions to the braceros. . . .
I bought my home during that period. . . . Some native-
born families moved north to Virginia Terrace. . . . That
shows how the bracero program benefited a few families.
Many people opened businesses during that period.

Ten of my informants who knew Daniel corroborate Tony's remembrances. They recall that Daniel was one of the wealthiest Mexicans in Santa Paula. Within the city he owned several parcels of land, apartment buildings, a grocery store, and a radio station. He is also remembered as a political activist. I will shortly return to this topic.

Mexican businessmen were also able to open shops by establishing business partnerships with Anglo Americans. In many cases when Mexican businessmen first started, they had to negotiate consignment contracts with Anglo American merchants because they were unable to fully stock their stores alone. These consignment agreements also benefited the Anglo American merchants. Since Santa Paula was a racially segregated society, braceros were not welcomed in the Anglo American stores. Anglo American merchants, therefore, were able to sell products to the braceros by leaving merchandise in the Mexican stores. If the goods sold, the profits were shared between the business partners. Organized prostitution also appears to have been a joint business affair between Mexican and Anglo American businessmen. Who the owners of this illegal activity were, however, is uncertain. According to Roney and Isabel, on a regular basis and on payday prostitutes from outside of Santa Paula came to the labor camps. Some of the prostitutes stayed in the labor camps while others visited the Mexican *cantinas*. Tony corroborated Roney and Isabel's remembrances and added that, although prostitution in the labor camps was not known to be a major source of income for the businesspeople, it nevertheless did occur. Tony also believed that in the mid-1940s his father was involved in this business venture. He recalled that Daniel held several meetings in which prostitution was discussed. Anglo Americans often attended these meetings. The occurrence of prostitution in Santa Paula labor camps is corroborated by a newspaper article in the *Santa Paula Chronicle*. Apparently, the police broke a prostitution ring that was organized by Anglo Americans. The local newspaper reported the criminal arrest of two Anglo Americans suspected of running the ring. A reporter wrote:

> *Roy Lee Smith and Billy Louis Smith, brothers charged*
> *with the transporting of a 15-year-old Rancho Sespe girl*
> *against her will to Ventura County citrus camps for*
> *purpose of prostitution, were heard by Judge Glenn D.*
> *Corey. . . . Both Roy, of Santa Paula, and Billy, of*
> *Fillmore, are held on $10,000 bail each. Billy's wife, Mary*
> *Lou, 18, is suspected of being an accomplice in the crime.*
> *(SPC, March 16, 1951, 64[260]:1)*

Other forms of illegal businesses did not flourish, apparently, during the bracero program. The occasional trafficking of marijuana appears to have been the only other type of criminal activity involving Mexicans in Santa Paula (*SPC*, October 8, 1929, 7[8]:1; *SPC*, July 19, 1932, 9[225]:1; *SPC*, December 14, 1938, 52[192]:1; *SPC*, August 5, 1943, 57[86]:1, 2; *SPC*, December 7, 1950, 64[194]:1; *SPDC*, November 1, 1963, 77[136]:1). However, my informants recall, and the *Santa Paula Chronicle* indicates, that selling marijuana was not a popular business there.

The economic changes in the Mexican community also appear to be related to non-commercial sources. José, Isabel, Linda, Tony, Roney, and Raymundo proposed that the economic diversification of the Mexican community should not be attributed solely to the growth of the business sector. When the Mexican veterans returned home, they triggered many social and economic changes. They, like the Mexican businesspeople, were able to promote reform because they no longer had to work in farm labor, since the GI Bill gave them the opportunities either to start a business or to return to school.[4] Several articles appearing in the *Santa Paula Chronicle* corroborate my informants' recollections and indicate that the veterans refused to work in farm labor (*SPC*, June 13, 1946, 60[37]:1, 2; *SPC*, September 6, 1947, 61[109]:1; *SPC*, May 7, 1948, 62[7]:1). One such article reported:

> *"Local labor is not interested in returning to agricultural*
> *work after having had a taste of other types of work during*
> *the war years," Hovley said. . . . The labor shortage*
> *throughout southern California is equally dire, Hovley*
> *said, with Orange county facing loss of the entire crop*
> *because of the scarcity [sic]. (SPC, June 13, 1946,*
> *60[37]:1, 2)*

A second article in the *Santa Paula Chronicle* commented that former agricultural workers were unwilling to return to the fields because they had entered other occupations after the war. The article noted that this was apparently a common pattern throughout the Southwest.

> *Local Growers to Be Helped by Importation of Workers.*
> *. . . A local citrus official said today the lemon houses*
> *could use some more pickers in the field, but it is primarily*
> *the orange crop which is desperate for pickers. He explained*
> *that the shortage of workers in the county is due to the fact*
> *that right now is the big harvest season not only for citrus*
> *crops but for many other agricultural products. Many*
> *former agricultural workers went into other lines of business*
> *during the war and have not returned, he said. . . . Ellis*
> *Coman, manager of the agricultural producers labor*
> *committee, explained, . . . "We have tried to recruit*
> *workers in the San Joaquin valley, Sacramento, New*
> *Mexico, and Texas, but the available supply is just not*
> *adequate to do the job. We have to save the crop and we*
> *wish we could do it." (SPC, May 7, 1948, 62[7]:1)*

In *Among the Valiant*, Morin (1963) identified a similar statewide labor pattern in California. After conducting oral history interviews with Mexican American veterans who participated in World War II or in the Korean War, Morin identified a common pattern among the respondents. Veterans stated that when they returned home they sought non-farm occupations after the war. Some of them also responded that the GI Bill allowed them to obtain government loans to attend college or trade school or to open a business.

José recalls that the GI Bill helped many veterans in Santa Paula finance their education in either technical school or college. For example, José's brother used the GI Bill to fund his entire college education, including law school. A few veterans also decided to use the GI Bill to obtain business loans. José, for example, decided to open a shoe repair shop. José stated:

> *When the GI veteran returned, he didn't want to work in*
> *the fields anymore. In the war they got exposed to different*
> *things, and they preferred to work in non-agricultural jobs.*
> *. . . After the war we had the GI Bill of Rights. A lot of*
> *us went to school. It was the biggest stepping stone that*
> *came our way. A lot of my friends after WW II took*
> *advantage of it. That's when we got the first level of*
> *professionals, such as my brother who became an attorney.*
> *. . . People who moved up did not lose their connections.*

Other institutional processes also gave Mexican American veterans the opportunity to move out of farm labor. At the end of World War II, the government opened eleven thousand civilian jobs in Port Hueneme and in Point Mugu (Triem 1985). These two military bases were located within twenty-five miles of Santa Paula and employed many Mexican American veterans. Linda recalled that her brother, Leon, and other local veterans were among the first Mexican Americans from Santa Paula who worked at the military bases. Linda stated:

> *Most Mexican boys went to war. Very few boys were left.*
> *. . . When they returned, they didn't have to work in the*
> *fields. They didn't want to do hard labor. They couldn't*
> *get a good job. The government supplemented their wages.*
> *Most boys went to school or got training. . . . My brother*
> *became a radio technician. . . . Our service boys didn't*
> *want to do hard work. The bases opened up, and for the*
> *first time a lot of our boys worked in [Port] Hueneme and*
> *Point Mugu.*

Thus, employment at nearby military bases and the availability of educational grants gave Mexican American veterans the opportunity to enter non-farm occupations. It also appears that the higher wages received in occupations such as television and radio repair, auto mechanics, trucking, carpentry, electrical work, barbering, and technical jobs at military bases allowed them to improve their economic position. Santa Paula property tax assessment records support this analysis, as a substantial number of Mexicans experienced economic mobility during the late 1940s to mid-1950s. By 1957, there were 646 people of Mexican descent who owned land on the East Side. This figure constituted 11 percent of the total Mexican community. In contrast, in 1938, a few years before World War II started, only 453 people owned property. There appears to have been a 43-percent increase in property ownership between 1938 to 1957. Also, in 1957, of the total number of property owners, ten people owned more than six parcels, indicating that an elite of small land owners had emerged in Santa Paula.

In summary, economic changes in Santa Paula generated the conditions that allowed people of Mexican descent to become independent of the citrus growers. Once this occurred, many members of the Mexican community were able to aggressively challenge racial discrimination in Santa Paula, and in particular social segregation.

CULTURAL AND CIVIL RIGHTS ORGANIZATIONS: A STRUGGLE TO FIGHT ANGLO AMERICAN DISCRIMINATION

On August 26, 1946, Mexican businessmen, Mexican American veterans, and other Mexican community men and women gathered in a town meeting to discuss the formation of a civic club that would address the social and racial problems that they experienced (Casa del Mexicano minutes, August 26, 1946). That evening, Daniel Guzman, Tony's father, announced to the audience that he had been attending civic meetings in Los Angeles where the Mexican Consulate recommended that a statewide Mexican network be established. The purpose of the network would be to promote cultural pride and to watch over the civil rights of Mexican people. Later, Daniel introduced a representative from the Mexican Consulate, who later asked the audience to establish La Casa del Mexicano. The consulate representative informed the participants that the Mexican government would assist the community in filing papers of incorporation and linking their Casa del Mexicano to other chapters statewide. The audience unanimously accepted the proposal and proceeded to elect a president and board members and to organize several committees. Daniel was nominated to be president, but he declined and instead accepted a position as a board member.[5] At the meeting, the first order of business was to raise funds for La Casa del Mexicano. The funds were to be used toward the construction of a building that would serve as their meeting place and as a cultural center where poetry readings, dances, and celebrations were to be held. Raymundo, who attended the first meeting, recalls how the idea of raising funds for the construction of La Casa del Mexicano began. He recalls that Daniel introduced the idea. Raymundo warmly remembered:

> *In the forties Mexicans used to celebrate the fiestas*
> *Mexicanas. We used to rent the park in front of the police*
> *station. . . . Immigrants and Mexicans born in the United*
> *States used to organize the fiestas, and the braceros would*
> *join us in our celebrations. Several men decided that instead*
> *of renting the park we should build a Casa del Mexicano to*
> *hold our reunions. [Daniel Guzman] and some other men*
> *got the idea from Mexicans in Los Angeles and Sacramento,*
> *where Casas del Mexicano were started with the help of the*
> *Mexican Consulate. . . . The Casa was built by twelve*

> *men who were construction workers, plumbers, businessmen,*
> *and carpenters. . . . The braceros were supposed to donate*
> *one day of labor, but the majority refused. Instead some of*
> *them donated money. . . . On the day of the inauguration*
> *of La Casa, over two thousand people attended.*

Apparently, the construction of a building was a major accomplishment for the Mexican community. In the past, if community members wanted to celebrate a public event, they needed to rent space from the city council. Unfortunately, their permits were often denied, and when they did acquire one, the city council typically allowed them to celebrate their fiestas only in the park located in front of the police station. In this way, the police would be able to keep an eye on them.

Raymundo also recalled that La Casa members, besides promoting cultural pride through their events, decided to organize a mutual aid committee. Raymundo's account of La Casa's philosophy was as follows:

> El objeto de la beneficencia Mexicana será auxiliar
> en forma y medios que los juezgue conveniente a los
> Mexicanos *[The purpose of the organization is to serve in*
> *any form our Mexican community]. . . . The first*
> *committees in the Casa were the* club de damas, club
> patriótico, *and the* comité de beneficencias *[ladies'*
> *club, patriotic club, and the mutual aid committee]. The*
> *fiestas were used to promote our Mexican culture. Someone*
> *read poetry, others presented skits, and others danced*
> bailes Mexicanos *[Mexican dances]. We also used to*
> *raise money for families who were poor.*

La Casa del Mexicano therefore served to strengthen the Mexican community's ethnic identity and to generate cultural bonds. The members' philosophy was to reinforce ethnic group unity and to assist those in financial distress.

Within a few years of the founding of La Casa del Mexicano, new organizations took root and branched out. Individuals who were interested in politics formed local chapters of the Alianza Hispana Americana, a statewide civil rights organization, and founded local organizations such as the Latin American Civic Club and the Latin American Veterans Association. Members of the Mexican community also became more assertive and demanded to hold their ethnic celebrations in public. In 1949, they obtained a permit to hold a parade in celebration of Mexico's independence. The *Santa Paula Chronicle* recorded this event.

*The parade consisted of floats and marching groups in
observance of Mexico's freedom from Spain 139 years ago.
Many citizens of Mexican descent turned out last night for
a program at La Casa del Mexicano on South Eleventh
street between Ventura and Harvard. A dance is slated for
tonight at 8:00 and will last until midnight. (SPC,
September 16, 1949, 63[113]:1)*

Gone were the days when the Mexican community was intimidated and
prevented from publicly celebrating their ethnic traditions. By taking their
celebrations to the streets, they sent a clear message to the Anglo American
community, showing them that their Mexican culture was also a source of pride.
Thus, the celebration of Mexican holidays served to reinforce their ethnic bonds
and reminded Anglo Americans that the public suppression of Mexican culture
would no longer be tolerated. To some readers, it may appear that these events
were insignificant. However, in a community such as Santa Paula, where
Mexicans were treated as inferiors and often ridiculed, the public celebration of
their culture was indeed a milestone. We need to remember that before then it
was unacceptable for Mexicans to display their culture in public and that only a
few years before the *Santa Paula Chronicle* referred to Mexicans as "wetbacks,"
"dogs," "cowards," "criminals," and "treacherous people."

By the late 1940s, the Santa Paula Anglo American community was becoming
more tolerant of the Mexican residents and began to recognize the contributions
of some of these citizens. For example, the *Santa Paula Chronicle* stopped using
derogatory labels when it referred to Mexicans. Moreover, it occasionally started
to include news articles about activities sponsored by the local Mexican American
veterans and even began to identify the prominent Mexican citizens of Santa Paula
(*SPC*, February 21, 1947, 60[247]:1; *SPC*, July 14, 1948, 63[63]:1; *SPC*,
September 21, 1950, 64[119]:1). In particular, news articles appeared about the
Mexican upper class. On one occasion, the *Santa Paula Chronicle* printed an article
about a party and community celebration sponsored by Daniel Guzman, the
owner of El Gusto restaurant. Daniel invited Pedro J. Gonzales, a famous civil
rights activist and singer, to perform at his radio station (KSPA). After performing
for the Mexican community, Pedro was scheduled to entertain people in an
exclusive party. The *Santa Paula Chronicle* reported this event.

*One of the most popular announcers, singers and composers
from south of the border visited . . . yesterday for the first
time in 15 years—and was nearly mobbed when he
appeared over station KSPA. . . . His name is Pedro J.*

> *Gonzales, whose group of recording artists known as "Los*
> *Madrugadores" has appeared in many western films. . . .*
> *He toured the city with an old friend, [Daniel Guzman]*
> *owner of [El Gusto]. . . . Gonzales was the first Spanish-*
> *descended radio announcer in California many years ago.*
> *Now between 55 and 60 years of age, he composed many*
> *of his best-known Mexican ballads while in prison. . . .*
> *Just prior to his appearance on KSPA last night, the singer*
> *was an honored guest at a dinner. . . . This morning he*
> *was a breakfast guest at the home of Mr. and [Mrs.*
> *Faustino Luera] of Santa Paula. (SPC, September 21,*
> *1950, 64[103]:1)*

In addition to Daniel Guzman, Henry Villa, Jr., and Martin Morales were considered by many Anglo Americans to be prominent Mexican citizens.[6] These wealthy men owned property and several businesses in Santa Paula and in other cities. One news article praised Mr. Villa's civic activism and commented that he was a distinguished and wealthy person. Mr. Villa apparently owned two construction companies and four ranches near Los Angeles. He was also commended for donating time and money to improve Santa Paula's streets and drainage system. A *Santa Paula Chronicle* reporter wrote:

> *[Villa's] business career is closely linked to the development*
> *of Santa Paula. Through both of his companies he*
> *participated in many civic development projects involving*
> *street and drainage improvement. . . . Today [Villa] owns*
> *citrus property in Fairview Valley near Moorpark, and has*
> *two ranches in the Santa Clara Valley, one about three*
> *miles east of Santa Paula and the other in the Sespe*
> *district west of Fillmore. On the latter property [Villa]*
> *settled with his family in 1941, where he makes his*
> *residence now. (SPC, February 21, 1947, 60[247]:1)*

Although Villa was a prominent Santa Paula resident, he did not live in the Anglo American upper-class residential zone; he also did not live on the Mexican East Side. Villa constructed a home on the outskirts of Santa Paula, apart from all the residential neighborhoods. Like Villa, Martin Morales was a respected and wealthy citizen. He owned over twelve parcels of property in Santa Paula and a tortilla factory ("Assessment Roll, City of Santa Paula, 1953–1957"). However, unlike Villa, Morales was considered to be a troublemaker. For example, Morales defied two of Santa Paula's sacred "rules" of interethnic social comportment. He ran for mayor of Santa Paula twice, and he repeatedly tried to buy property in the Anglo American residential zones. For Mexicans to run for political office and to purchase property in Anglo American neighborhoods was in essence to break social taboos, to violate the political and social boundaries imposed by members of the Anglo American community. Morales' political activism in Santa Paula takes us to the period when Mexican businessmen and Mexican American veterans attempted to desegregate the town's city politics. Morales launched the first attack, and the Mexican community fervently continued his defiant stance.

CITY COUNCIL POLITICS
AND THE EXCLUSION OF
MEXICAN-ORIGIN PEOPLE

In Santa Paula, the citrus growers have traditionally controlled the city council, and the at-large district electoral system has obstructed the election of Mexican candidates. Therefore, before I describe the first activities of the Mexican community against unfair political practices, I need to explain why these two factors have historically prevented this community from obtaining equitable representation within the city council. This section is important, as it will illustrate the procedures used by Anglo Americans to exclude Mexicans from city council politics.

Belknap (1968), a former resident of Santa Paula and currently a historian, wrote an account of the political power held by Santa Paula's citrus growers from the 1870s to 1964. His analysis of city council politics elucidates why the local government has favored the interests of the growers and helped them to maintain Mexicans in a peonage position. Focusing exclusively on interviews with Anglo Americans (in particular with the founding families) and on historical records, Belknap observes that, since the founding of Santa Paula, the growers have dominated the city council. For the growers, controlling the city council has been one of their most effective methods to protect their interests. Belknap comments:

> During the first seventy years of Santa Paula's history,
> then, not only did citrus come to dominate the town's
> economy, but the families who owed their wealth to citrus
> came to dominate its political and social life. . . . Many
> ranchers played active and important roles in city and
> school district government. The first man to serve as mayor
> of Santa Paula was Louis A. Hardison. Perhaps the best

> *known of all of Santa Paula's mayors was M. L. Steckel,*
> *another rancher. He was followed in office by William L.*
> *Ramsey, a leading figure in the co-operative movement.*
> *Ramsey not only served as mayor for eight years, but also*
> *spent an additional nine years on the city council. . . . A*
> *prominent member of the city council in the years following*
> *the war was Nathan W. Blanchard III. As recently as*
> *1958 another rancher, Ernest Richardson, was serving as*
> *mayor. Since 1954 the Congressional district has been*
> *represented by Charles McKevett Teague, a son of the*
> *citrus pioneer. (Belknap 1968:128–131)*

As outlined by Belknap, starting with the first mayor of Santa Paula and continuing until 1958, all mayors were leading citrus growers and controlled city politics. Belknap also notes that, since 1954, Santa Paula citrus growers have been able to protect their agricultural interests within congressional politics. Charles M. Teague, the son of the founder of Limoneira Ranch, served as the district's congressman from 1954 until his death in 1969.

Belknap further writes that, because the city council has traditionally been dominated by the citrus growers, Santa Paula's merchants and the Mexican community have been adversely affected:

> *Though the domination of the local economy by a few big*
> *ranchers and the absence of industry saved Santa Paula*
> *from the horrors of the Great Depression, these factors were*
> *the cause of an increasing dissatisfaction among the*
> *merchants of the town. . . . Even as late as 1962 . . .*
> *many of them [merchants] were convinced that ranchers on*
> *the city council were working to keep industry out of Santa*
> *Paula. . . . In addition, the lemon farmers required their*
> *workers to buy through company stores. Workers' bills*
> *were deducted from their wages, and failure to make an*
> *adequate number of purchases from the ranch store could*
> *result in the loss of a job. (Belknap 1968:125, 126)*

According to Belknap, city council members repeatedly voted against the introduction of any type of industry to Santa Paula because it would threaten the growers' control over Mexican labor. In other words, Anglo American merchants and other town people favored the introduction of light industry to the area, the goal being to diversify the Mexican labor force so that better-paid workers would help stimulate the merchant economy. The citrus growers, on the other hand, were against the introduction of industry for the simple reason that they would have to compete for the local labor force. Hypothetically, if light industry was introduced, the growers would have to raise farm wages to maintain their work force. This obviously threatened the growers' cheap labor pool. Belknap states:

> Since the merchants could do little business with either farmers or farm workers, they naturally came to hope that industrial concerns might locate in Santa Paula. The advent of industry would produce an expansion in the nonfarm population, and hence an increase in the number of their customers. No industry, however, came to Santa Paula. For this the merchants blamed the ranchers. . . . The ranchers were motivated, these businessmen assumed, by a desire to keep down farm wages. The big citrus companies, they believed, feared industry because manufacturing plants would enter the local labor market and bid up the price of workers. The citrus growers had given the merchants good cause to suspect them, for throughout the history of Santa Paula they had consistently and successfully worked to keep agricultural wages low. (Belknap 1968:125–127)

Concurring with Belknap's analysis of city council politics, Jesus Ornelas, in an unpublished paper (1984) on Santa Paula's voting patterns, adds that the growers had been able to maintain control of the city's politics by discouraging the Mexican community to participate. Jesus Ornelas is a second-generation resident of Santa Paula. He is also a political activist and manager of the Cabrillo Farm Worker Housing Cooperative. According to Ornelas, in the 1940s, Mexican Americans and immigrants had persistently constituted approximately 40 percent of Santa Paula's population. However, a history of political and economic repression subtly forbade Mexican Americans from participating in elections. Mexican Americans were not apathetic toward voting or running for office. Rather, their lack of involvement was an expression of their perceived reality. They knew their entrance into politics was not allowed by the status quo and that if they participated they would be punished. Ornelas explained it this way:

> While the profits of the citrus industry continued to increase in the 1940s the economic status of the Mexican worker remained at its low level. The growers were determined to

> *keep this relationship stabilized. . . . The Chicano*
> *population of Santa Paula had experienced a form of*
> *displacement. The traditional Chicano laborer was unable*
> *to establish a firm economic base in the city because of his*
> *exploitation as a "cheap labor" force for the citrus industry.*
> *. . . The American obsession with race has indeed had a*
> *powerful influence on the Chicano people. . . . One of the*
> *effects of the majority's racial ideologies has been the social,*
> *political and economic suppression of Chicanos. Politics has*
> *been one of the main arenas of competition in which*
> *Chicanos have long been unable to act with maximum*
> *effectiveness. This failure, often attributed to political*
> *apathy, in fact seems to reflect clear knowledge of Anglo*
> *institutional repression. Apathy implies a choice not to act*
> *while knowing that action is possible. . . . Chicanos did*
> *not vote, not because voting was an Anglo thing, but*
> *because Anglos forbade Chicano involvement at the polls.*
> *American society imposed clear restrictions based on law*
> *and custom. . . . The political socialization of a minority*
> *group is retarded when the host society is perceived to be, or*
> *is indeed, hostile. (Ornelas 1984:6–8)*

Further, the Mexican community's ongoing lack of political power has traditionally been exacerbated by the institutionalization of the at-large district electoral system, an unfair political practice that guarantees Anglo American candidates' success at the election polls. In Santa Paula, as in many farm communities in the United States, for generations it has been common for at-large district elections to be used to make the Mexican American vote ineffective (Takash-Cruz 1990). In the absence of more democratic electoral practices—such as single-member district elections—the Mexican American vote has traditionally been fragmented and weakened. Let me illustrate these two different political scenarios, the at-large and the single-member district electoral systems. In a community where an at-large district election is held, candidates who receive the highest number of votes are elected to city council. The problem with this system is that there is no assurance that all the residential districts of a city will be represented. In contrast, a single-member district election ensures that the different districts of a city are equitably represented. Within this electoral process, a person who runs for office must reside in the district for which she or he ran. This system guarantees that the entire city council will not be elected by one side of town or by one constituency because every district in a community will have the opportunity to elect a representative. Also, in a single-member district election, the gerrymandering of racial minority communities into separate voting districts is prohibited (Takash-Cruz 1990).

In Santa Paula, Mexicans began running for public office on March 14, 1941, but the at-large district electoral system worked against them. That year, for the first time in Santa Paula's history, a Mexican, Martin Morales, challenged the political structure and ran for city council (*SPC,* March 14, 1941, 55[256]:1). Suffice it to say that Morales received the least number of votes and came in last. Morales ran for office again in 1956. This time he received a larger number of votes, yet they were insufficient to elect him to city council (see Minute Book 1953, Letter K, pp. 260–261, in City of Santa Paula 1914–1989). Simply put, if Santa Paula had held a single-member district election, the Mexican East Side would have been better represented because part of the city council would have had to be elected from that area. Several of the city council persons, if not half of them, would have resided on the East Side because historically approximately 40 to 50 percent of Santa Paula's population has lived in that area.

The election of Anglo American candidates through the at-large system has also been historically facilitated by the fact that, although the Mexican community has traditionally constituted close to half of Santa Paula's total residents, a large number of these people are Mexican nationals and are not eligible to vote.[7] In contrast, most Anglo Americans are eligible to vote, and their voting constituency is larger than that of the Mexican-origin population, therefore ensuring that their preferred candidates will be elected.

CHALLENGING ANGLO AMERICAN CITY POLITICS: EARLY MEXICAN AMERICAN SUCCESSES

In spite of the city council's persistent practice of implementing unfair political policies in Santa Paula, the Mexican community continued to try to make the council responsive toward their needs. Morales' political defeats were not wasted. He was a naturalized Mexican immigrant who was economically successful, and he constantly challenged the Anglo Americans. Morales became a role model in the community. My informant Linda recalls that Morales was not intimidated by the Anglo Americans because he was wealthier than most of them. He was the first Mexican to run for political office, and he even had the audacity to challenge residential segregation by persisting in attempts to buy the home of an Anglo American. Therefore, Morales' political candidacies are today remembered as challenges to the Anglo American political structure, rather than as defeats. In short, he was admired for his defiance of social conventions. He encouraged others to voice their concerns against unjust political practices and racial discrimination.

One such occasion took place on May 21, 1957, when the city council unjustly attempted to levy a discriminatory racial tax against Mexican businessmen. The city council planned to place an annual tax of five hundred dollars on any business that sold liquor or provided dancing facilities to the braceros. This tax was directed against the Mexican businessmen because Anglo American businessmen did not provide recreational services to braceros. Essentially, this was a Mexican *cantina* tax. As usual, the city council thought that they would be able to treat the Mexican community disrespectfully and impose a discriminatory tax. To their surprise, however, Mexicans responded angrily and launched a protest. Political activists took it upon themselves to represent the social needs of the braceros and the economic interests of the Mexican businessmen. In a city council meeting, Hap Sonora, a Mexican American veteran, took the role of spokesman. Sonora argued that the tax was unfair and that, furthermore, the policy exposed the hypocrisy and racism of the city council. He concurred with the city council that the braceros needed supervised recreational activities and that perhaps levying a tax to pay for increased police surveillance might be useful. However, Sonora demanded that the tax burden be placed on the growers and not the businesses because the growers were responsible for importing the braceros to Santa Paula. Sonora argued that, since the bracero program had begun in Santa Paula, the burden of providing the workers with recreational activities had fallen solely to the Mexican community. He noted that two thousand braceros would visit the *barrios* on Saturdays and Sundays, searching for leisure activities. Sonora did not blame them because they needed some type of entertainment. However, he stated that it was the growers' responsibility—not the Mexican community's—to entertain the braceros. Sonora eloquently defended the Mexican community by presenting indisputable facts. A Santa Paula reporter captured this event in a news article:

> *Supervised recreation facilities are badly needed for the 2,000 Mexican nationals brought here to pick citrus each season, the City Council was told last night during a discussion of the proposed $500 dancing fee for night spots serving liquor in Santa Paula. "They're only human," the council was told by [Hap] Sonora, who himself was a candidate for the City Council several years back. "They have good housing, good food and jobs which keep them busy five days a week. But what about Saturday and*

> *Sunday? They're turned loose on the town, just like GI's*
> *from a near-by Army camp.*
>   *Nobody makes any arrangements for their leisure*
> *time—not the citrus ranchers nor the city. They let the bars*
> *worry about them. They head for Santa Paula's night*
> *spots, and naturally some of them get into trouble.*
>   *What we need is an ordinance saying, if you bring 500*
> *Mexican nationals into Santa Paula, you'll have to foot*
> *the bill for more policemen to ride herd on them. Either*
> *that or some sort of supervised recreation, similar to the*
> *USO in wartime camp towns. (SPDC, May 21, 1957,*
> *71[21]:1)*

Sonora's forceful statement showed concern for the entire Mexican community, including the braceros who, he said, should be provided recreational activities. Furthermore, for their safety and the safety of others, these men should not be turned loose after a night of partying. More important, following in the footsteps of activist Martin Morales, Sonora stood up to the city council and demanded an end to unfair political practices. He also demonstrated to the Anglo American city council that the Mexican community was prepared to fight them on this issue. Thus, for the first time in Santa Paula's history the city council backed down, and the Mexican community won the fight. The city council decided to rescind the entire tax proposal.

One year after the infamous *cantina* tax battle, thirty Mexican American political activists launched a civic campaign to elect Mexican Americans to city council. The organization was called the Latin American Civic Organization (LACO), and its leadership was composed primarily of Mexican American veterans.[8] Hap Sonora was elected president of LACO. In the constitution the organization listed as its main objective to improve and defend the civil rights of the Mexican American community by exercising the right to vote. The *Santa Paula Daily Chronicle* summarized this event:

> *About 30 members of the newly organized Latin American*
> *Civic Organization of Santa Paula met last night to hear*
> *the first reading of their constitution and talks by several*
> *candidates for city and county posts. . . . The constitution,*
> *which received tentative approval, was read to the member-*
> *ship by Secretary Treasurer [Henry Villa, Jr.]. . . .*
> *Objectives listed . . . [include] to improve the social,*

> *educational, economic and spiritual conditions of Mexican*
> *Americans residing in the United States of America*
> *through an active participation in local affairs by exercising*
> *the right to vote. (SPDC, April 2, 1958, 71[245]:1)*

Interestingly, this news article also suggests that some of the Mexican-origin residents were changing their ethnic label to "Mexican American" and to "Latin American." This change is communicated in the name of their organization and in the language they used to draft its constitution. In the constitution, they refer to the Mexican-origin community as "Mexican American," and in the title of the organization they use the term "Latin American" rather than "Mexican."

In that evening of 1958, LACO nominated three Mexican American candidates to run for office. Richard Mena ran on an economic development platform. He addressed a concern held by many Mexican and Anglo American merchants: the need to introduce light industry into Santa Paula. Hap Sonora and Jack Lopez ran on controversial platforms. They addressed Mexican community issues, long neglected by the city government, that could easily be interpreted by Anglo Americans to be radical minority politics. Sonora pushed for urban renewal in the Mexican neighborhoods, and Lopez for a playground in the *barrios*. What follows summarizes the candidates' platforms.

> *At intervals during the meeting, four different candidates in*
> *coming city and county elections were asked by President*
> *Hap Sonora to express their platforms before the member-*
> *ship. . . . Richard Mena . . . said his platform "is simple*
> *sound progressive city government. I'd like to see some*
> *light industry in Santa Paula." . . . Sonora said, "I'd*
> *rather see the money spent down below Harvard where*
> *they don't have any sidewalks and drains. They have to*
> *break out boats down there every time it rains," he said.*
> *Jack Lopez, former Santa Paula police officer, . . . cited a*
> *need for playground facilities to keep children off the streets*
> *at night. "Oxnard and Ventura have playgrounds, why*
> *can't we?" (SPDC, April 2, 1958, 71[245]:1, 3)*

Following the endorsement of candidates and a campaign to get out the Mexican vote, LACO succeeded in electing one of its candidates to the city council. Richard Mena, the candidate who did not run on an ethnic interest group platform, was elected to office (Minute Book 1958, Letter L, p. 262, in City of

Santa Paula 1914–1989). Apparently, his platform for broader economic development was attractive to a wider constituency. For the first time in Santa Paula's history a person of Mexican descent was elected to the city council.

Although Mena became a city councilman, Santa Paula's interethnic politics remained the same. The voice of one Mexican American elected official lacked the power to change local government attitudes and policies. That is, in the Mexican *barrios* the status quo continued. No parks or recreational facilities were constructed, street drainage continued to be a major source of flooding during the rainy season, streets remained unpaved or in need of repair, and school segregation continued. At this time, Mexicans could not change the local political process because the at-large district electoral system was entrenched. Thus, for the Mexican community to gain representation in proportion to its population size was nearly impossible. The continued political underrepresentation of the Mexican-origin community was the outcome of this process. Its worst repercussion was the unbalanced funding of urban renewal projects on the East Side. City council budgetary allocations were a priority only in the Anglo American neighborhoods, to the extent that the East Side was practically abandoned.

Notwithstanding the neglect of the Mexican community by the Anglo American power structure, there were some positive social changes in the 1950s. In the sphere of "American politics," the Mexican community was able to chisel a very small piece off the citrus growers' political monopoly. Furthermore, Mexicans demonstrated that some members of their community were willing to challenge the Anglo Americans' abusive use of power. Their main success was the breakdown of segregation in public places and in the neighborhoods, a topic to which we now turn.

THE DESEGREGATION OF THE PUBLIC CONSUMER MARKET AND THE ANGLO AMERICAN NEIGHBORHOODS

The Mexican-origin community actively began to challenge social segregation in Santa Paula during the early 1950s. Attempts to desegregate Santa Paula began in the local theater, were followed by the department stores, and concluded with the residential areas. There does not appear to have been any movement to desegregate the schools. This may be partially explained by the fact that in California the desegregation of Mexican students was not implemented by the state until 1964. Although in 1947, in *Mendez v. Westminster,* California courts ruled that it was unconstitutional to racially segregate Mexican students, school boards across the state did not enforce the state supreme court ruling until nearly two decades later (Hendrick 1977; Wollenberg 1976).

The struggle to desegregate Santa Paula's social sphere must be attributed to the Mexican-origin community in its entirety. The stores were desegregated by men and women alike, the theater by a group of young men, and the residential areas by the Mexican businessmen and Mexican American veterans. None of my informants recalls which individual or which civic group introduced the idea that it was time to challenge segregation. People were generally inspired by the desegregation movements that were taking place around the country. In the early 1950s, Mexican people began questioning the ethical basis of social segregation in Santa Paula: Why should they all have to sit on one side of the theater? Why couldn't they shop in the Anglo American department stores? Quite suddenly, Mexicans started defying the social space norms imposed upon them by the Anglo Americans. Linda recalls that Mexicans first challenged social segregation in the theater. Apparently, a group of young men went to see a movie and sat on the Anglo American side. The usher asked them to move, but they refused. The usher then threatened to call the police if they did not leave the theater. The young Mexican males complied and left the theater. The next Sunday the young men returned and once again sat on the Anglo American side. The same scene was repeated. The following Sunday the same group of young men sat on the Anglo American side. This time, Hal Urias and Vicente Rodríguez refused to move and told the usher to call the police. The usher backed down and left the two young men alone. On the fourth Sunday, a group of young Mexican men sat on the Anglo American side, and they all refused to move.

Linda believes that the owners of the theater eventually allowed Mexicans to sit wherever they wanted because they feared a Mexican boycott. Because Santa Paula's moviegoing population was relatively small, the owners of the theater could not afford to alienate their Mexican clientele. That is, because there was only one theater in Santa Paula, the Anglo Americans knew that if Mexicans stopped coming to the movies the theater would close. Consequently, the possibility of an economic crisis encouraged the Anglo American owners to be tolerant. Tony concurs with Linda's analysis but adds that, since many Mexican boys had fought in World War II and in the Korean War, some Anglo Americans felt that Mexicans should be treated more politely.

The desegregation of the stores followed a similar pattern. After the theater was desegregated, Mexicans began frequenting the Anglo American stores. J. C. Penney appears to have been the main target since it was the store with the most merchandise and the lowest prices in town. In the case of the stores, however, Tony believes that it was the Mexican American middle class that initiated the desegregation process. As he states:

*In the 50s people began to get feelings. It was the time of
the pachuco era. The time of equal rights. Mexicans
weren't political the way they did it [challenged segrega-
tion]. They just moved in. That's the way they did it.
That's the way they do it today. They're just there. They
move in. What can the Anglos say? . . . The Mexican
American middle class began to say, Why should we shop
at Rosa's and Hector's? Let's go to J. C. Penney's. The
Anglos saw them coming. . . . They didn't say anything.
They just hoped someone would tell them to go back to the
Mexican stores.*

Tony added that Anglo American patrons resented being around Mexicans and
were often rude to them. However, since the store owners did not ask them to
leave, Mexicans continued patronizing the Anglo American stores. Most Mexicans, however, continued going to the Mexican stores because they were offered
credit there and the sales clerks spoke Spanish. The braceros, in particular,
continued to patronize the Mexican stores and only on a few occasions purchased
items at J. C. Penney.

The struggle to desegregate the residential zones was more difficult, dramatic,
and complicated. On occasion, Anglo Americans tolerated the presence of
Mexicans in the theater or in the stores. To have a Mexican neighbor, however,
was quite a different matter. This was unheard of. Residential segregation had
been practiced since the late 1800s, and racial mixing in the neighborhoods had
not been permitted. Not even in the low-income Anglo American neighborhoods were Mexicans allowed to rent or buy property. Nonetheless, the struggle
for residential desegregation began in the early 1950s. During this period,
residential desegregation is best described as occasional interethnic mixing rather
than integration, in that most Anglo American neighborhoods remained exclusively White until the early 1960s ("Assessment Roll, City of Santa Paula, 1953–
1957"). The Mexican neighborhoods also remained exclusively Mexican. To this
date, very few Anglo Americans have moved into the Mexican neighborhoods—
an issue I will later return to.[9]

The struggle to desegregate Santa Paula's residential zones once again began
with the efforts of businessman Martin Morales. In 1953, Morales offered to buy
the homes of several Anglo Americans who resided in Virginia Terrace, an affluent
Anglo American neighborhood. Morales wanted to move from the East Side into
an upper-class Anglo American neighborhood. At first, every homeowner
Morales spoke to refused to sell his property. Eventually, Morales was able to
convince one person. When Morales initiated the real estate transaction, the news

spread throughout Virginia Terrace, and local residents were angered and immediately attempted to stop Morales from moving in. They circulated a petition asking residents to prohibit Mexicans from buying homes in Virginia Terrace. The petition was then sent to the Santa Paula Chamber of Commerce for its endorsement. In an unprecedented move, the Santa Paula Chamber of Commerce sided with Morales and supported his right to live in Virginia Terrace. To most Anglo Americans this was a devastating blow, as this incident threatened the foundation of their racial beliefs. On the other hand, to the Mexican community Morales' success symbolized the onset of the breakdown of social segregation. One of my informants, Linda, vividly summarized how the initial dismantling of residential segregation began. She recalls that when Morales obtained the support of the Anglo American business community no one could stop him from moving to Virginia Terrace. Linda stated:

> *During the Korean War segregation began to break down.*
> *The attitudes of Anglos began to change. . . . As long as*
> *they [Mexicans] had money they could buy a home*
> *anywhere. [Martin Morales] was the first* Mejicano *to*
> *buy a home in Virginia Terrace. They [Anglos] made it*
> *very difficult for him, but he knew how to fight them. . . .*
> *They circulated a petition to try to stop him, but he was a*
> *grand marshal [in the parades], he was a businessman with*
> *a lot of money, he had a lot of backers. That's what he*
> *did. He knew a lot of Anglos who helped him, . . . and*
> *they said you have a lot of money, now you can do what*
> *you want. . . . You can live where you want. The Anglo*
> *businessmen helped him.*

I must add that Morales' success must be attributed to two major factors: (1) he was wealthy and was able to afford property wherever he wanted, and (2) he was an influential member of the Santa Paula Chamber of Commerce. He also often donated money to city projects and charities. Therefore, it was good business for the chamber to support Morales.

Although Morales' action initiated the first stage of residential desegregation, most Mexicans continued to be segregated on the East Side ("Assessment Roll, City of Santa Paula, 1953–1957"). Santa Paula property tax assessment records indicate that for the next three years no other Mexican moved into the Anglo American neighborhoods. It was not until 1957 that Santa Paula's tax records indicate that the desegregation of some Anglo American neighborhoods began at a grand scale. In 1957, 19 percent of the 646 Mexican-origin landowners bought homes in Anglo American neighborhoods ("Assessment Roll, City of Santa Paula, 1953–1957"). These homes were located near the border of the Anglo American and Mexican neighborhoods. Exactly how or why this process occurred is unclear. I believe, however, that it may be related to "White flight." That is, when Mexicans began to move into the White neighborhoods located on the border zones, many Anglo Americans responded by moving out. These neighborhoods were located on Ojai Road, South Mills Street, and South Tenth Street ("Assessment Roll, City of Santa Paula, 1953–1957"). It is also unclear why Mexicans bought property only along the interethnic borders and not in other Anglo American neighborhoods. Most likely, this may be attributed to the Anglo Americans' refusal to allow the interior of the West Side to be integrated.

Resistance toward selling West Side property to Mexicans was finally overcome in 1959. The desegregation of some of the neighborhoods on the West Side appears to be related to policies enacted by the Santa Paula Realty Board and by the federal government. In 1959, the Santa Paula Realty Board proposed to build thirteen hundred new homes in an undeveloped area of the West Side (Belknap 1968:132). The real estate company speculated that these homes could be sold to veterans who qualified to receive federal housing loans. The city council enthusiastically approved the plan (*SPDC,* August 18, 1959, 73[65]:1). Contrary to local expectations, the Santa Paula Realty Board broke with tradition and sold homes to any veteran who qualified, irrespective of race. My informant, Linda, recalls that the construction of a new housing development on the West Side was an attractive opportunity to many veterans.[10] The homes were new, moderately priced, and backed up by the federal government's veteran home loan program. Consequently, many Mexicans bought property on the West Side, and the desegregation of the Anglo American neighborhoods proceeded.

Although by the early 1960s Mexicans had been able to successfully challenge several racist practices and desegregation proceeded on a grand scale, most Mexicans continued to be discriminated against. The city council continued to disregard the needs of the East Side residents and did not fund urban renewal projects in the Mexican neighborhoods. On the contrary, in 1963 the city council approved the construction of Santa Paula's first freeway (Freeway 126; see Triem 1985) and, without regard for the Mexican community's health and psychological comfort, voted that it be constructed on the East Side. Rather than tearing down citrus orchards on the outskirts of town, the city council callously chose to place the new freeway in the Mexican neighborhoods, thereby dislocating hundreds of residents. The construction of the freeway came at a big cost to the East Side. It created noise and air pollution problems, led to the devaluation of property, destroyed the rustic aesthetic environment of several East Side neighborhoods, and laid the foundation for future environmental problems. Segregation may have ended in Santa Paula, but racial discrimination did not. We will now turn to one of these unfair practices and examine how part of the Mexican community was discriminated against by the citrus growers following the termination of the bracero program in 1964.

SIX

The Segmentation of the Farm Labor Market, 1965 to 1976

By 1970, the quality of life for the Mexican-origin community of Santa Paula improved. Residential segregation had completely broken down, and many Mexicans often resided on the West Side.[1] Moreover, people of Mexican descent were no longer entirely dependent on the agricultural industry, for non-farm employment had become available in the nearby cities of Santa Barbara, Oxnard, Ventura, and Los Angeles (Santa Paula Chamber of Commerce 1986; Triem 1985). As seen in Table 2, approximately half of the Mexican-origin working-age population had obtained non-agricultural employment (United States Census Bureau 1973:779). Although these social advances contributed to improved interethnic relations, people of Mexican descent continued to be treated as second-class citizens. School segregation had not been dismantled, the at-large district electoral system continued to obstruct the election of Mexican American candidates, and the East Side was in dire need of urban renewal projects (Menchaca and Valencia 1991; Santa Paula School District Board of Trustees 1979). Moreover, half of the Mexican-origin community remained under the economic control of the citrus growers because agriculture continued to be a major employment source in Santa Paula.

This chapter will be concerned with a discussion of some of the social problems affecting the Mexican-origin community of Santa Paula. The focus will be on the unjust economic and political dilemmas confronting the Mexican people who continued to work in the citrus industry during the aftermath of the bracero program and until 1976. Issues dealing with schooling and the city council will be dealt with in later chapters. As will be demonstrated, many Santa Paula citrus growers practiced unfair labor policies against Mexicans by paying low farm labor wages and at all costs obstructing union organization. These policies adversely

TABLE 2   *Occupations of Mexican-Origin People in*
Santa Paula, 1970
Total Mexican-Origin Population = *7,328*[a]
Total Employed = *2,401*[b]

Occupation	Number
Professionals and Technicians	119
Managers and Administrators (non-farm)	58
Sales Workers	55
Clerical and Kindred Workers	232
Craftspeople	215
Operatives and Transportation Operators[c]	618
Farm Laborers	614
Laborers (non-farm)	249
Service Workers	204
Private Household Workers	29
Farmers and Farm Foremen	8

a. Median family income $ 7,384 (United States Census Bureau 1973:985).
b. United States Census Bureau 1973:779.
c. This category includes packinghouse workers and truckers who transport citrus products.

affected the economic welfare of farm workers by serving to keep them in a subservient position. In reconstructing this historical period, I rely on scholarly writings, oral histories, and farm labor reports. Unfortunately, in this discussion, I am unable to corroborate my field research by frequently drawing upon newspaper articles from the *Santa Paula Daily Chronicle*. For some unknown reason, from the mid-1960s to the late 1970s, this source failed to report news about the political activities of the Mexican-origin community. Only occasionally do a few newspaper articles describe farm labor unrest. These news articles, however, reflect the type of reporting that occurred from the 1920s to the late 1940s, when Mexicans were depicted as irrational and violent troublemakers. The style of reporting appearing in the 1950s—when Mexican-origin people were depicted favorably—was short-lived and not present by the early 1960s.

During my discussion of the 1960s, I use the term "Mexican American" in reference to people of Mexican descent who were born in the United States. This ethnic label is used because most of my informants recall that in this period the native-born preferred to call themselves "Mexican American" rather than "Mexican." Individuals who preferred to call themselves "Mexican" were primarily senior citizens or people born in Mexico. In reference to the oral

histories of this period, Roney, Tony, José, Linda, and Isabel continued to provide
valuable accounts; the main informants, however, were farm workers, agribusiness
managers, labor contractors, and farm labor crew leaders. Therefore, this chapter
is a composite of the memories of sixty-five people. These respondents included
seven individuals representing Santa Paula's agribusiness interests, one person who
was the office manager of the United Farm Workers union (in 1986), thirty-seven
farm workers, and twenty Mexicans who did not work in farm labor but recall the
farm labor unrest of the late 1960s to mid-1970s. I begin this account with the
growers' responses to the closure of the bracero program.

THE AFTERMATH OF THE
BRACERO PROGRAM:
THE SEGMENTATION OF THE
FARM LABOR FORCE

Throughout the United States, church organizations,
unions, and political activists launched a long campaign in the early 1960s to end
the bracero program. The main issue raised by the organizations opposing the
program was the fundamental moral threat that imported contract labor posed to
the American free labor market (Craig 1971). Many political activists challenged
the alleged benefits of the bracero program. The most successful spokesperson was
César Chávez, a labor organizer from Delano, California. Chávez took his
campaign to the people and obtained popular support against the program. He
organized several tours throughout the Southwest and spoke about the inhumane
work conditions that the bracero program had produced for domestic farm
workers (National Advisory Committee on Farm Labor 1967). Among the main
problems were static domestic wages, the farm workers' inability to obtain
improved working conditions (such as the availability of drinking water and toilets
in the fields), and the growers' refusal to pay time and a half for overtime work.
The most serious issue was the farm workers' inability to obtain the right to
collective bargaining or, in other words, the legal right to have union representation (Taylor 1975). Chávez also testified in front of federal committees
investigating the benefits and problems posed by the bracero program. He
effectively argued that the bracero program was a danger to the American free
labor market system because it was setting a precedent that could be replicated in
other non-agricultural industries (National Advisory Committee on Farm Labor
1967). Agribusiness lobbyists countered Chávez' arguments by stressing that the
bracero program benefited the American public. Allegedly, farmers were able to

keep the cost of production down by importing low-cost Mexican labor and subsequently passing the savings on to consumers. Agricultural lobbyists, however, were unable to convince the federal government that the benefits outweighed the adverse effects. Finally, on December 31, 1964, the federal government terminated the bracero program.

When the bracero program ended in Ventura County, Santa Paula's citrus industry was among the many agricultural-producing areas that experienced a temporary setback. By the mid-1960s Ventura County had become one of the major citrus-producing zones in the United States (Mines and Anzaldúa 1982), and Santa Paula had become the county's major citrus producing city (Triem 1985). Over 73 million dollars worth of citrus was marketed worldwide from Ventura County farms (Ventura County Crop Report 1964, cited in Ventura County Agricultural Commission 1921–1986). Thus, the termination of the bracero program prompted a labor shortage that required agribusinessmen to immediately restructure the industry's hiring practices in order to control domestic wages. In response to the labor shortage, Santa Paula and other Ventura County growers joined forces to protect their interests through the Ventura County Citrus Growers Committee (VCCGC) (see chapter 4). Their first strategy was to replace imported contract labor with urban workers from Los Angeles County (Mines and Anzaldúa 1982).[2] The recruitment of a new work force would fill the labor shortages and prevent local labor from demanding higher wages. This strategy, however, proved to be disastrous. One year after the bracero program ended, the citrus industry employed 27,082 manual laborers to replace three thousand braceros (*SPDC*, Tuesday, May 24, 1966, 80[22]: special agricultural edition, section 2, p. 1). Unlike the braceros, who had proved to be a stable and dependable labor force, the newly hired workers were inexperienced and inept at picking citrus (Mines and Anzaldúa 1982:37). This problem was further exacerbated by the fact that the new farm labor force, though apparently large in numbers, was not actually large enough to harvest the fields. An article appearing in the *Santa Paula Daily Chronicle* highlighted the growers' severe farm labor problems. Apparently, the workers who were hired to replace the braceros were unskilled and unqualified to harvest the fields. The *Santa Paula Daily Chronicle* reporter wrote:

> *In 1964 the Citrus growers committee was able to keep a pick force of 3,000 pickers. . . . Yet one year later, with the shut-down of the bracero program, it was required to hire 27,082 pickers to maintain the 3,000 level at peak.*
>
> *Result, was the well known distress of local growers,*

> *especially at the beginning of the 1965 season. Labor turn-*
> *over was immense due to unqualified workers supplied by*
> *outside agencies, most of which proved unusable.*
>
> *Growers were thus unable to time harvesting properly*
> *and meet shipping schedules for export.*
>
> *Loss of quality in the harvest was also suffered.*
>
> *A general decline was felt to the extent that many*
> *growers posted a net loss for their efforts at the end of the*
> *1965 season. (SPDC, May 24, 1966, 80[22]: special*
> *agricultural edition, section 2, p. 1)*

Because the new labor force proved to be untrained in picking citrus, the large number of workers needed to replace braceros dramatically pushed up the cost of production to such an extent that many growers lost money one year after the bracero program ended. In 1965, the Ventura County agricultural commissioner reported a farm crop valuation decline of seven million dollars from 1964. According to the commissioner, the change was largely associated with the high cost of labor in 1965. The agricultural commissioner reported:

> *"Highlighting 1965 was the loss of some crops due to rains,*
> *the shortage of experienced labor and the problems of*
> *extended seasons," states the annual report of agricultural*
> *commissioner, C. J. Barrett.*
>
> *"Citrus," said Barrett, "felt the shortage of labor more*
> *than did some of the other crops," considered significant*
> *because citrus accounts for almost half the total values dealt*
> *with in the report. . . . Result of these and other difficulties*
> *was a sharp turn downward in farm crop valuation for*
> *Ventura County in 1965, a decline of $7 million from*
> *1964. The drop marked the end of a long steady climb in*
> *annual total valuation, but probably does not signify a*
> *trend, since forces influencing the change were mostly*
> *accidental or temporary in character, and effective measures*
> *have been employed to over come labor difficulties arising*
> *from shutdown of the bracero program. (SPDC, May 24,*
> *1966, 80[22]: special agricultural edition, section 1, p. 1)*

Though the shutdown of the bracero program set back citrus profits, the problem was viewed as temporary by the commissioner, in that Ventura County growers were in the midst of initiating a plan to replenish the farm labor force. As part of this strategy, a campaign was set in motion to recruit Mexican nationals and former braceros to Ventura County. Unfortunately for domestic farm labor, this campaign set the conditions for the segmentation of Santa Paula's farm labor force and the eventual creation of occupational conflicts between the workers. The growers benefited from this event, while most farm workers were adversely affected.

Following the termination of the bracero program, Santa Paula and other Ventura County growers gradually replenished their farm labor force by going into Mexico and actively recruiting Mexican nationals to the United States.[3] The VCCGC sent representatives to Mexico and advertised on the radio and in the newspapers of the areas that traditionally sent workers; Limoneira Ranch sent recruiters to visit former braceros in villages and small towns in rural Michoacan (Mines and Anzaldúa 1982:37). Two of my informants, Ralph López and Lencho Velásquez, who were farm labor managers during the time of the campaign, recall that they were among the recruiters who took several trips to Mexico. Furthermore, in an attempt to bring back its former braceros, Coastal Growers Association (CGA), the largest harvesting company in Ventura County, sent them invitations encouraging them to return the following season (Mines and Anzaldúa 1982:39). In Mexico, as word spread of the labor shortages in Ventura County, many Mexican nationals and former braceros migrated back, regardless of whether they had legal documentation.[4] Thus, between 1965 and 1968, Ventura County—and in particular Santa Paula—experienced a gradual, yet massive influx of Mexican nationals.[5]

While the campaign to recruit Mexican nationals to Ventura County was set in motion, citrus growers were actively competing to retain their skilled farm labor in the county. For example, Limoneira Ranch and CGA (which managed the labor needs for numerous Ventura County farmers) began to offer much more attractive wages and benefits than farmers from other areas of California (Mamer and Rosedale 1981; Mines and Anzaldúa 1982). In the mid-1960s, both companies paid their pickers approximately $2.15 to $2.45 an hour (Mines and Anzaldúa 1982:33), in contrast to the low wages of $1.20 to $1.40 an hour paid in the Coachella Valley and other parts of California (National Advisory Committee on Farm Labor 1967:47). The wages offered by both companies were among the highest in the Southwest. Furthermore, Limoneira Ranch not only offered slightly higher wages than CGA but also offered housing and expanded benefits that included added vacation pay, pension benefits, and health insurance. Limoneira Ranch also provided its workers free picking equipment and transportation to the fields (Mines and Anzaldúa 1982). When news about these optimal working conditions spread among Mexican nationals, interested applicants migrated to Santa Paula and to other cities in Ventura County. However, because only two companies were offering these employment terms, an oversupply of migrant labor competed for the jobs at Limoneira and CGA, and only some of them were able to obtain work. The majority of the workers who migrated to Ventura County were hired by growers who paid lower wages and did not offer employment benefits (Mines and Anzaldúa 1982).

It is ironic that the high wages and benefits paid by Limoneira Ranch and CGA eventually generated the conditions that created conflict among Santa Paula's farm workers and resulted in segmenting the labor force. Farm workers were segmented into a primary sector that was well paid and a secondary sector that was offered undesirable wages and working conditions. Although the segmentation of the labor force occurred, whether the growers had planned for their recruitment campaign to eventually generate the conditions for the division is uncertain. Irrespective of this, it is clear that the segmentation benefited the growers, because the oversupply of labor served to stabilize farm wages as well as generate disunity among the workers. The oversupply of labor, however, most adversely affected the Mexican migrants. Most of them were forced to accept employment within the secondary sector. Moreover, the labor force segmentation made union organization nearly impossible in the country because primary- and secondary-sector employees did not have the same occupational interests.

In the case of Santa Paula, Ralph López' and Lencho Velásquez' personal experiences shed light on how the workers were impacted by the segmentation of the labor force. According to them, as farm labor managers they were able to observe how the workers were affected. Both of them offered a similar analysis and proposed that, when the farm workers were given vastly different employment terms, they no longer shared the same workers' interests. Primary-sector farm workers became loyal company employees and were against organizing a union. A similar analysis was provided by Juan Vásquez, the office manager of Ventura County's United Farm Workers union. According to Juan, the well-paid labor force was against unionization, as they had nothing to gain and everything to lose. If they supported their underpaid co-workers, their salaries would not be raised because they already received among the highest hourly wages in the state. On the other hand, they potentially could be fired if they participated in union activities. The executive manager of Limoneira Ranch, Alfredo Gutiérrez, offered an alternate analysis. Although he also believed that occupational conflicts emerged among the workers as a result of vastly different employment conditions, he considered the segmentation of the labor force to be the outcome of a natural labor market process. In his opinion, Limoneira Ranch had traditionally increased its wages in order to compete for the best workers. If other growers refused to follow its example, Limoneira management could not be blamed for this. According to Alfredo, Limoneira was a reputable company and had always raised wages when needed. If this practice produced a surplus of labor in Santa Paula, this was a problem of the "law of supply and demand." Alfredo stated:

> *It is not our fault that workers are attracted to Limoneira.*
> *They come as part of the law of supply and demand.*
> *There are a lot of factors that have attracted workers to the*
> *area. I really don't know how surplus labor affects our*
> *hiring practices, but I try to keep our wages high.*

Based on Alfredo's analysis, the occasional problem of a farm labor surplus in Santa Paula might have been prompted by Limoneira's employment practices. However, the company's intent was not to generate disunity among the workers but rather to ensure that the company had efficient and skilled labor at all times.

Lisa McGarat, the 1986 president of the Ventura County chapter of the Women in Agriculture association and the daughter of a prominent citrus rancher, only partly agreed with Alfredo's analysis regarding why Mexican nationals were attracted to the county farms. Lisa recalled that in the mid- to late 1960s growers unintentionally generated the conditions that flooded the labor market when they invited their former bracero employees back to work. The braceros returned, and so did many other workers. This recruitment practice, however, ended in the late 1960s when the growers realized that there was an oversupply of labor in the county. Later, economic problems in Mexico—and not farm labor employment practices—continued to stimulate migration from Mexico to Ventura County. Although Lisa believes Mexicans are no longer recruited, she and other growers have formed a committee within Women in Agriculture to discourage growers from recruiting farm labor from Mexico.

Adding ethnographic descriptions to the analyses offered by Ralph, Lencho, Juan, Alfredo, and Lisa, political scientists Richard Mines and Ricardo Anzaldúa (1982) comment that when they studied Santa Paula's agricultural industry they found that primary-sector employees consisted of former braceros who had been previously employed by Limoneira Ranch. My interview data support their analysis. When I interviewed thirty-seven farm workers, I found that they had either moved to Santa Paula immediately after the bracero program ended or within a few years afterward. My respondents recalled that they or their parents chose to live in Santa Paula because Limoneira Ranch was offering high wages and comfortable company housing. Not all of my informants, however, were employed by Limoneira Ranch. Only those braceros who had formerly worked within the company were hired. One of my most interesting interviews corroborating Mines and Anzaldúa's analysis was the information provided by Gloria López, the daughter of a farm labor crew leader employed by Limoneira

Ranch. Gloria's father was also appointed by Limoneira's management to be housing supervisor of one of the labor camps. She recalled that after the bracero program ended, the apartments and houses were reserved for the braceros and their families who were en route to Santa Paula. Within a year and a half after the bracero program ended, all employment positions and housing vacancies were filled to capacity. Gloria also commented that Limoneira Ranch assisted its former braceros in obtaining their green cards.

In retrospect, although it appears that many former braceros and their families were employed by Limoneira Ranch, not all the Mexican nationals who came to Santa Paula fared as well. Once the jobs in Limoneira were filled, the farm workers had to find other employment or migrate someplace else. My farm worker informants recall that many Mexican families decided to settle in Santa Paula and therefore sought employment with the small-scale growers or with the local cooperative agricultural association. These employers paid substantially lower wages and offered only seasonal work. Thus, these workers were incorporated within the secondary labor market. A case in point was the farm workers employed by the Santa Paula Growers Association (SPGA).[6] The association was composed of several small-scale farmers who hired an agribusiness firm to manage and employ their labor. After Limoneira Ranch, the SPGA was the second-largest employer of farm labor in the city. In comparison to Limoneira Ranch, the association offered inferior wages, bad working conditions, and no benefits (Mines and Anzaldúa 1982). For example, the farm workers hired by the SPGA were employed for less than eight months out of the year and were required to supply their own picking equipment. They also did not receive holiday or vacation pay. The severest disparity between Limoneira Ranch and SPGA, however, was the type of housing they offered their employees. Unlike Limoneira Ranch, which voluntarily complied with state housing regulations, SPGA made no attempt to improve its old, substandard family labor camp, known as El Campito (the Little Camp). Whereas Limoneira Ranch employees were housed in two- to three-bedroom homes with large kitchens and functioning bathrooms, in El Campito there were no such comforts. The SPGA camp was constructed on the East Side in 1920 and during the 1940s was used as provisionary housing for the braceros and some local farm worker families (*Ventura County Star Free Press,* February 2, 1983: A-12). During the late 1960s, approximately over one thousand adults and children inhabited the same housing units that five hundred braceros had previously occupied.

By the late 1960s, the 130 houses in El Campito were in need of major repairs.[7] Windows were broken, the paint on the walls was chipping, wood floors were splintering, the ceilings of some homes were cracking, and the plumbing in most of the houses often backed up. Furthermore, the children were forced to play in the dirt streets, as there was no local park. The camp also had no street lights or sidewalks, and only two main roads were paved. Suffice it to say, El Campito was deplorable and an embarrassment to the city of Santa Paula, Mexicans and Anglo Americans alike. In contrast to El Campito, Limoneira Ranch provided its employees with a modest, yet safe and well-landscaped park, the roads to the homes were paved, and the company parceled a small yard for each household.

Exacerbating the deplorable housing conditions at El Campito were the employment terms that forced SPGA farm workers to become migrant laborers. Since the association did not offer them year-round employment, after the harvest season they were forced to migrate to other parts of California in search of work. In contrast, Limoneira Ranch offered many of its workers year-round employment. Men were hired to harvest the fields, and women were employed in the packing house to wash, sort, and pack citrus products. When the work in the packing house slowed down, some of the women were transferred to the fields to work alongside the men. However, although Limoneira Ranch management offered optimal employment terms to many of its workers, it also treated part of its labor force much as did the SPGA (Mines and Anzaldúa 1982). During the harvest season, Limoneira Ranch hired temporary workers for approximately four to eight months and did not offer them the same benefits as it did its year-round employees.

In retrospect, according to Ralph and Lencho, the two former farm labor managers, by the late 1960s approximately 40 percent of Santa Paula's farm worker population was employed by Limoneira Ranch within its primary sector, while the rest of the farm workers were hired on a part-time basis either by Limoneira Ranch or by the SPGA. This labor force segmentation, they recall, successfully diffused all movements to unionize labor. Corroborating their analyses were similar recollections offered by most of my farm worker informants.

THE SANTA PAULA GROWERS ASSOCIATION FARM WORKERS AND THEIR STRUGGLE TO UNIONIZE FARM LABOR

By the mid-1970s, in Santa Paula, the problems posed by the termination of the bracero program had long been resolved to the satisfaction of the citrus growers. Differing working and living conditions had segmented Santa Paula's farm workers into primary and secondary labor sectors. The better-paid Limoneira Ranch employees appeared to be satisfied with their terms of employment, while the SPGA farm workers wanted to upgrade their benefits and housing conditions. Eventually, differing occupational interests among the workers were manifested in conflicting attitudes toward unionization. Many SPGA employees favored unionization because they needed representatives to arbitrate their grievances, while most Limoneira Ranch employees remained faithful to their employer. These conditions, therefore, sparked a bitter struggle between the farm workers who favored and those who opposed joining the United Farm Workers union. We must now examine how the segmentation of the farm labor force unfolded in Santa Paula.

In 1974, two events converged in Santa Paula to set the political climate that mobilized the SPGA employees toward political militancy. One spark was the occupational abuses that they had been tolerating since the termination of the bracero program. The workers were no longer satisfied with merely having a job. After having worked nearly ten years in Santa Paula, they wanted higher wages, year-round employment, and better housing. Another event that simultaneously occurred was César Chávez' campaign to establish a local base for the United Farm Workers union (UFW) in Ventura County.

The UFW had grown from its central California home base in the grape fields of Delano, stretching southward to the orange orchards in the Imperial Valley and northward to the tomato fields of Sacramento (Taylor 1975). In 1974, as part of its recruitment drive, the UFW visited farm communities in Ventura County. Many Santa Paula farm employees attended these UFW meetings and became convinced that they should join the union. Chávez' successful lobbying accomplishments at the state and federal levels evidently helped to persuade thousands of farm workers throughout California, including Santa Paula, that the UFW could upgrade their employment standards. For example, at the state level, in 1973 the state of California passed the California Occupational Safety Act, which mandated three provisions: (1) portable rest rooms must be provided to the farm workers in the fields, (2) drinking water must also be available in the work place, and (3) employers must adhere to safety standards to protect their workers from pesticides (Shulman 1986). Also, of utmost success for Chávez was his effective 1974 lobbying campaign in which he obtained the support of California governor Edmund G. Brown and many state legislators to enact a law giving farm workers the right to union representation (Decierdo 1980). In 1975, such a law was passed under the Agricultural Labor Relations Act (ALRA) (Alatorre, Zenovich, Dunlap, and Berman 1975). For the first time in California history, growers were mandated by law to allow their workers to hold union elections.[8] Under the ALRA, farm workers were given the right to decide if they should be represented by a union or if they wished to deal directly with the growers. The ALRA also stipulated that if the growers refused to comply with the law, the farm workers had the right to have their grievances arbitrated by the judicial courts. And, if the courts ruled in favor of the farm workers, the growers would have to pay a settlement, rehire workers that had been fired, pay wages lost by the workers during the labor dispute, and recognize the union as the workers' legitimate bargaining agent. Thus, the passage of the ALRA was a major achievement for the farm labor movement in California, as farm workers now had the right to vote for union elections and to bargain collectively.

At the federal level, Chávez and the UFW were also successful in having two significant pieces of legislation passed. In 1967, a minimum wage was set for farm workers, requiring employers to pay at least an hourly wage forty cents below the federal minimum (Sosnick 1978:38). Though farm workers were not extended the same minimum wage as industrial workers, the new farm labor wage protected them from severe forms of exploitation. Moreover, in 1974 the federal government extended federal unemployment insurance to farm workers (Shulman 1986). For the first time in United States history, farm workers would be able to claim unemployment insurance during periods of economic distress.

Throughout California, including Sacramento, the San Joaquin Valley, and the Imperial Valley, the UFW had been able to negotiate many favorable contracts for the workers. These contracts guaranteed workers increased wages, time-and-a-half payment for overtime work, and extension of employment benefits (e.g., medical care) to farm workers (Gonzalez 1985). Therefore, when union organizers arrived in Ventura County, many Santa Paula farm workers, in particular those who belonged to the secondary labor market, favored joining the UFW. Likewise, a great number of the farm workers were against initiating a union movement because, they argued, the working conditions in Santa Paula had radically improved and it was only a matter of time before all the citrus growers would offer comparable employment terms as Limoneira Ranch.[9] Those who opposed the movement also did not believe they could pressure the growers into allowing them to join the UFW.

In spite of the opposition, one evening a group of SPGA farm workers executed a plan to persuade others to join the UFW (Mines and Anzaldúa 1982). These organizers believed that to convince the farm workers to confront the growers and demand union elections would be difficult unless their political consciousness was raised. Thus, their first strategy to arouse the workers was to launch a strike against the SPGA. If management reacted favorably toward the labor grievances, then it would be unnecessary to proceed with the union movement. However, if management did not accommodate their demands, this would prove that the company did not have any intentions of raising wages or improving working conditions. On January 25, 1974, hundreds of SPGA employees went out on strike and demanded improved employment conditions. Among the demands they presented were: (1) all workers would receive a wage increase, (2) workers would be informed before starting work what the hourly wage or price was per box, (3) all workers would receive a printed employment contract written in both English and Spanish, (4) housing improvements would be made to El Campito, (5) labor camp rents would be frozen for a year, and (6) the SPGA would recognize El Comité de Campesinos Santa Paula Growers as the bargaining agent for the strikers (*SPDC,* January 30, 1974, 87[190]:1; *SPDC,* February 8, 1974, 87[197]:1). The strike committee, popularly known as "El Comité," was composed of three farm workers, a Mexican American business-man, the pastor of Our Lady of Guadalupe Church, and two attorneys from the American Civil Liberties Union.

Seven days after the strike began, the SPGA responded to the strikers' demands. They asked Lee Chancey, manager of the Ventura County Citrus Growers Committee (VCCGC), to be their spokesman. Chancey communicated to the strikers that the growers would agree to all demands except two. Wages would not be raised, nor would the growers recognize El Comité as the bargaining agent (*SPDC,* January 31, 1974, 87[191]:1). The workers took the growers' response as an insult and refused to end the strike. Therefore, the strike continued for six more days until Chancey announced that the growers were willing to increase wages but would not allow El Comité to be the workers' negotiating agent. Chancey added that El Comité was not needed, in that the workers and the SPGA had found a peaceful means of negotiating. On February 7, the strikers voted to end the work stoppage and to accept the growers' terms. El Comité was also immediately disbanded (*SPDC,* February 8, 1974, 87[197]:1). At this time, the outcome of the strike appeared to be successful for both the workers and the growers. The workers obtained most of their demands, and the growers were able to avert union activity.

Although the farm workers won the strike, many were disappointed that the union movement was abandoned. Consequently, a small group decided to continue their struggle to unionize labor (Mines and Anzaldúa 1982). These individuals knew their task would be difficult because many farm workers feared losing their jobs if they joined the movement. To gain community support, they sought advice from Father Dennis, the pastor of Our Lady of Guadalupe Church. Father Dennis had previously helped them when he participated in El Comité. He was also known as a longtime sympathizer and supporter of UFW activities. When approached by union supporters, Father Dennis agreed to help them by allowing them to hold meetings and rallies at the church.

Several of my informants recall that, when Father Dennis began to lobby actively in support of the UFW movement, many parishioners were dismayed. Rosalinda, Alberta, María, and Sally were among my many informants who offered a similar account of Father Dennis' activities. They recall being surprised that Father Dennis became involved with the labor movement, because he was an Anglo American and a newcomer to Santa Paula. They could not understand why he did not behave like the previous Spanish priests, who never criticized the growers. My informants recall that the Mexican-origin congregation initially rejected Father Dennis because many people thought that he was a communist. The congregation was suspicious of him. People used to gossip and wonder: Was Father Dennis a racist? Was he a communist? Was he mentally ill? Was he a boozer? After the initial shock of having an Anglo American priest preach about the UFW and liberation theology, the Mexican-origin community soon came to love and trust him. He was a kind man and dedicated to his congregation. Although he was well liked, Father Dennis remained a controversial figure in Santa Paula. He was rather eccentric and dramatic, especially during Sunday masses when he ended the services by switching his clerical robe for another one that had an embroidered eagle, the symbol of the UFW. His last words were always, "Go in peace—Chicano power!" Father Dennis also hung a black and white UFW flag on the wooden podium while he gave his sermons. He did this to demonstrate to the congregation that there was nothing wrong with supporting the UFW.

The momentum to obtain union representation resumed on February 28, 1975, when the SPGA laid off senior women harvesters and replaced them with single male pickers (*SPDC,* February 28, 1975, 87[216]:1). Firing the women was the growers' method of only partially complying with the previous year's labor strike concessions. Because wages had increased to $3.80 an hour, the growers hired new workers who would begin their contract at a lower wage scale. This angered the farm workers because one-third of the labor force was laid off. In efforts to protect themselves from further abuses, the farm workers decided to immediately reconstitute El Comité and discuss a plan of action. As part of the discussions, the workers deliberated over whether they should vote to hold union elections. In spite of the mass layoffs, the farm workers decided to have El Comité represent them and to hold off on the vote. At this time their concern was to launch a series of strikes to protest the layoffs. Although those who favored joining the UFW were unable to convince the majority of the workers to vote in favor of holding union elections, the group instead voted to develop close ties with the UFW and to ask César Chávez for advice. Immediately after the meeting, the SPGA farm workers began the strike activity, and three-fourths of them walked out on strike (*SPDC,* February 28, 1975, 87[216]:1).

Anticipating a work stoppage, the growers had prepared themselves to deal with their angry employees. Weeks before the strike began, the growers envisioned that the workers would go on strike. Therefore, one week after the strike began, SPGA management was able to replace many of the striking workers with a group of temporary laborers from outside Santa Paula (*SPDC,* February 28, 1975, 87[216]:1). Scab labor had been previously contacted and told to be prepared to come to Santa Paula immediately. Ralph López, one of the association's farm managers, was asked to recruit and hire the strikebreakers. The association also selected Ralph to be its spokesman because he was Mexican. When I interviewed Ralph, he informed me that he reluctantly represented the growers, and he personally felt that the layoffs were unfair. However, because he was part of the management team, it was his duty to side with the growers. According to Ralph, he was selected as the spokesman because the growers expected to gain public sympathy by having a Mexican represent them. He was used as an example of the fair working conditions available within the company. For instance, after having worked as a field harvester, Ralph had been promoted to farm labor crew leader and eventually to manager supervising several crews. The association also expected Ralph to be able to divide the workers and end the strike merely because people liked him and owed him favors. Ralph was well liked because he often acted as a broker between the growers and the employees, and whenever his co-workers got in trouble with the police, he would serve as their interpreter and often bail them out of jail.

Ralph recalls that the association had false perceptions of the farm workers. Laying off the women had been a serious mistake that would unavoidably spark the union movement. The growers' decision to renege on the previous year's labor agreement was poorly timed, occurring when Chávez' popularity was increasing around the county. He also recalls that management unrealistically expected the strike to end merely because he would threaten to fire the strikers. Ralph had no such power. Instead of listening to Ralph's threats, the strikers met with UFW advisors and scheduled a meeting with César Chávez.

When Chávez arrived in Santa Paula in early March, he advised the farm workers to "hold the line" at all costs (Mines and Anzaldúa 1982). Chávez also assessed the situation and informed the strikers that they had a strong chance of winning. In order to succeed, however, they needed to gain more support. They would need to convince the farm workers from Limoneira Ranch and employees of the city's packing house to join them. In this way, they would achieve a complete work stoppage and cripple the citrus industry in Santa Paula. The plan was to put pressure on all the growers in order that they, in turn, would pressure the SPGA to negotiate with El Comité.

As a means of initiating a work stoppage, the strikers attempted to convince packing house workers to join them. Many responded by offering financial assistance, but they refused to join the strike. The lack of support angered the striking farm workers. Compounding their anger were rumors that spread throughout the farm worker labor camps. Several of my informants recall that there were many packing house employees who advised their co-workers to ignore the strikers because they were UFW spies. They also told their co-workers that the strike was a plot to gain support for the UFW, at their expense. In retaliation for the lack of support demonstrated by the packing house employees, many angry strikers launched an attack against those individuals who refused to support them. On March 4, 1975, Briggs Packing House was selected as the first protest site. At 4:00 P.M., when it was time for Briggs employees to quit work, the angry strikers blocked all the exits to prevent the workers from leaving the facility. Some strikers also broke the headlights of several of the cars in the parking lot. Those few packing house employees who dared cross the picket line were called vicious names by the strikers. Despite these actions, only a few of the packing house workers walked out and joined the picket line. Out of the 150 packing house workers, few dared to approach the crowd, instead remaining within the confines of the packing house until 4:45 P.M., when the strikers dispersed. The *Santa Paula Daily Chronicle* described part of the events that occurred that evening.

> *"This is terrorism," [Jim Beyer], manager of the Briggs Packing House, said this morning after striking fruit pickers Tuesday damaged several vehicles and allegedly kept packing house employees from leaving the facility on Peck Road for almost an hour after the normal quitting time. . . . Employees were afraid to leave the safety of the plant. About 150 workers, who usually leave at 4:00 P.M., waited until about 4:45 P.M. to leave. By that time the strikers had left the area. [Beyer] said . . . "It is a shame that people working in the packing house should have to suffer. . . . They are totally innocent." . . . [Beyer] added that he did not understand why the pickers chose to picket Briggs packing house because the facility has nothing to do with the strikers' grievances. (SPDC, March 5, 1975, 87[219]:1)*

Two of my informants, Raúl and Hilda, recall that the Briggs Packing House demonstration failed to gain the results the strikers expected. Hilda, who was an employee at the packing house, recalls that very few packers walked out in support of the picket line. Instead, most of the packers became very angry and lost all sympathy for the strikers. Raúl and Hilda also recall that, in the *barrios* that evening, rumors spread that the attack launched against the packing house workers had angered many husbands whose wives were employed there. Allegedly through this indirect process, husbands who were not employed in farm occupations stopped supporting the strikers. Mechanics, plumbers, and service workers were angry that the strikers harassed their wives and called them vicious names. Raúl remembers that after this incident occurred many people stopped attending the strike meetings, and support for joining the UFW declined among the farm worker community. Raúl also blamed the UFW for causing all the Mexican workers' interpersonal conflicts. He accused the UFW of advising the strikers to become violent against their co-workers. His interpretation of the strike is underscored in this recollection.

> *Cuándo la unión se metió, o la metieron, todo en Santa Paula se jodió. Esos liderillos no sabían qué hacer y nada más traían como pendejos a los trabajadores. No es nada malo con que haya una unión, pero el problema es que los achichincles que se hacen líderes con la ayuda de la unión no son estudiados y solamente son bocones. . . . Lo que necesitamos es que los hijos de los campesinos que van al colegio regresen al pueblo, y ellos se metan a pelear al ranchero, pero a la buena. . . . Con respeto, datos, y mucho coraje.*

> *When the Union came to Santa Paula or someone invited them to come, everything in Santa Paula got messed up. The labor organizers didn't know what they were doing and just had the workers running around like idiots. There isn't anything wrong if we have a union, but the problem is that local people who are made leaders don't have any education and the only thing they know how to do is talk too much. . . . What we need is for the children of the immigrants who are in college to return home, and they should be the ones who [represent the farm workers and] fight with the growers. . . . They need to do it with respect, facts, and a lot of courage. [My translation]*

Raúl's opinion of the UFW's involvement appears to be overcritical. He blamed solely the union and the SPGA strikers for the interpersonal conflicts that occurred during the strike, yet he neglected to examine how the growers were involved in creating the conditions that sparked the labor conflict. For example, he failed to acknowledge that many of the strikers were angry and launched the attack on the packing house because the previous day an immigration raid had been carried out in El Campito and many of the striking families were appre-hended (*SPDC,* March 4, 1975, 87[218]:1). Furthermore, it was rumored that the SPGA had called the INS and had the families deported (Mines and Anzaldúa 1982).

In the second week of the strike, that the farm workers were evenly divided into supporters and non-supporters became apparent. It was also obvious that a citywide agricultural work stoppage was improbable because most packing house workers and Limoneira Ranch employees refused to walk out on strike. Gloria, the second-generation Limoneira Ranch employee, offered the following analy-sis, explaining why her co-workers preferred to remain neutral during the labor dispute. Gloria was in full spiritual support of the strikers and sympathized with their problems. She had many friends and *comadres* (her children's godmothers) living in El Campito. Nonetheless, she was not in favor of joining the strike or holding union elections. According to Gloria, the working conditions on Limoneira Ranch were excellent and the growers treated the workers with respect. She believed, however, that if any Limoneira employee supported the strike she or he would immediately lose any placement within the company's retirement program and possibly lose her or his pension plan. The workers, particularly those who were in their late thirties to early forties, therefore, had to be loyal to the company if they wanted to protect their retirement pensions. She added that, unlike the SPGA, Limoneira Ranch practiced a fair promotion system and never replaced seniority employees with newcomers. To illustrate her analysis, Gloria shared one of her memories. In 1962, at sixteen years of age, she was employed sorting Sunkist lemons at the Limoneira Ranch packing house. At that time, several teenage girls who picked citrus were waiting to be promoted to cannery work. Because of the fifteen-hour shifts at peak harvest season, a turnover of female packing house workers was expected, given the slower productivity of several older women. At age fifty, the older women complained that the long shifts were making their varicose veins flare up, straining their eyes and backs, and causing bladder problems (because they were not allowed to use the rest rooms as needed). Consequently, these older women defied company rules and took several unauthorized breaks. The employees thought it was only a matter of time before management would replace the senior women with young girls who were quicker with their hands. Management surprised everyone by choosing to keep the older women at the same wages and instead hired only two teenage girls. This event was quite unexpected by labor because management would have paid the entry-level girls lower wages and at the same time the company would have received a higher work output. Analyzing this case, Gloria believed that the company kept the older women for two reasons. First, Limoneira Ranch was following its traditional policy of taking care of its senior workers. Second, if the company had fired or retired the older women, this incident might have lowered the employees' morale and perhaps would have eventually slowed down production. According to Gloria, management paid stable wages, provided year-round employment and housing, and offered a pension plan and health benefits in order to maintain high employee productivity. Gloria captured Limoneira Ranch's apparent motto toward labor in this way: "A happy worker is a productive worker." When I interviewed five other Limoneira Ranch employees, they relayed similar accounts to explain why they considered themselves to be company workers.

By the end of the second week of the strike, interpersonal conflicts between supporters and non-supporters erupted into violence. One evening a strike leader was murdered in his home (Mines and Anzaldúa 1982: 49). Once again, rumors surfaced. Most people said that the incident was related to the strike activities in the fields, and others said that an angry husband of one of the packing house workers shot the labor leader. Yet others said that the man was shot because he was having an adulterous affair with a married woman. The last account rumored that an anonymous caller telephoned the husband of the adulterous wife and ignited the shooting. No one knew what had really happened. The violence did not end there, as a second labor leader was brutally beaten on his way home from a labor meeting (Mines and Anzaldúa 1982:49).

With the escalating violence directed toward the strike leaders and the workers' inability to resolve the labor protest, the strikers were forced to seek legal recourse. On March 12, 1975, attorneys from the Ventura County Legal Aid filed a class action suit on behalf of the strikers against the SPGA. Counsel for the strikers alleged that the association had hired strikebreakers during the labor dispute and that this constituted an unfair labor practice under federal and state labor codes (California Labor Code Section 1140c, cited in Shulman 1986:19).

When the class action suit was filed, the strike officially ended. The growers were unwilling to have anything more to do with the strikers. The strikers had lost the struggle in the fields. At that point, the labor dispute took on a new direction. It moved into the courtrooms. Therefore, the growers, unable to win the strike, decided to get rid of the strikers through other means: by expelling them from Santa Paula in order to set an example for the rest of the farm workers. To do so, the growers issued housing eviction notices to all striking residents of El Campito and ordered them off of SPGA property (Mines and Anzaldúa 1982). The strikers' legal counsel immediately filed a second lawsuit stipulating that the eviction notices were retaliatory and were an attempt on the part of the growers to intimidate the strikers and prevent them from continuing with their suit. Counsel argued that this act was illegal and an unfair labor and housing practice.

Most strikers responded to the eviction notices by refusing to move out of El Campito.

The strike may have officially ended, but the labor movement continued in Santa Paula. Many of my informants recall that one night people were awakened by the siren sounds of an outdated fire truck speeding through the empty streets. Furthermore, the howling city whistle—set in motion by the fire department— alerted the Santa Paula community that it was in the midst of a crisis. The next morning, people were dismayed to find that someone had set fire to the SPGA packing house. Rumors began. Accusations were made that either the growers, the former strikers, or the UFW had started the fire. Two main speculations emerged to explain who the culprits might be. The first conjecture was that the association burned the packing house because it had lost thousands of dollars in the strike. Thus, if the packing house were destroyed, the association would be able to collect monetary damages from its fire insurance and therefore recoup part of the losses incurred during the strike. The second speculation was that the UFW burned the packing house in order to frighten the growers in Santa Paula. The fire was the union's way of sending a message to the growers: "If you want to play dirty, we'll also play dirty." Other people, who disagreed with these conjectures, said irresponsible strikers burned the packing house because they were angry. To this date, no one knows who burned the packing house. We do know, however, that the growers collected the insurance and the movement to hold union elections continued.

THE LABOR UNREST CONTINUES AND THE SANTA PAULA GROWERS ASSOCIATION LAWSUIT ENTERS THE COURTROOMS

For weeks, the Mexican-origin community, regardless of past attitudes toward the strikers, mourned the outcome of the strike. It was a moral defeat for the entire community, and that its political militancy would be suppressed by the growers was clearly understood. Once again history repeated itself, and the farm worker labor movement was temporarily suppressed. Paradoxically, in late May, two months after the strike had ended, a new development occurred. Hundreds of Santa Paula packing house workers walked out on strike and joined the former SPGA strikers in their struggle to obtain collective bargaining representation (*SPDC,* May 22, 1975, 88[22]:1; *SPDC,* May 30, 1975, 88[26]:1). Moreover, in the nearby cities of Fillmore, Sespe, Saticoy, Oxnard, and Ventura, thousands of workers went out on strike, and movements to hold union elections began (Mines and Anzaldúa 1982; *SPDC,* July 10, 1975, 88[54]:1; *SPDC,* August 13, 1975, 88[78]:1).

Although many packing house workers in Santa Paula changed their attitude toward the UFW, more than half of these workers refused to strike or support holding union elections. Limoneira Ranch employees also refused to get involved in the labor activities. Therefore, confrontations began between the workers, and the conflicts spread from the workplace to the private homes of individuals. Some angry strikers decided to picket the homes of individuals who refused to join the labor struggle. The *Santa Paula Daily Chronicle* reported one such incident:

> *Pickets . . . carried their picket lines to the homes of the strike breakers. There have been complaints from people currently working as packers that pickets have followed them to their homes to set up picket lines on the sidewalks fronting the houses. News of this development came as a surprise to legal representatives of the strikers, but indications are that as long as pickets remain on public property and cause no trouble no laws are being violated. (SPDC, May 30, 1975, 88[26]:1)*

For months interpersonal conflicts continued to escalate from the private homes of individuals to public places frequented by the farm workers. Hector, a businessman, recalled how the family store became involved in the strike. Hector's father, Samuel, owned a grocery store in Santa Paula and sold food on credit to the farm workers. Samuel also helped newly arrived immigrant families by referring them to farm employers and assisting them in finding housing. He was respected by the farm workers and was a personal friend of the growers. When the labor unrest began, many strikers expected Samuel to be part of El Comité. Samuel, however, decided to stay out of the labor dispute for several reasons. First of all, he did not want to lose the clients who were opposed to the strike, and second, he did not want any picket lines near the store. Consequently, many farm workers bitterly criticized Samuel for not getting involved. Hector recalled that the farm workers were unfair because his father donated large amounts of food to the striking families:

> *When the workers went on strike, many farm workers criticized my father. They got mad because he didn't get involved. He couldn't because it would hurt the store, and besides many of his friends were growers. . . . If he became a leader he probably would have been kicked out of the*

Rotary. . . . They [the farm workers] called him names.
The same people that called him names came to pick up
boxes of food for the striking families.

As a result of the labor unrest in the county, Chávez once again came to offer moral support and to advise the farm workers on how they could join the UFW. On July 10, 1975, in a tour throughout the county, Chávez spoke to thousands of farm workers. He informed them about their collective bargaining rights under the Agricultural Labor Relations Act (*SPDC,* July 10, 1975, 88[54]:1). He explained to them that the state government of California gave agricultural employees the freedom to associate for the purpose of discussing labor organization. Farm workers also had the right to hold a secret ballot election, and if they obtained a majority vote in favor of joining a union, they could elect officials to represent them. After they obtained a majority consensus, they then needed to file a petition with the state government. The government would afterward enforce the workers' right to obtain union representation. At that point, Chávez informed the workers that the growers were legally bound to enact a contract with the union. The contract could not be broken unless agreed upon by the union members and the growers.

Although César Chávez' visit to Ventura County served to boost morale among the county's farm laborers, he was unable to convince the majority of them to hold union elections. His visit primarily served to establish close lines of communication between supporters of the UFW and the home office in Delano, California. Eventually, though, Chávez' persistent unionization campaign paid off. By 1978, the UFW was able to unionize over 80 percent of the citrus pickers in Ventura County.[10] In Santa Paula, however, the UFW was unsuccessful. The majority of the farm laborers did not favor holding elections, and unionization movements temporarily stopped in 1976. Many of my informants attribute this event to the intimidating messages that they received from the growers, in particular from the SPGA. In late autumn of 1975, the SPGA officially decided to fire all of its workers and disband their own association. Their goals were twofold: (1) to blacklist all the strikers and force them to move out of Santa Paula and (2) to minimize the impact of the lawsuit filed against them. That is, in case the farm workers won the suit, the growers would not have to rehire them or pay back wages because the association would had been disbanded. Moreover, the farm workers would have to move out of El Campito because the property would be sold.

At first, disbanding the SPGA appeared to be a brilliant strategy because if the association no longer existed, the lawsuit would be a moot point. Moreover, this situation would force the majority of the strikers to move out of town. To the dismay of most Santa Paula residents, however, on May 10, 1976, a federal judge ruled in favor of the strikers and found the SPGA guilty of breaking federal and state labor laws (*SPDC,* May 10, 1976, 89[133]:1). The court ruled against the association and concluded that their legal defense was unjustifiable. The association had argued that it did not hire scab labor during the dispute nor was it responsible for negotiating with the strikers. According to the association, labor was hired through independent contractors and not by the association itself; therefore, the growers were not responsible for unfair labor practices committed by the strike arbitrators, such as Ralph. The judge found all of these arguments invalid and ruled that the association had broken three laws (1) by hiring scab labor during the strike, (2) by refusing to allow workers to associate for the pupose of initiating collective bargaining, and (3) in being responsible for the misconduct of any manager or labor contractor who acted on behalf of the association (California Labor Code Section 1140c, cited in Shulman 1986:19).[11] In sum, the association was found guilty of unfair labor practices. Ironically, although the strikers won the ruling, the initial problem that had sparked the strike was concluded to be a legal action. The court ruled that the association had the right to lay off the women pickers and rehire new labor because the workers did not have a contract prohibiting the growers from proceeding with such an action. It had been illegal, however, for the association to replace strikers with scab labor during the dispute. Finally, in 1977 and 1980, the strikers also won their housing eviction suit against the association. The Supreme Court of California ruled that the eviction notices were illegal and constituted unfair labor practices (Mines and Anzaldúa 1982). Thus, even though the association was dissolved and its members were now independent growers, the former association was responsible for paying back wages and compensating the strikers for all damages.

Ultimately, although the strikers finally won their lawsuits, the growers were able to divide the farm workers in Santa Paula and to convince their loyal employees not to join the UFW. Without a united farm worker community, a total agricultural work stoppage in Santa Paula was impossible. Consequently, many of Santa Paula's farm workers continued to be discriminated against by the growers. I will next examine how the farm workers who were evicted from their homes adroitly responded to the crisis and discuss why this incident sparked other political movements in Santa Paula. Once again, members of the Mexican-origin community tried to make Santa Paula a more harmonious place to live by alleviating racial discrimination in the city.

SEVEN

Interethnic City Council Politics

The Case of the Housing Cooperative Movement

By 1970, the growers' ability to dominate Santa Paula's social life declined when they lost control of the city council (Belknap 1968). For the Mexican-origin community and, in particular, the farm workers, this change alleviated their marginalized status, as the council became more responsive to them. Once the growers did not control the city council, urban renewal projects were implemented on the East Side and in the labor camps. Without this change in political structure, these urban renewal projects probably would not have been instituted because these activities did not benefit the growers. This chapter will examine the changing political relations between the city council and the people of Mexican descent. Particular attention is paid to the farm worker housing cooperative movement, since this was the main social advancement that affected the Mexican-origin community after the growers lost control of Santa Paula's city council. In reconstructing these events, I rely on nineteen interviews. Sixteen interviews were conducted with Mexican-origin people and three with Anglo Americans.

THE CHANGING POLITICAL STRUCTURE

In the late 1960s, Anglo American merchants who were not involved in citrus production broke the political monopoly the citrus growers had exercised over Santa Paula's city council for nearly a century (Belknap 1968). To explain how this event occurred and how it benefited the Mexican-origin community, it is necessary first to examine the social conditions that contributed to the changing political structure and thereby clarify why council members eventually became more responsive toward their Mexican-origin constituency and actively implemented urgently needed urban renewal projects. When the growers lost political control of the city council, three factors that ran against their interests were converging: (1) demographic changes, (2) the new political significance of the Mexican American vote,[1] and (3) land tenure changes prompted by aging citrus orchards.

In regard to demographic changes in Santa Paula, by 1970 the growers' political power had eroded because the majority of the residents did not owe them political allegiance. In the case of the Mexican community, since industrial jobs had become available in the nearby cities of Los Angeles, Santa Barbara, Ventura, and Oxnard, nearly half of the community was able to obtain non-agricultural jobs (Triem 1985; United States Census Bureau 1973:779) (see Table 2). Therefore, those who worked outside the agricultural industry became independent of the growers. Within the Anglo American community, the citrus growers' political support also declined. This was largely associated with the influx of thousands of newcomers to Santa Paula. From 1960 to 1970, the city's population increased by 36 percent, growth that was due largely to 4,766 new residents moving into Santa Paula (United States Census Bureau 1963:6–384; 1973:6–779, 6–836, 6–931). Many of these people were Anglo Americans who had no close ties to the citrus families (Keefe 1979; Keefe and Padilla 1986). New residents were able to move to Santa Paula because Freeway 126 was constructed in 1963 (Triem 1985). For the first time in the city's history, Santa Paula was connected to California's main freeway and highway systems (e.g., freeways 101 and 1, and Highway 5). By car, Santa Paula was now approximately forty-five minutes from Los Angeles and fifteen minutes from other major coastal cities. Before the construction of Freeway 126, people had to travel via either a mountainous route or a desolate country road to reach Santa Paula. Therefore, when the freeway was constructed, Santa Paula became an attractive residential bedroom community area for people who preferred the ambiance of an agrarian city (Keefe 1979; Keefe and Padilla 1986).

Thus, by the late 1960s, as Santa Paula had many residents who did not owe political allegiance to the citrus growers, it became possible for individuals without agricultural interests to be elected to the city council. Three of my informants, José, Tony, and Robert, also recalled that the growers' political power declined when several Anglo American merchants sought the support of Mexican American voters. This was a second major factor contributing to Santa Paula's changing political structure. This change occurred in the late 1960s and benefited the Mexican-origin community. In return for the Mexican American vote, Anglo

Santa Paula Mountains.

Santa Paula.

American merchants who ran for the city council began to promise that, if elected to office, they would appoint Mexican Americans to the city planning commission. They also promised to support Mexican American candidates who ran for high school or elementary school board positions. In other words, a number of Anglo Americans began practicing interethnic coalition politics in order to dismantle the growers' hold over the city council.

Interestingly, once the merchants obtained political control of the city council, real estate changes within Santa Paula's land tenure structure apparently served to keep them in office. This was a third factor that served to dismantle the growers' political power. That is, in the early 1970s many citrus families began selling their farm land to real estate developers, thus prompting the entrance of more newcomers to Santa Paula. Real estate developers built new housing tracts where old citrus orchards were once located. The housing developments became attractive homesites for outsiders who preferred to live in small agrarian cities yet be close enough to commute to work in the nearby larger urban areas. Santa Paula's rustic environment of oak, palm, sycamore, cottonwood, and eucalyptus trees was quite attractive. The city was also surrounded by mountains covered with citrus orchards (Santa Paula Chamber of Commerce 1986). Alfredo Gutiérrez, a board member of the Santa Paula Savings and Loan Company, and Hank Levin, the president of the Teague-McKevett Corporation, offered valuable insights regarding why several Santa Paula farmers sold their land. Both informants identified four similar reasons. First, after the freeway was constructed, Santa Paula became an excellent commuter community for people who worked in the outskirts of Los Angeles. Second, the children and grandchildren of many citrus growers became uninterested in managing their families' citrus businesses and consequently sold their land. Third, several large aging orchards became unprofitable to maintain. The owners of the orchards had the option of replanting or selling the land to real estate developers. Selling the property was a more reasonable alternative for those landowners who preferred not to invest in replanting. Fourth, after the bracero program ended, the UFW began to actively recruit members in Santa Paula, which made farming a risk. Some farmers decided to sell their orchards rather than deal with the UFW. In turn, after the tracts of land were sold, the orchards were torn down and homes were constructed to make room for new residents. The end result of the newcomers' settling in Santa Paula was that the pool of residents who did not support the growers increased.

In sum, demographic changes, coalition politics, and real estate projects collectively served to change the makeup of Santa Paula's city council.

NEW CITY COUNCIL
MEMBERS AND THEIR
CAMPAIGN PROMISES

Changes within Santa Paula's political structure benefited the Mexican-origin community in various ways. For example, beginning in 1970, the representation of Mexican Americans increased within the city planning commission because the newly elected officials fulfilled their campaign promises. For the first time in Santa Paula's history, Mexican Americans came to constitute 25 percent of the planning commission and, between 1972 and 1980, their presence increased from 25 to 38 percent (Salas 1984; see Minute Book 1965–1970, letters L, M, and N, in City of Santa Paula 1914–1989). My informant Tony was among the several Mexican Americans appointed to the commission. He served between 1972 and 1980. There also appeared to be a slight increase in the election of Mexican American candidates within the Santa Paula school boards (Salas 1984). A case in point is the experience of my informant Robert, who was elected to Santa Paula's elementary school board between 1973 and 1977. Robert attributes part of his success to endorsements from two Anglo American city council members. Though most of his votes came from Mexican Americans, the Anglo Americans' political support helped him gain enough votes to be elected. Furthermore, the changing political structure of Santa Paula benefited the Mexican-origin community because the new council members fulfilled their campaign promises. For example, urban renewal projects were funded for the Mexican neighborhoods. In 1969, Las Piedras Park was constructed on the East Side (*SPDC,* June 9, 1969, 83[33]:1). It was the first park built in a Mexican neighborhood. The city council also allocated funds to install more street lights on the East Side, to repair and construct sidewalks, and to repave a few streets that were covered with potholes.

Tony also recalls that, although for the first time in Santa Paula's history council members implemented urgently needed projects on the East Side, city policies remained practically unchanged. According to Tony, the East Side needed major repairs, not just a few "bandage projects." For example, when he served on the planning commission, he presented several proposals to improve living conditions on the East Side. He was most concerned with removing the pesticide, chemical, and oil plants from the East Side and rezoning them to the outskirts of the city limits. Each time he introduced a rezoning proposal, it would be turned down by the planning commission because it was judged to be unfeasible or expensive. When Tony's proposals were turned down, he was outraged. He could not believe the city planners were unable to develop a plan to improve environmental conditions on the East Side. Tony's proposal to construct a new drainage system on the East Side was also turned down because of the cost, although the existing drainage system was over a hundred years old. He couldn't convince the commission that the drainage problems on the East Side were urgent, although it was common knowledge that during the rainy season the drainage pipes would overflow in the streets and cause major traffic congestion problems. One year, Tony almost resigned from the commission when his colleagues voted in favor of restoring several storm drainage pipes on the West Side instead of repairing the system on the East Side. Once again he was outraged that the commission voted in favor of repairing pipes that were less than forty years old. In his opinion, the drainage system on the West Side needed some improvements, but in comparison with what was needed on the East Side, it was not an emergency situation. At that time he decided not to resign because he needed to continue arguing in favor of urban renewal projects for the East Side.

In spite of Tony's disappointments, on one occasion his lobbying efforts paid off: he suggested that the landscaping of Las Piedras Park be upgraded. It was an idea shared by many Mexican American civic leaders. The planning commission endorsed the proposal, and the city council voted unanimously in favor of the landscaping project. Although this was a monumental achievement, Tony recalls that the building materials used to landscape the park were of low quality in comparison with those used to build the six parks on the West Side. When the city council approved the proposed Las Piedras Park landscape budget, he was angry but not surprised because the use of cheap building materials for East Side projects was an accepted practice. For example, when the city council approved the construction of the light fixtures on the East Side, cheap wooden posts were purchased. However, when new light fixtures were needed on the West Side, attractive metal posts were installed. Moreover, when several streets were repaved on the East Side, they were improperly tarred and left unleveled. This type of sloppy construction work never occurred on the West Side.

Tony also believes that city maintenance policies for the East Side and West Side were unbalanced. For example, the maintenance crew kept the West Side streets properly clean and the parks well manicured and landscaped. On the East Side, however, besides the weekly trash-day pickup, it was uncommon to find a maintenance worker cleaning the streets. Furthermore, after Las Piedras Park was constructed, weeds were allowed to grow throughout the grounds. According to Tony, the unevenness in the city maintenance policies contributed to the beautification of the West Side as well as to the progressive physical deterioration of the East Side.

Unfortunately, although East Side–West Side city policies were obviously unbalanced, very few people formally complained. No one organized a protest rally or jammed the city council during budget hearings. The only public protest was launched by Jimeno, a retired Mexican American veteran. For years, Jimeno parked his truck in front of city hall and displayed some political commentary— often accusing council members of racism and stealing money—on a poster placed on the truck's cabin. And every time a new council was elected, Jimeno drove around town with his poster, criticizing the new council members. He would later park his truck in front of the police station or in front of city hall. On one occasion, Jimeno offered the following commentary:

> *MAYBE OUR 3 NEW INCOMING*
> *COUNCILMEN WILL HAVE GUTS AND*
> *TAKE CARE OF THIS PROBLEM. LIKE*
> *YOU SHOULD HAVE 2 1/2 YEARS AGO.*
> *DEMOCRACY DEPENDS ON INFORMATION*
> *CIRCULATING FREELY.*

To this day, Jimeno parks his truck in front of city hall or the police station. He changes the political commentary every two weeks.

When I spoke to Tony, I asked him why people of Mexican descent did not protest against the council's policies. He responded that he did not know, and instead offered an analysis as to why Mexican American civic leaders did not launch an outright attack against the city planning commission or the city council. Tony believes that Mexican Americans did not confront the city council because they were afraid. Tony also believes that they do not confront the city council because such a confrontation would be futile. The council merely ignores them when they complain. In the past, when Mexican American civic leaders criticized the council for not making all the needed urban renewal changes on the East Side, they were treated cordially, but no resolution was offered. Instead, complicated budgetary arguments and environmental impact reports were introduced by the city officials, and the Mexican American leaders were informed that the city was doing its best. Tony attributes the problem also to the difference in the level of education between the Anglo American council members and themselves. Most of the Mexican American leaders were high school dropouts and a few of them had less than an elementary education.[2] On the other hand, most of the Anglo Americans were college graduates. When council members presented their counterarguments, they did so in a complicated and commanding tone. Their arguments were based on projected budgetary estimates which were difficult to dispute. Also, the city council was often represented by legal counsel or engineers who supported the positions of council members. Tony recalls that, several times after the Mexican American leaders met with the council, they vowed not to support any more Anglo American politicians. After their anger subsided,

A Mexican American criticizing city hall.

however, they concurred that a city council that was dominated by merchants was better than one dominated by citrus growers. Also, Mexican American leaders acknowledged the fact that some of the Anglo American council members were politically useful to the Mexican-origin community. For example, with Anglo American support the Mexican American representation had increased within city hall. Beginning in the early 1970s, several Mexican Americans had been elected to office, and others were appointed to the city planning commission (see Minute Book 1970, in City of Santa Paula 1921–1986).

Moving on to another topic of Santa Paula's politics, Tony warmly noted that although the Mexican American leadership traditionally had not practiced confrontational interethnic politics, Mexican youth became more politically aggressive in the 1970s. According to Tony, this youthful attitude benefited them all, for the youth placed pressure on the city council to do something about the deplorable living conditions in the farm worker labor camps. We now turn to this issue.

CHICANO YOUTH AND
THEIR POLITICAL VOICES:
THE CASE OF EL CAMPITO

By 1972, many of the Mexican-origin youth of Santa Paula were influenced by the political philosophy of the Chicano Movement, and they publicly became vocal against unfair farm labor practices and against the city government's minimal efforts to fund urban renewal projects on the East Side (*Ventura County Star Free Press,* July 30, 1972, 97[268]: section B-6). With respect to the city council, the Mexican-origin youth were particularly critical of the council members' ignoring the housing problems affecting the farm workers who resided in the labor camps located within the city limits.

To a large extent, the political consciousness of the Mexican-origin youth of Santa Paula was part of a larger national political movement—the Chicano Movement. At the national level, the seminal forces that sparked the Chicano Movement were the United Farm Workers, the Alianza Federal de Pueblos Libres (Federal Alliance of Free City States), the Crusade for Justice, the Brown Berets, and the Chicano Student Movement.[3] The crystallization of these subgroups created a national social movement in the late 1960s which came to be known as the Chicano Movement. The various Chicano political organizations became concerned with understanding how Anglo American racism had shaped the Mexican experience in the United States. Demonstrations, boycotts, strikes, and sit-ins became political vehicles that brought to national attention the Mexican-origin people's poverty level, the farm workers' struggle against servitude wages and working conditions, and certain perceived inequalities (e.g., police brutality; limited access to higher education). Such ethnic consciousness was also manifested in the birth of the self-imposed label "Chicano" (Gómez-Quiñonez 1978).[4]

In Santa Paula, many people changed their ethnic label to "Chicano" during the early phase of the Chicano Movement (Keefe and Padilla 1986). The main Chicano political organization established in the city was a Brown Beret chapter founded in 1972 (*Ventura County Star Free Press,* July 30, 1972, 97[268]: section B-6). The organization was primarily composed of Chicano youth who were concerned with improving farm worker conditions and initiating an urban renewal program on the East Side. Lourdes was among my informants who attended the Brown Beret meetings and rallies. She recalled that once a month the Brown Berets marched in military style around the East Side. They wore tan-and-brown uniforms with brown berets and shouted political propaganda while they marched. They would end their peaceful marches in local Las Piedras Park, where a large crowd gathered to hear political speeches on class oppression. She also remembers that many of the farm workers employed by the Santa Paula Growers Association (SPGA) attended the rallies and listened attentively to the speeches. The main themes discussed by the Brown Berets were the deplorable employment and housing conditions endured by the SPGA farm workers. Lourdes recalls that farm workers also often spoke during the Brown Beret rallies. The youth and the farm workers would use El Campito labor camp as an example of the class exploitation experienced by the Chicano community. Since the rallies were held in Las Piedras Park, which was located adjacent to El Campito, the speakers would point to the labor camp during the political speeches and shout: "Is it fair for people to live in shacks? Look at how the growers treat us." What follows is Lourdes' remembrance of a Brown Beret rally held in Las Piedras Park.

> *After they marched around the* barrio, *I went to the park to listen. . . . He [a Brown Beret speaker] was a young college student who believed in democracy and social reform and was trying to help the* raza *[people of Mexican descent] in Santa Paula by raising their people's consciousness and telling them there was something wrong if most of the Mexicans were poor and the Anglos were middle class or rich. He wanted the Mexicans to do something about their poverty, and that meant confronting the growers and the police.*

Lourdes also recalled that, during the same period that the Brown Berets were holding their rallies in Las Piedras Park, the farm workers employed by the SPGA went out on strike (see chapter 6). In turn, the farm worker activity served to heighten the political consciousness of many Chicano youth. In response to the labor activity, many young Chicanos supported the farm workers by participating in the picket lines. Lourdes also recalled that Chicano youth displayed their moral support for the farm workers by cruising the streets in the evening. For several weeks over a hundred cars—each piled with at least seven teenagers—honked their horns and formed enormously long caravans beginning on the East Side. The caravans would then cruise over to the downtown area. On each car a Mexican flag was pasted on the rear window, and when the Chicano youth saw a policeman, they would shout political slogans such as "Chicano power," "Viva la raza," or "Viva César Chávez." Lourdes described one such evening when Chicano youth formed a car caravan to demonstrate their ethnic solidarity with the farm labor activities. Lourdes stated:

> *Cholos,[5] farm workers, college students . . . fourteen-year-olds to their mid-twenties cruised the streets. . . . We didn't know what we were doing, but we felt that we had to make our presence known. . . . It was the political climate. Our consciousness was being raised by the Chicano Movement.*

Corroborating Lourdes' remembrances, Tony also recalled that the car caravans and the political rallies at Las Piedras Park were important events. The caravans served to bring urgent political attention to the social needs of the East Side, in particular to the problems of El Campito. The farm workers' protest against the living conditions in El Campito was an ongoing complaint that was ignored by the growers. However, when hundreds of Chicano youth and political activists also began to voice similar complaints, the situation at El Campito became a more serious matter that had to be investigated by the city council. It was not in the interest of the city council to have Chicano youth organizing protest rallies in Santa Paula, as this would disrupt the city's peaceful ambiance and frighten residents.

Although the political activism of the Chicano youth was widespread in Santa Paula, it ended suddenly in 1976. Lourdes and Tony both attributed this change to a decline in the city's farm labor strike activity (see chapter 6).[6] Apparently, when the farm workers employed by the SPGA lost the strike of 1975, one of the Chicano youths' main goals was defeated. At that point, they began to lose their political momentum. Although the youth activism ended, Lourdes and Tony both agreed that it served to bring citywide attention to the housing problems on the East Side, and in particular to El Campito labor camp.

FARM WORKER HOUSING MOVEMENTS TO REHABILITATE THE LABOR CAMPS

In Santa Paula, El Campito labor camp constituted the worst substandard housing division in the city. It was Santa Paula's most infamous slum and an embarrassment to the city residents.[7] Although Santa Paula residents had felt for decades that the city council should intervene on behalf of the farm workers and demand some improvements in the camp, it was common knowledge that changes would not be implemented. That is, because the city council was dominated by the growers until 1969, no one expected council members to pass a policy against the growers' interests (Belknap 1968). However, when control shifted on the council from the citrus growers to the merchants, the possibilities for improving the living conditions in El Campito increased. This section will discuss why the city council took on the charge of pressuring the citrus growers to renovate the labor camp.

El Campito was constructed in 1920 by a group of citrus growers (Black 1984; *Ventura County Star Free Press,* February 2, 1983: A-12). The purpose of the camp was to house the field pickers employed by the growers. In 1965, the camp was owned by the SPGA and occupied by the associations' farm employees. Although this housing was provided to the farm workers, it was clearly substandard. The homes were constructed out of plywood, lacked insulation, and did not have standard housing foundations (*Los Angeles Times,* March 6, 1983:1, 15). They had been constructed on cement blocks rather than placed on cement slabs as required by standard housing regulations. In the mid-1960s, during the rainy seasons, the cement blocks began to disintegrate in many of the homes. Many houses also tilted sideways during the rainy season. The residents of El Campito repaired the damages by balancing the houses on large piles of rocks placed underneath the floors (*Los Angeles Times,* March 6, 1983:1, 15). Furthermore, when the floors collapsed, the renters would fill the holes or make new floors by placing more rocks underneath their homes. In spite of the ongoing housing complaints filed by the farm workers, the growers neglected to listen to their tenants and refused to repair the camp (*SPDC,* January 30, 1974, 87[190]:1; Mines and Anzaldúa 1982). El Campito also lacked any street lights and had only a few paved roads. Throughout the history of the labor camp, major improvements were not funded by the growers.

As explained in chapter 6, the residents of El Campito launched a strike in 1975 against their employers—who were also their landlords. The farm workers voiced complaints against low wages and unfair landlord practices. In retaliation for their going out on strike, the SPGA evicted the tenants. The growers envisioned that the eviction notices would force the farm workers to end the strike. To the contrary, the farm workers reacted by refusing to vacate the premises and instead filing an agricultural workers housing discrimination lawsuit (Mines and Anzaldúa 1982). After the suit was filed, the growers demanded that the farm workers vacate the premises immediately. In turn, the farm workers asked the courts for protection. The courts intervened and ruled that the farm workers could remain in the labor camp until the case was adjudicated. In 1977, two years after the suit was filed, the judicial courts offered a final judgment on the housing dispute. The courts ruled that the eviction notices had been illegal and the farm workers did not have to vacate the premises. The owners of the labor camp also had to compensate the renters for damages and legal fees. Ironically, though the farm workers won the suit, the courts did not force the growers to renovate the camp because at that time agricultural labor camps were exempt from state and federal housing regulations (Shulman 1986). The federal government did not require agricultural labor housing to comply with health and safety standards until 1982 (Migrant and Seasonal Agricultural Worker Protection Act 1982, 29 U.S.C. sec. 1823, cited in Shulman 1986:3).

Following the court proceedings, the owners of El Campito decided to sell the camp. At this point, the city council intervened on behalf of the residents of El

Campito. The position taken by the city council was apparently a result of community pressure. Several of my informants recall that the actions of the growers were perceived by the Mexican-origin and Anglo American communities as an example of extreme neglect and cruelty. Therefore, the city council was expected to intervene. Moreover, since the Santa Paula city council was no longer controlled by the citrus growers, its members were not pressured to pass policies solely favoring the growers' interests. To help the residents of the labor camp, the city council made a provision ordering that whoever bought the camp had to renovate it. This made finding a buyer difficult for the growers. The new owner of the camp would also face two additional problems: (1) the city council made it publicly known that it would not approve any real estate plan that would displace the residents, such as rezoning the land for industrial purposes or converting it into a middle- or upper-class housing district, and (2) the labor camp was inhabited by residents who were unwilling to vacate the premises (*SPDC,* December 14, 1983:1; *Ventura County Star Free Press,* February 2, 1983: A-12).

In 1979, El Campito was finally sold to Blue Goose Corporation, an agricultural business (Black 1984). The new owner purchased a total of twenty acres that contained one hundred houses. A few months later, Blue Goose Corporation decided to sell the houses to the residents or to any interested buyers, although they had not renovated the houses as required by the city council (*Ventura County Star Free Press,* February 2, 1983: A-12). The residents were given a few months to purchase the houses, otherwise the dwellings would be sold on the open market. Because most farm workers could not raise the money within the designated period, they formed an organization with the intent of preventing the corporation from selling their homes. The farm workers called themselves "La Colonia Santa Paula Comité." Disgusted with the actions of the new owner, the city council also decided to step in and protect the rights of the farm workers. In order to prevent Blue Goose from selling El Campito to non-residents, council members passed an ordinance mandating that the houses be sold to the farm workers (*Ventura County Star Free Press,* December 14, 1983: A-8). The city council also required Blue Goose to rehabilitate the camp before any house could be sold (*SPDC,* December 14, 1983: 1). Blue Goose refused to comply with the city's requirements. In response, the council members filed a lawsuit against the corporation (*Ventura County Star Free Press,* February 2, 1983: A-12). One year later, the judicial courts ruled in favor of Blue Goose and stated that the city council did not have any right to intervene in the corporation's affairs. After the city lost the court battle, Blue Goose obtained the right to evict the tenants of El Campito.

The residents did not lose hope of remaining in El Campito and becoming its legal owners. Instead, they sought legal assistance from a Ventura County non-profit farm worker housing agency called the Cabrillo Economic Development Corporation (CEDC) (Black 1984). CEDC had recently been established in Ventura County to assist farm workers who had been displaced from labor camp housing.[8] Evidently, the housing crisis experienced by the residents of El Campito was a common problem facing many Ventura County farm workers. According to many of my informants, a countywide housing crisis emerged in the late 1970s, when many growers decided to sell their labor camps to real estate developers.[9] Apparently, when César Chávez' labor movement succeeded in Ventura County and over 80 percent of the farm workers joined the UFW, many growers decided that it was time to sell the labor camps (Mines and Anzaldúa 1982). After decades of neglect many labor camps had virtually turned into slums, and the growers anticipated that Chávez would pressure them to build new housing. Hence, selling the camps rather than demolishing them and building new housing was more profitable for the growers. Throughout Ventura County the farm workers responded to their housing crisis by forming housing cooperatives.

In the case of the residents of El Campito, CEDC recommended that they too organize themselves into a farm worker housing cooperative. If they formed a cooperative, their organization would be eligible to obtain loans from either the UFW or the state government's Farm Home Administration Department in order to buy the camp. And, if they were successful in obtaining the loans, both institutions would oversee the sales transaction between Blue Goose Corporation and the farm workers.[10]

The residents of El Campito followed the advice of the CEDC and reconstituted La Colonia Santa Paula Comité into La Colonia de Santa Paula Board of Directors. After acquiring UFW and state government assistance, they approached Blue Goose and offered to buy the camp. Immediately and without hesitation, Blue Goose offered a counterproposal and attempted to reach a compromise without having the UFW involved. Apparently it was in Blue Goose's best interest not to involve the union because the corporation had many investments in agricultural production. To the surprise of the farm workers, Blue Goose's offer was better than expected. Blue Goose proposed that if the residents did not ask the UFW or the government for assistance, it would sell El Campito to a real estate developer that would construct low-income housing and sell houses only to the residents. Moreover, to ensure that the developer would comply with all agreements, Blue Goose agreed to reduce the price of El Campito by 50 percent. In turn, the residents would agree to abandon their housing cooperative plans and act as conventional homeowners (*Resources* 1984:4, 5 ; *Ventura County Magazine,* July 1983:5). CEDC advised them to accept the offer. Blue Goose

Renovating El Campito labor camp.
Courtesy Ventura County Star Free Press.

subsequently sold the property to Ramos and Jensen Developers for just over half the value of the land (Black 1984). The property, assessed at $1,060,000, was sold for $650,000.

In 1982, the residents of El Campito reached a final agreement with Blue Goose and Ramos and Jensen Developers, and plans were made to begin construction. CEDC and Santa Paula's city council then assisted the farm workers in obtaining mortgage loans, referring them to banks in Los Angeles that had recently begun offering loans to farm workers. Over two-thirds of the applicants qualified for the housing loans. Those families who did not qualify were allowed to rent the homes with the option of buying when they did qualify. In 1983, the developers commenced construction, and in less than a year 128 homes had replaced the former El Campito shacks. The homes were sold to the farm workers for $43,000.

When the construction of the houses began, the city council also offered to reduce the development costs by modifying the city's housing-standard requirements. The purpose was to reduce the cost of building the homes and thereby help the farm workers to qualify for the mortgage loans. The city council exempted the farm worker houses from having two-car garages and permitted the installation of utility lines aboveground (Black 1983). This reduced the price of constructing the homes, and the savings were passed on to the farm workers. The

El Campito becomes La Colonia Santa Paula.

city council also agreed to reduce the sewer charges by 25 percent. Thus, through the joint efforts of the Mexican-origin community, the city council, and the CEDC, El Campito was transformed from a labor camp into a working-class residential community. In 1983, the name of El Campito was changed to La Colonia Santa Paula.

THE GROWTH OF THE FARM WORKER HOUSING COOPERATIVE MOVEMENT IN SANTA PAULA

The transformation of El Campito into a residential community inspired other farm workers in Santa Paula to convert their labor camps into Mexican *colonias* (neighborhoods) also. In these cases, Santa Paula's city council was again instrumental in facilitating the transitions. Ralph López, one of the former managers of the SPGA, emerged as the leader of the second phase of the farm worker housing cooperative movement in Santa Paula. For a moment it is necessary to explain why Ralph became a representative of the farm workers, as this will explain how the second phase of the housing cooperative movement began.

La Colonia Santa Paula Neighborhood Watch foot patrol.

As mentioned in chapter 6, Ralph had been a broker between the farm workers and the growers. His job was to advocate on the growers' behalf. In 1975, Ralph attempted to break the strike launched by the farm workers employed by the SPGA and tried to convince them to concede to the growers. Afterward, when the farm workers lost the strike and the SPGA disbanded, Ralph took advantage of the situation. He organized nearly two-thirds of the employees who had been fired by the association and, with them, formed a for-profit farm worker agricultural association called Sistemas Agrícolas Mexicanos (Mexican Agricultural Systems)(SAMCO).[11] Ralph also invited other farm workers who had not been employed by the SPGA to join SAMCO. Together, Ralph and the farm workers pooled their financial resources and bought the disbanded association's equipment and buses. Ralph became the president of SAMCO and the main share holder. Out of this venture Ralph became a millionaire, and the farm workers profited because the wages they obtained were among the highest in Ventura County. The farm workers also organized a credit union so that they could extend themselves loans. Therefore, in 1983, when the former residents of El Campito succeeded in transforming the camp into a residential community, Ralph suggested that SAMCO farm workers proceed in a similar manner. The city council, to facilitate the conversion of the labor camps into Mexican *colonias,* placed subtle political pressure on the citrus growers. It began to enforce the 1982

Las Piedras Condominiums.

state housing laws that required agricultural housing to comply with state housing regulations. Farm worker housing was no longer legally exempt from the state's safety and health housing codes (Shulman 1986).

Following a similar organizational committee process as had the residents of El Campito, seventy-four farm worker families associated with SAMCO organized themselves into two non-profit farm worker housing cooperatives. The first group comprised thirty-two families. In the winter of 1984, this group of families bought several low-income apartment complexes located adjacent to La Colonia Santa Paula and converted them into Las Piedras Condominiums. The property was formerly owned by local growers, and the apartments had previously functioned as labor camps. To purchase the property, SAMCO associates obtained mortgage loans from the state government and the same banks that had assisted the former El Campito residents. And in 1985, the second group, composed of forty-two more families, initiated the conversion of a labor camp into a working-class residential community (*SPDC,* April 5, 1985, 98[133]:1). For $140,000 they purchased a camp, adjacent to La Colonia Santa Paula and to Las Piedras Condominiums, from local Santa Paula growers who were about to lose the camp as a result of a defaulted loan. The farm workers were able to purchase the property through SAMCO's credit union. After the real estate transaction was completed, Ramos and Jensen Developers built forty-two new homes. The

La Colonia Las Piedras.

builders asked the city council to waive several housing construction codes in order to reduce the cost of the houses (*SPDC,* April 5, 1985, 98[133]:1). The city council agreed. During the winter of 1985, forty-two farm workers' families became homeowners, and they renamed their housing development La Colonia Las Piedras.

RETURNING HOME: MY FIRST ETHNOGRAPHIC OBSERVATIONS

In 1985, I arrived in Santa Paula to collect my ethnographic dissertation field research. I returned to my former hometown, which I had left in 1974 to attend college. I was, therefore, able to observe the last phase of the housing cooperative movement in Santa Paula. When I arrived, I was amazed to find that all the labor camps located on the East Side had been demolished and replaced by Mexican *colonias.* I also arrived in time to attend a festivity celebrating the transformation of the labor camps. The celebration commenced with a Catholic mass held in La Colonia Las Piedras. Following the mass, a series of speeches were presented by city council members and Mexican-origin community leaders, including Ralph. After the speeches, a Mexican band played *cumbias* while the attendants gathered around the picnic tables to eat their *birria* (barbecue).

At the celebration I spoke to several farm workers. They informed me that this event not only represented the conversion of their labor camps into decent housing, but also marked the culmination of the SPGA labor struggle. According to these informants, over three-fourths of the residents of the new Mexican *colonias* had been formerly employed by the SPGA and had participated in the strike of 1975. As they related their version of the strike of 1975 and told me about the housing cooperative movements, they stressed how much they had suffered. My informants attentively counted the major phases of their struggle. First, they had launched two strikes that they lost. Second, they had entered a long and bitter court battle that they finally won. And third, the majority of the former SPGA employees had filed a second lawsuit against the eviction notices at El Campito. Throughout their struggle, the farm workers had suffered economic deprivation and experienced constant fear because they were afraid of being physically harmed by the growers. However, throughout their struggle they did not give up. Only a few families decided to abandon the fight and search for work elsewhere. Changing their voices from the sad tone of their account of the labor struggle, they suddenly shifted to a more rapid and higher-pitched tone when they talked about Ralph: "El Don," as they sarcastically referred to him. They agreed that Ralph was a *diablo* (devil). They described him as a man full of contradictions, yet extremely *aguzado* (intelligent). On the one hand, he was always out for himself. He was a brown capitalist. On the other hand, Ralph was proud of his people and had always tried to help them. For example, they told the account of Ralph's valiant efforts when he organized SAMCO. He did the impossible. Ralph convinced the farm workers to trust him even though he had sided with the growers during the strike of 1975. And, afterward, Ralph was able to convince the SPGA to sell him their equipment at a very low price. At first my informants acted perplexed over how Ralph was able to convince the growers to sell the equipment. Interrupting the conversation, one of the farm workers said: "Of course we know. He cordially forced them." Allegedly, the growers knew that Ralph had become a labor boss in Santa Paula and that he controlled almost half of the farm workers. The growers knew that in the future if they wanted their orchards to be harvested by Ralph's men they needed to be his business associates and not his enemies. In concluding their oral history of Ralph's activities, the farm workers explained how SAMCO became the economic foundation for the second phase of the housing cooperative movements. Overall, they agreed their struggle took ten painful years—but it was worth it. They now enjoy among the best employment conditions in Ventura County and live in nice homes.

Three views of a Catholic celebration blessing the Mexican colonias.

At the celebration, my informants also compared themselves to the farm workers employed by Limoneira Ranch. Their general sentiments expressed resentment and empathy. They angrily remembered that Limoneira employees refused to help them during their labor struggle. However, they also felt sorry for those workers. They were concerned that the Limoneira farm workers would never become homeowners because they lived in labor camps. Though, at this time, they agreed that Limoneira's labor camps were comfortable, they concurred that in less than ten years the houses would be run-down. Allegedly, the deteriorating housing conditions would force the growers either to renovate the labor camps or to evict the residents. They predicted that Limoneira growers would eventually evict the farm workers from the camps because it would become unprofitable to house labor. They also sarcastically commented that, in the end, the Limoneira employees' loyalty would be compensated by a pension plan that might be sufficient only for a taxicab ride to the poorhouse. In sum, my informants agreed that Limoneira farm workers had to begin fighting for themselves and also cast aside the illusion that the growers actually cared for them.[12]

These conversations with Santa Paula farm workers offered valuable insights into a long and complicated labor struggle that I needed to document. I arrived in Santa Paula during a period that appeared to indicate that many social changes had taken place. For example, the farm workers had launched a successful labor

movement against the growers, and the city council had become more responsive toward the Mexican-origin constituency. I also observed that people of Mexican descent had begun to exercise political power in Santa Paula. On the other hand, I saw that, although interethnic relations in Santa Paula appeared to be less hostile, modern forms of racism persisted. In the public sphere, many Anglo Americans continued to display their ideology of superiority by being paternalistic toward Mexican-origin people and retaining their social distance from them. Moreover, the city council continued to be dominated by Anglo Americans, and the elementary schools continued to be racially segregated (Santa Paula School District Board of Trustees 1979). I also observed that these modern forms of racism had affected the Mexican-origin community in both positive and negative ways. Therefore, I will now examine these issues and illustrate how dominant group racism is currently manifested in Santa Paula.

EIGHT

Modern Racism

*Social Apartness and the Evolution
of a Segregated Society*

When I conducted my ethnographic research in Santa
Paula from October 1985 to October 1986 and revisited the city in 1990 and 1991
for approximately one month each time, I observed that the racial and ethnic
discrimination experienced by the Mexican-origin community was subtle, yet
pervasive. Santa Paula residents are divided into two distinct ethnic communities:
the Anglo American and the Mexican-origin enclaves. And it appears that the
social boundaries separating these two peoples are maintained by the Anglo
Americans. Mexican-origin residents are willing to interact socially with the
dominant ethnic group, yet a reciprocal attitude is not shared by many Anglo
Americans. Anglo Americans maintain their social apartness by remaining distant
from the Mexican-origin people in the churches, schools, and neighborhoods. By
"social apartness" I mean that there is a cultural system in place by which Anglo
Americans determine the social space in Santa Paula. Cultural norms have been
institutionalized to designate the proper times and places in which Mexican-
origin people may socially interact with Anglo Americans.

When an outsider observes this interethnic system of social apartness, on the
surface it does not appear to be a harmful process, as people in Santa Paula maintain
distant, yet cordial interethnic relations. An observer may also agree that this type
of system is merely a reflection of an "ethclass" community structure, as identified
by sociologist Milton Gordon. According to Gordon, social apartness is a
common process practiced by people of different ethnic backgrounds and social
classes (Gordon 1964, 1978). Gordon also stresses that in multiethnic societies it
is natural for people of diverse ethnic backgrounds to remain among their own
kind because different ethnic groups do not share the same value systems,
traditions, or lifestyles (Gordon 1978). Though I partly concur with Gordon in
that social apartness between ethnic groups is to a large extent a voluntary process,

my field research led me to observe that it is primarily a voluntary process on the part of the ethnic group that imposes and maintains the social boundaries. However, for the most part, it is an involuntary process imposed upon a politically subordinated ethnic group. As a case in point, the Mexican-origin community in Santa Paula is cordially coerced into accepting the social boundaries. Social apartness in Santa Paula is a form of racial discrimination (the action), and it derives from prejudicial views (the attitude). For over a century in this city, Anglo Americans have been socialized to view people of Mexican descent as social inferiors and uncultured foreigners who are expected to retain their physical distance from dominant group members. Of course, the social boundaries that characterize social apartness are no longer maintained by violence or physical coercion, as they were during the late 1800s and through the end of the Korean War. Rather, interethnic social apartness is maintained by the institutionalization of rules of correct interethnic social comportment.

The question still remains: What harm is there in practicing interethnic social apartness if no violent measures are used and if interethnic peace is maintained? Although interethnic social relations differ in particular communities and different measures are used to maintain social apartness, my analysis informs us that, in Santa Paula, interethnic boundaries have served to confer social disadvantages upon the Mexican-origin community. Therefore, social apartness has led to deleterious outcomes. I concur with Fredrik Barth's (1969) analysis that in most multiethnic communities social boundaries are consciously or unconsciously used to perpetuate an unbalanced system of social rewards that benefit those who impose the boundaries. In Santa Paula, the social disadvantages experienced by the Mexican-origin community are manifested in (1) the perpetuation of school segregation, (2) the unbalanced urban development of the East and West sides, (3) the forced social isolation of Mexican-origin people, and (4) the belief of racist Anglo Americans that Mexican-origin people can be humiliated when the groups come into contact.

Another question also needs to be raised regarding the complicated role(s) that social class differences play within multiethnic societies. This is a line of inquiry that I often thought about and discussed with my informants. I pondered: Perhaps in Santa Paula the social distance between the Anglo American and Mexican-origin peoples is not related to racist attitudes or ethnic antagonisms. That is, Can their social distance be attributed to social class differences? My ethnographic observations indicated, however, that in Santa Paula interethnic social apartness is complicated but is not caused by social class differences. Quite the contrary. I found that social class differences or similarities were not the main variables determining whether cohesive or distant relations developed between people of Mexican descent and Anglo American residents. My findings did not support

Milton Gordon's ethclass thesis or similar analyses by other scholars who propose that interethnic conflict diminishes between people of the same social class (Gordon 1964; Madsen 1964; Ransford 1977).

In Santa Paula, Anglo American and Mexican-origin people of the same social classes did not share any sense of solidarity. Let us take the working class. In spite of the demographic data from the U.S. Census Bureau indicating that 63 percent of Santa Paula residents are working class (United States Census Bureau 1983b:108), the common social class background did not generate interethnic cohesion. I also did not observe any shared sense of social class solidarity among the Mexican-origin and Anglo American middle or upper classes. My ethnographic observations were further confirmed by my Mexican-origin informants. Unanimously, they stated that the absence of social interaction between Anglo Americans and themselves was not based on social class differences.

To elucidate this system of social apartness, I will now turn to my ethnographic descriptions and findings. This discussion will be based on seventy-six interviews, sixty-four conducted with Mexican-origin people and twelve with Anglo Americans. I also rely on school records and census reports to provide the contextual background.

SOCIAL PRIVILEGE AND SOCIAL APARTNESS

Throughout the late 1800s and until the mid-1950s, Mexican-origin people were socially segregated in Santa Paula. Mexicans were forced to remain among their own kind by the use of violent and repressive methods. Anglo Americans intimidated Mexicans by threatening them with Ku Klux Klan rituals and with police harassment. Economics also played a major role in the subordination of Mexicans in that they were dependent on the citrus growers for employment. This dependency coerced Mexicans into accepting the Anglo Americans' prescribed and proscribed interethnic social norms. At all times, Mexicans were expected to defer to the Anglo Americans.

At present, dominant group racism is not manifested in the same manner as in the past because most residents no longer tolerate or endorse the old segregated system. In Santa Paula, as in many American communities, the belief that non-White people should be segregated and treated inhumanely is considered today to be a bigoted position inconsistent with a modern democracy. Moreover, since the passage of the Civil Rights Act of 1964—which prohibits discrimination on the basis of race, religion, color, or national origin—no community can legislate local laws that confer unequal racial treatment (Takaki 1987). Although this legislation was passed with the intention of eradicating past social injustices, previous racist practices have had long-term effects. Today we have not yet been able to dismantle the effects of a history of racial segregation. Schools and neighborhoods continue to be segregated, and there is no immediate solution in sight (Donato, Menchaca, and Valencia 1991). We also cannot ignore the fact that discrimination against racial minorities continues. One of the most pervasive and subtle methods to perpetuate racism is to subscribe to the popular belief that Anglo Americans have the right to special privileges. This I consider to be a modern manifestation of racism and the basis of many forms of discrimination, including the practice of social apartness. These manifestations of Anglo American demands for special privileges take on different forms in different communities.

For many people who belong to the dominant culture, becoming adjusted to a legal system that no longer confers upon them political or social privileges has been difficult. In particular, this occurs because these privileges historically have been consciously or unconsciously perceived to be "the way things are," "common sense," or the "proper" rules of social comportment (Forgacs 1988; Hall 1986). Although discrimination against non-Whites may be perceived by many people of the dominant culture to be wrong, to them this liberal belief in no way appears to be contradictory to the notion that "their people" deserve special privileges (e.g., that they be served first in restaurants or stores; that the best jobs be reserved for Whites; that no college enacts affirmative action admission policies). Privilege is often justified as a reasonable reward for being a decent and hardworking people, or merely for being White Americans.

In Santa Paula, as in other U.S. communities, in order to preserve and rationalize the social privileges enjoyed by many Anglo Americans, it has become necessary to ignore the long-term impacts of past racial policies and practices. Such rationales as "No one is holding those people back" or "Those people prefer to be among their kind" are often used. "Selective amnesia" characterizes how many people of the dominant culture remember the past and disengage its long-term effects on present social conditions (Frisch 1981). To do this, the dominant culture has imposed cultural mechanisms to justify the way things are (Siegel, Vogt, Watson, and Broom 1954). Cultural measures of social control vary among communities but everywhere subtly serve to rationalize the special privileges enjoyed by those in power. The type of privilege demanded by the dominant culture also varies by community.

In the case of Santa Paula, a system of social apartness has been used to ascribe Anglo Americans special privileges. Social apartness is there characterized as a system of social control by which Mexican-origin people are expected to interact with Anglo Americans on the terms of the latter group. Anglo Americans determine the proper times and places in which both groups can come into contact. There are clear social boundaries that define where the Mexican-origin population is unwanted and displaced. This system is maintained by the enforcement of interethnic norms of correct social comportment. In other words, there is a set of prescribed and proscribed interethnic rules that serve to maintain cordial, yet socially distant relations. Indeed, this system is a manifestation of modern racism and ensures a type of privilege enjoyed by the Anglo Americans of Santa Paula. This system, however, cannot be labeled "segregation" because neither laws nor violence is used to confine Mexican-origin people in particular social spaces. Social apartness is different from segregation because segregation against non-Whites was sanctioned by federal law (*Robinson and Wife v. Memphis and Charleston Railroad Co.* 1883; *Plessy v. Ferguson* 1896) and enforced by local police departments. Violence was also used by White Americans to terrorize non-Whites and thereby prevent them from breaking segregationist laws. Today, in many rural communities of the United States, segregation still exists because violent and coercive actions are practiced by White Americans against non-Whites, in order to ensure that they remain within their ethnic neighborhoods (see Feagin 1989). In Santa Paula, however, social segregation in its traditional form evolved into a system of social apartness. As in the past, Anglo Americans continue to determine the community's social space—but now they use new methods of enforcement. The problem with this system is that it is a subtle type of oppression, as it serves to humiliate, debase, and marginalize people of Mexican descent. It also leads to unbalanced economic rewards that favor the Anglo American community.

SOCIAL CLASS AND
SOCIAL APARTNESS

Before I move on to my description of Santa Paula's system of social apartness, I will address the issue of social class differences. This analysis is necessary because while I conducted my field research and reviewed city reports I found that some Anglo Americans attributed their community's social apartness to difference in income. They assumed Mexican-origin people were poor and Anglo Americans upper or middle class. Therefore, this perceived economic bifurcation allegedly set the groups apart.

Santa Paula is a biracial ethnic community with a population of 26,000 (United States Census Bureau 1983b:33). Approximately 50 percent of the residents are of Mexican ancestry and 50 percent of Anglo American descent (United States Census Bureau 1983b:137). Seventy-seven percent of the Anglo Americans are of Anglo-Saxon, German, or Irish descent (United States Census Bureau 1983b:52).

TABLE 3   *Santa Paula Households*[a] *by Ethnicity and Social Class,*[b]
                                  1983

Ethnicity	Working Class	Middle Class	Upper Class
Mexican and Anglo American	4,342	2,306	213
Mexican	1,807	822	45
Anglo American	2,535	1,484	168

a. Total households in Santa Paula are 6,861.
b. Income description: Working Class under $20,000, Middle Class $20,000 to $49,000, Upper Class $50,000 and over. Source: United States Census Bureau 1983b; 108,149.
Source: United States Census Bureau 1983b: 108, 149.

Santa Paula is composed of 6,861 households (United States Census Bureau 1983b:108), with 40 percent of the households classified as Mexican-origin and 60 percent as Anglo American.[1] In general, the residents are characterized as working class, in that 63 percent of the households earn under $20,000 ($N = 4,342$ out of 6,861; see Table 3). The working-class sector is ethnically composed of 42 percent Mexican-origin households ($N = 1,807$ out of 4,342) and 58 percent Anglo American households ($N = 2,535$ out of 4,342) (United States Census Bureau 1983b:108).[2]

The middle class is much smaller and consists of 34 percent of the total households in Santa Paula ($N = 2,306$ out of 6,861). The household income for this sector ranges from $20,000 to $49,000. Sixty-four percent of the middle-class households are Anglo American ($N = 1,484$ out of 2,306), and 36 percent Mexican-origin ($N = 822$ out of 2,306). The upper-class sector is relatively small and is composed of only 3 percent of the total residents of Santa Paula ($N = 213$ out of 6,861). The household income for this sector consists of earnings of $50,000 and over. Seventy-nine percent of the upper class is composed of Anglo Americans ($N = 168$ out of 213) and 21 percent of Mexican-origin people ($N = 45$ out of 213) (United States Census Bureau 1983b:108, 149).

The main conclusion that can be drawn from the census statistics is that the majority of the residents—Anglo Americans and Mexican-origin people alike—belong to the working class. Based on this finding, it cannot, therefore, be assumed that most Mexican-origin people are poor and that most Anglo Americans are wealthy. This is an important demographic fact because census data clearly indicate that social class differences between Anglo Americans and Mexican-origin people cannot be used to explain why interethnic social apartness exists in this community. Social class differences may be useful in explicating why the Anglo American upper class does not socialize with the majority of the Mexican-origin working class (e.g., as related to social class snobbery or because the social class circles of both sectors are different). A social class analysis applies, however, only to a very small number of Anglo American families ($N = 168$ households). A similar social class argument cannot be used to explain why interethnic social apartness exists within the working class. Therefore, my ethnographic interviews will attempt to offer competing explanations for the social apartness existing between the Mexican-origin and Anglo American communities. We will now turn to this discussion. The elementary schools will be our starting point.

SOCIAL APARTNESS IN THE EDUCATIONAL CONTEXT: SCHOOL SEGREGATION

A system of social apartness is apparent in Santa Paula's elementary schools. In this case, the practice has been classified by the state of California as "school segregation." I agree. School segregation in Santa Paula is a vestige of past racist practices that are firmly rooted in the city's social structure. It is part of Santa Paula's system of social apartness, as it serves to maintain distance between most Mexicans and Anglo Americans. Initially, it was imposed upon the people of Mexican descent, and presently it is maintained by local uncodified rules implemented by the Anglo American–dominated school board. In 1978 the State of California notified the Santa Paula School District Board of Trustees that their elementary schools were racially segregated (Riles 1978). In reaction to the state's findings, the Santa Paula school board responded that the schools were not segregated, but rather that they were ethnically isolated as a result of socioeconomic differences between Mexicans and Anglo Americans (Santa Paula School District Board of Trustees 1979). That is, the school district argued, ethnic isolation in the public schools was due to residential housing patterns influenced by buying power, which in turn dictated where students went to school. In any event, the state then required that an investigation be conducted on the status of Santa Paula's elementary schools. An advisory committee was formed to investigate the state's concerns and to prepare a report as to why Mexican-origin students were concentrated on the East Side of Santa Paula.

In "1979 State of California Department of Education Desegregation Report," the Santa Paula School District Board of Trustees presented its findings (Santa Paula School District Board of Trustees 1979). Based on the advisory committee's investigation, the school board concluded that because most Mexicans were poor they were concentrated in different sections of Santa Paula (on the East Side) and therefore their schools had become ethnically isolated. Thus, the ethnic isolation in the schools was alleged to have resulted from a natural economic process and not from racial or ethnic discrimination. The school board and the advisory committee stated:

> *In the past months we have spent a great deal of time,*
> *energy and patience considering all possible factors relevant*
> *to the task we were appointed to study. It would appear*
> *that we are about to conclude the first part of our obliga-*
> *tion—determination of the existence of racial/ethnic*
> *isolation in our school district. . . . Without question, the*
> *children in our community whose language is other than*
> *English have needs that demand a large part of our*
> *concern, but [we] believe that is only a part of our task.*
> *. . . It is our opinion that the "problem" we should be*
> *dealing with reaches beyond racial/ethnic and cultural*
> *differences. We believe that it is to a great extent a socio-*
> *economic problem. (Santa Paula School District Board of*
> *Trustees 1979:4, 5)*

The school board and the advisory committee also felt that, because the ethnic isolation was attributable to de facto (natural) causes, they felt no obligation or intention to desegregate the schools. Therefore, they rejected any strategy to change the schools' racial composition as inappropriate and unnecessary. They also felt that if a desegregation plan were implemented, it would produce problems for the Anglo American students and, consequently, the parents of the Anglo American students would oppose any change. Thus, neither busing nor redistrict-ing was recommended as a strategy to solve the city's school racial/ethnic imbalance. By their own admission, the school board and the advisory committee did not consider school segregation to be wrong. They stated:

> *We believe the alternatives of bussing and changing the*
> *district boundaries are not in the best interest of those*
> *involved. Although these alternatives may satisfy the*
> *"letter" of the law by shifting "numbers" we feel the*
> *"spirit" of the law . . . will not be served. Nothing will*
> *improve if it's just used to move children around. . . .*
> *Those communities that have dealt with segregation only*
> *from a racial/ethnic point—thereby isolating the special*
> *needs of one aspect of their student population [the Anglo*
> *American students] from the special needs of the other*
> *aspects of their student population . . . created additional*

> *problems. . . . It would be our hope that we could find*
> *creative and effective ways to benefit all the children in our*
> *school district. (Santa Paula School District Board of*
> *Trustees 1979:4, 5)*

In sum, the school board's response to the State Department of Education was that it would contest any mandatory desegregation action required by the state of California.

In 1985–1986, when I conducted my field research, I found that the State Department of Education issued a mandate to desegregate the schools after the report was complete but did not enforce it. School segregation continued in Santa Paula. Furthermore, it even increased after the desegregation report was written. Based on the most recent data available, the vast majority of the Mexican-origin and Anglo American students in Santa Paula continue to attend racially and ethnically segregated schools (Menchaca and Valencia 1990). Data from the *California Basic Educational Data System* (California State Department of Education 1985) show that three of the six elementary schools are very high-density Mexican-origin, one is high-density Anglo American, and two are borderline segregated. In fact, the three schools that were dubbed "minority schools" in "1979 State of California Department of Education Desegregation Report" have increased their Mexican-origin student enrollment substantially. The 1979 minority percentages for Grace S. Thille, McKevett, and Barbara Webster were 90 percent, 82 percent, and 81 percent, respectively. In 1985, the minority enrollment percentages for these segregated schools had climbed to 96 percent, 88 percent, and 89 percent.[3]

In addition, when I analyzed the findings presented in the desegregation report alleging that school segregation in Santa Paula was the outcome of socioeconomic differences between the Mexican-origin and Anglo American peoples, I found that the report contained no data to support this position. In an attempt to investigate the validity of this conclusion, I examined city census data. Because the census data indicate that 58 percent of the Anglo American households in Santa Paula can be characterized as working class (United States Census Bureau 1983b:108), my analysis informs us that the social class allegation made in the "1979 State of California Department of Education Desegregation Report" was incorrect (Santa Paula School District Board of Trustees 1979). That is, if the socioeconomic analysis were correct, working-class Anglo American students who reside in low-income neighborhoods should be isolated in working-class schools. In Santa Paula, however, Anglo American students from different social classes are mixed in the schools (California State Department of Education 1985). Anglo American students attend three predominantly White schools—Glen City,

Blanchard, and Thelma B. Bedell (Santa Paula School District Board of Trustees 1979; California State Department of Education 1985). In short, the argument made by the school board that ethnic isolation of its public schools is attributable to a natural socioeconomic process is a dubious and tenuous contention. A more plausible explanation is that ethnicity transcends socioeconomic status as a marker for school segregation in Santa Paula.

As discussed in chapter 3, Santa Paula school records, oral histories, the local newspaper, and academic studies provide substantial evidence indicating that the ethnic isolation of Mexican students in separate schools has been the outcome of historical school segregative practices (e.g., *Santa Paula Chronicle* and *Santa Paula Daily Chronicle;* Belknap 1968; Menchaca and Valencia 1990; Santa Paula School District Board of Trustees 1963; Triem 1985; *VCHSQ* 1955, 1957, 1958, 1959; Webster 1967). These documents also indicate that between 1925 and 1953 the school segregation of Mexican students was closely associated with two factors: (1) the growth of the Mexican population and (2) the residential segregation of the Mexican community. A brief review of the founding of Santa Paula's elementary schools will elucidate these issues (see Table 4).

When Santa Paula's first two schools were established in 1872, only Anglo American students were enrolled (*VCHSQ* 1959). One of the schools was private, and the second was public. Both schools were located in Anglo American neighborhoods, far from the Mexican residential zones. The public school was called Briggs, and the private school was not assigned a name. In the late 1800s, two new schools were established in the downtown area—Ventura Street School and South Grammar School. Both schools offered public education (see chapter 3). At South Grammar School both Mexican and Anglo American students often attended (Webster 1967). On the other hand, when Ventura Street School first opened, it was reserved for Anglo American students, and not until the early 1920s were a few Mexican students allowed to enroll. In these two schools interethnic mixing was permitted because Mexicans helped to raise the average daily attendance counts required to receive state funds (Santa Paula School District Board of Trustees 1963). Though Mexican students were encouraged to enroll in school, they were subjected to racial discrimination. For example, before attending class, they were required to bathe in showers constructed especially for them. Mexican students were also segregated in separate classrooms (*SPC,* September 4, 1914, 27[24]:1; *SPC,* June 26, 1919, 29[14]:1; Santa Paula School District Board of Trustees 1963).

Unlike Ventura Street School and South Grammar School, the White school located toward the west of Santa Paula did not admit Mexican students (*VCHSQ* 1957, 1959). At that time, Briggs School, which accommodated the students residing on the outskirts of town, did not allow Mexican students to register

TABLE 4   *Founding Dates of Santa Paula Elementary Schools*

School	Year Established	Neighborhood	Ethnic Makeup of School during Founding
Private[a]	1872	White	White
Briggs	1872	White	White
Ventura Street School	1892	Downtown	White[b]
South Grammar School	1898	Downtown	Ethnically mixed
McKevett	1911	White	White
Olivelands	1913	Mexican	Mexican
Barbara Webster (Canyon School)	1925–1926	Mexican	Mexican
Isbell	1925–1926	White	White
Grace S. Thille	1952	Mexican	Mexican
Glen City	1952	White	White
Blanchard	1960	Ethnically mixed	Ethnically mixed
Thelma B. Bedell	1963	White	White

a. The first school had no official name.

b. Ventura Street School began admitting Mexican students in the 1920s. During its first years in operation only White students were admitted.

Sources: Santa Paula School District Board of Trustees (1963); Ventura County Historical Society Quarterly 1958, 1959; Webster (1967).

(*VCHSQ* 1959). In 1913, Olivelands School was built specifically for the Mexican students who were unable to attend the downtown schools.[4] Olivelands School therefore became Santa Paula's first Mexican school, which was built because Limoneira Ranch had recruited a large number of farm worker families to Santa Paula (*VCHSQ* 1959). Allegedly, an increase in the size of the Mexican population necessitated a separate school for Mexican students.

As a result of the overall growth of Santa Paula's population, in the mid- to late 1920s, Mexican students were no longer needed at the downtown schools to augment the attendance figures required to receive state funds (see chapter 3). The Anglo American and Mexican student populations became large enough to require two state-funded schools. In 1925–1926, two new schools were constructed. However, Mexican and Anglo American students were no longer allowed to attend the same schools (Santa Paula School District Board of Trustees 1963; Webster 1967). Mexican students were moved to Canyon School (later renamed Barbara Webster), and the Anglo American students were sent to Isbell School. One of the rationales used to justify the school segregation of Mexican students was that it was better for them to attend school near their homes. This argument was merely a smoke screen for racial prejudice, as the Anglo American community did not want Mexicans to be present on the West Side. That is, by 1925 the Anglo American community had subjected the Mexican population to religious and residential segregation, and the schools were the only place where the ethnic groups came together. With the relocation of the Mexican students, the social segregation of the Mexican community—which was confined to the East Side of Santa Paula—was now complete.

In 1952, two new schools were constructed to accommodate the growing elementary school population, resulting in increased segregation of the Mexican students (Santa Paula School District Board of Trustees 1963; Webster 1967). Grace S. Thille School was located in the heart of the East Side and Glen City in the West Side. The rationale for building the schools in those zones is unclear, but it appears to be associated with the town's population growth and persistent Anglo American beliefs in residential segregation. Racial differences determined where Santa Paula's population could reside and where the students attended school.

During the early 1960s the school segregation of Mexican students entered a new phase. Most Mexican students continued to attend the East Side schools. However, in 1960 Blanchard School was built, and it accommodated both Mexican-origin and Anglo American students. This racial mixing was not implemented for altruistic purposes, however. Rather, it was a response to the breakdown of residential segregation in Santa Paula, which, beginning in 1957, gradually disintegrated as 127 Mexicans bought homes along the dividing boundary between the East Side and the West Side (see chapter 5). And then in 1959 new neighborhoods were built on the West Side and Mexicans were allowed to buy property there. Therefore, as the population increased in the new West Side neighborhoods, it became necessary to build a school near this location. The result was Blanchard School, located in the racially mixed residential zone (Santa Paula School District Board of Trustees 1979). With the exception of Blanchard, Santa Paula's schools continued to reflect the town's segregated residential patterns.

In 1963 Thelma B. Bedell School was founded. It was constructed toward northeast Santa Paula to accommodate the growing number of students who moved into the new housing developments. The area where Thelma B. Bedell School is located was originally a predominantly White residential zone (see Table 2).[5] In the mid-1970s, however, many Mexican-origin families moved to northeast Santa Paula, and their presence subsequently transformed Thelma B. Bedell into an ethnically balanced school.[6] Today Thelma B. Bedell has somehow once again become ethnically segregated and is now a high-density Anglo American school. The number of Anglo American students enrolled exceeds the government's statistical formula for an ethnically/racially balanced school (see note 3).

Given the aforementioned facts, the placement of the schools in Santa Paula is clearly and firmly rooted in the town's residential patterns. In my analysis I contend that, if residential segregation had not been practiced in the past, school segregation would not be a contemporary problem. The Anglo American and Mexican-origin communities would not have been separated in different sections of the city. Unfortunately, the long-term effects of current residential segregation are difficult to dismantle. Notwithstanding the fact that residential segregation is no longer imposed upon Santa Paula's residents, the majority of the people continue to follow past residential patterns. Today, 95 percent of the Anglo American residents live on the West Side, and 68 percent of the Mexican-origin population continues to reside on the East Side (United States Census Bureau 1983b:66). Therefore, because the majority of Santa Paula residents continue to cluster in the traditional ethnic zones, residential segregation has not completely broken down, and the school board has done little to desegregate the schools.

At present, the only ways to desegregate the schools are (1) busing or (2) redistricting. However, as previously discussed, the school board of trustees and the desegregation advisory committee rejected both plans. They considered the two proposed solutions disruptive to the current system and to the benefit of no one. I fail to understand the alleged fundamental problems with either response. The only problem I envision is that many Anglo American parents may not like to have their children attend predominantly Mexican schools. In my analysis, redistricting and busing would not pose economic problems for the school district because Santa Paula is a very small city, approximately eight miles wide (east to west) and six miles long (north to south). Since the Anglo American students are concentrated in three schools (Glen City, Thelma B. Bedell, and Blanchard), some of them could be transferred to the Mexican schools, thereby desegregating the school district. Barbara Webster School (89 percent Mexican-origin and 11 percent Anglo American), for example, could be desegregated by changing its district boundaries. Because Thelma B. Bedell (49 percent Anglo and 51 percent Mexican-origin/other)[7] and Barbara Webster are located approximately two miles from each other, these two schools have the capacity to serve the same residential neighborhoods. Some of the Anglo American students who live less than a half mile (four blocks) from Barbara Webster School and who attend Thelma B. Bedell could be transferred to Barbara Webster. Likewise, Mexican students could be easily transferred to Thelma B. Bedell.

In other schools, busing could be implemented as an alternate way to desegregate the Mexican schools. Because many children are currently bused from their homes to their schools already, rerouting the bus system would mix students of different ethnicities in the schools. This should not be an inconvenience because it would increase the commute time by only a few minutes. The students most likely would have to be on the bus only five minutes longer than they currently are. For example, Glen City School (46 percent Anglo American and 54 percent Mexican-origin/other) could be paired with either Grace S. Thille School (4 percent Anglo American and 96 percent Mexican-origin) or McKevett School (12 percent Anglo American and 88 percent Mexican-origin). Glen City School is located approximately four miles from the predominantly Mexican schools. Blanchard School, which is ethnically balanced, could also be used to desegregate one of the Mexican schools because it is located approximately four miles from each of them.

In conclusion, the position taken by the school board not to desegregate the schools appears to reflect a perspective that "it is better to leave things as they are." Most Mexican-origin elementary students traditionally attend school on their side of town, and the school board does not want to institute any new changes. In sum, the current school segregation of the Mexican-origin students is merely another example of Santa Paula's norms of interethnic social apartness.[8] Interethnic mixing takes place only when Anglo Americans determine how much and when.

THE CHURCHES

The churches represent another area in which my informants ($N = 76$) identified interethnic social apartness to be blatantly obvious. Once again, in this context Anglo Americans determine when Mexican-origin people can and cannot share Anglo social spaces. In Santa Paula there are thirty churches, two of them Catholic and the rest Protestant (Santa Paula Chamber of Commerce 1986). With the exception of one Catholic parish, Mexican-origin people and Anglo Americans attend different churches. It also appears that Protestants are the most highly ethnically isolated religious group.

When I conducted my field research, I visited the Protestant churches and observed that there was no interethnic mixing. On only one occasion did I observe an Anglo American couple attend a Sunday service in El Niño Pastor, the Mexican Protestant church. Furthermore, when I visited the Anglo American Protestant churches, I noticed that Mexican-origin people were not present. When I conducted the latter observations, however, I was advised by several informants that I should wait outside and observe whether any Mexicans entered or exited the buildings. They suggested that because I was not a member of the

Anglo American congregations I should not attend the services, as I might upset some parishioners.

In trying to understand why Anglo American and Mexican-origin Protestants attended separate churches I interviewed Reverend Manuel Salazar and Reverend Adrian Gonzalez—both Protestants. They frankly stated that the problem was that Mexican Americans were not welcomed by Anglo American congregations. Reverends Salazar and Gonzalez explained that if Mexicans went to the Anglo American churches they would not be asked to leave, but they would be treated rudely. In general, Mexican Americans did not visit the Anglo American churches because they did not want to place themselves in a position to be humiliated. Reverend Salazar, the pastor of El Niño Pastor, also remarked that his congregation's current ethnic isolation is a direct outgrowth of religious segregation. In 1915, church documents clearly indicate that Anglo Americans intentionally segregated Mexicans in a separate church because they believed the Mexicans were inferior (see chapter 2).

Reverend Gonzalez, a Pentecostal pastor from El Templo de Jesús, offered similar observations. His congregation, as Mexican-origin people, have been forced to attend a separate church since 1929. Before then they were expected to hold Sunday services in tents and were not allowed to enter the Anglo American churches (see chapter 2). In our conversation I asked him if perhaps Mexicans historically have been expected to attend separate churches because of language differences. He responded that language differences in the past were used as polite excuses to justify religious segregation. Mexicans were said to prefer attending services in which Spanish was spoken. Today, however, language cannot be used to conceal the real reason why Mexicans are not welcome, for very few Protestants are Spanish monolinguals. Reverend Salazar offered the same response when I asked him about the role that language possibly played in the history of El Niño Pastor.

Furthermore, when I asked seven Protestants of Mexican descent why interethnic social apartness exists in the churches, they commented that Anglo American racism was the main reason. Iris succinctly summarized the sentiments of these informants:

> *Most of the Anglo American Protestants are rednecks and they don't like Mexicans. . . . I don't believe that they are all racist because I have several Anglo American friends from different churches. . . . I think that we're kept out of their churches because most of the leaders are old people and they have redneck views. In the future it's going to change*

because the younger Anglo Americans get along with the
Mexican Americans. . . . For now we have to be patient.
Although I don't like being discriminated [against], I don't
think about it. I love my church and my people. Going to
church with Mexicans helps us keep loving our people. . . .
I try not to think about the rednecks.

In sum, Iris resents being discriminated against and does not like being excluded from the Anglo American churches. Interestingly, her comments also reveal that she has built an emotional defense mechanism to alleviate the pain she experiences. That is, although Iris is discriminated against, she enjoys attending services with other Mexican American Protestants. Apparently, the ethnic affinity that results from such religious contacts helps her not to think about the racial discrimination she has experienced.

In comparison to the Protestants, the process of interethnic social apartness is apparently not as rigid among Catholics. In the mid-1970s, the religious separation of the Mexican-origin and Anglo American Catholics began to break down. Some Mexican-origin people from Our Lady of Guadalupe Church parish gradually began to attend Sunday services in Saint Peter's Church, the Anglo American parish. Ironically, this process was not reciprocated by the Anglo American Catholics. To this date they do not attend Our Lady of Guadalupe, the Mexican Catholic church. Apparently, the interethnic mixing of Saint Peter's Church was associated with policies instituted by the Los Angeles Catholic Archdiocese. In 1975, the archdiocese placed Father Dennis, an Anglo American, as the senior pastor of Our Lady of Guadalupe Church. Conversely, Father Tomás, a Spanish priest, was transferred from Our Lady of Guadalupe to Saint Peter's. Father Tomás was not promoted, however, to senior pastor. Both Catholic churches were headed by Anglo American priests. When Father Tomás left his parish, part of the Mexican-origin congregation followed him and joined Saint Peter's Church. A similar pattern did not occur in Our Lady of Guadalupe Church. When Father Dennis became the head pastor of the Mexican church, he was unable to attract any Anglo American parishioners.

Father Dennis was later replaced by Father Ignacio, in 1985. When I interviewed Father Ignacio, I asked him why Anglo Americans did not attend this parish. He responded that his parish has historically been perceived by most Catholics to be for Mexican people.[9] Father Ignacio did not believe racism was a motivating factor. He added that it was difficult for Catholics to break with tradition. In his opinion, that was the reason Father Dennis had been unable to recruit Anglo Americans to attend Our Lady of Guadalupe Church. When I asked Father Ignacio why Mexican people were able to break with tradition and the

Our Lady of Guadalupe Church.

Saint Peter's Church.

Anglo Americans were not, he was unable to respond. Instead, he spoke about
why many Mexican Catholics prefer to be part of Saint Peter's Parish. He offered
three main observations. First, Saint Peter's is a large church with a luxurious
setting. It is sumptuously decorated with large stained-glass windows, and its walls
are artistically sculptured with Roman iconic carvings. Saint Peter's also has
expensive furnishings including a large marble pulpit, chandeliers, rosewood
benches, and tile floors. In contrast, Our Lady of Guadalupe Church is a humble
mission with only a few comforts. Its interior is modestly furnished with a wooden
pulpit, wooden benches, and four inexpensive Spanish-style chandeliers. Its
furnishings give it an appearance of austerity. To Father Ignacio, for most people
to attend Saint Peter's Church because of its accommodations was only common
sense. This was the main reason to which he attributed the movement of
Mexican-origin people to the Anglo American church. Second, he assumed that
it was primarily Mexican American middle-class parishioners who left Our Lady
of Guadalupe Church. Third, Father Tomás' presence probably contributed to
the ethnic mixture of Saint Peter's.

Father Ignacio also offered unkind comments regarding why Our Lady of
Guadalupe Church is an essentially Mexican parish. I was rather surprised to hear
such generalizations and condescending views. Overall, he believed that his
Mexican parishioners were uneducated, mostly undocumented, often did not
bathe before they came to church, took their shoes off while attending services,

and always brought along their "screaming kids." To Father Ignacio, those were plenty of reasons why most Anglo Americans would not want to attend Our Lady of Guadalupe Church. Simply put, Father Ignacio believed that Our Lady of Guadalupe Church only attracted poor Mexican people.

Not wanting to cross Father Ignacio by asking him to verify his social class analysis with concrete examples, I left his office somewhat upset. I had attended Our Lady of Guadalupe Church on a regular basis for approximately eight months, and I had not observed the unpleasant images and negative behaviors he described. It was also the parish I had attended as a child and a teenager. I concurred with him that many parents brought their screaming babies to church, but I disagreed that most of the Mexican people were poverty-stricken or undocumented. From my past residence in Santa Paula, I was able to recognize a large number of the parishioners and knew that they were neither undocumented nor poor. Many of these people were Mexican Americans, not Spanish monolinguals. In addition, nearly all of my Catholic Mexican-origin informants ($N = 55$) disagreed with Father Ignacio's stereotypes, as indicated by their own observations and recollections.

Following my interview with Father Ignacio, I decided to investigate further why Our Lady of Guadalupe Church was ethnically isolated. I thought perhaps Father Ignacio's analysis was correct regarding why Anglo Americans have traditionally avoided the Mexican church. I then attempted to interview the head pastor of Saint Peter's Church. After three telephone calls and two visits to the rectory, I was unable to obtain an appointment with Father Murphy. Finally, on my second visit to the rectory, the office administrator, Rose, informed me that she had been instructed to assist me. Father Murphy would be unable to meet with me. Rose was very helpful and analytical in her account of the Catholic churches.

Rose explained that Our Lady of Guadalupe Church was currently ethnically isolated, whereas Saint Peter's Parish was ethnically mixed. To substantiate her analysis, she examined Saint Peter's membership records. Based on these records, Rose estimated that nearly 40 percent of the parishioners in Saint Peter's were of Mexican origin. Not all of these members, however, were from Santa Paula; many people from nearby towns also attended Saint Peter's Church. When I asked Rose why Our Lady of Guadalupe Church was ethnically isolated, she offered a social class analysis. According to Rose, poor people attend Sunday services at Our Lady of Guadalupe, middle-class people at Saint Peter's, and wealthy people at St. Thomas Aquinas, a parish in the nearby city of Ojai. I then asked, "Since only middle-class people attend Saint Peter's Church and no Anglo Americans attend Our Lady of Guadalupe Church, are we to assume that there are no poor or working-class Anglo American Catholics in Santa Paula?" Embarrassed by the generalization she had made but unwilling to retract the statement, Rose responded that there are many Anglo Americans on a fixed income, but they should not be considered poor. Allegedly, Anglo American senior citizens cannot be considered working class because they receive social security. In her opinion, they do not attend Our Lady of Guadalupe Church because they do not consider themselves to be part of the working class. Rose then added that even if they wanted to attend the Mexican church they couldn't because English language services were not offered. Rose commented:

> *We [Saint Peter's Church] offer four masses in English and Our Lady of Guadalupe offers four masses in Spanish. People know that if they want to hear mass in English they can come to Saint Peter's and if they want to hear mass in Spanish they can go to Our Lady of Guadalupe.*

When I informed Rose that Our Lady of Guadalupe Church offered English-language services, she was surprised. I then decided to probe further into the language issue. I asked, "In the past, might the absence of Spanish-language services have discouraged Mexican people from attending Saint Peter's?" Rose commented that she did not think so. She recalled that before 1970 Saint Peter's always had a few middle-class Mexicans who regularly attended services. She did not know why in the past most Mexican Catholics preferred to attend Our Lady of Guadalupe Church. She assumed that they chose to be among their own people. For example, she recalled that when Our Lady of Guadalupe Church was built, Mexicans voluntarily stopped attending Saint Peter's Church and only a few middle-class Mexican families remained. To Rose, this worked out well for all involved. Rose stated:

> *Although the Mexican congregation has recently increased, we have always had Mexicans attend our church. For example, [Joe Becerra] and his family have been members of our parish. . . . Before Our Lady of Guadalupe Church was founded, Mexicans came to our church, but they preferred their own parish. . . . When Mexicans asked for their church, that's when we had the ethnic church attendance separate. . . . I think it worked well.*

In short, Rose attributed the ethnic isolation of Our Lady of Guadalupe Church to social class differences between the Anglo American and Mexican-origin peoples. Also, she was unwilling to admit that there were any Anglo

American Catholics who were working class, for if she had, her social class analysis would be weakened. Rose also refused to accept that segregation was ever practiced within the Catholic church. In her analysis, Mexican people chose to separate themselves.

Rose's analysis paralleled the majority view of my Anglo American informants. Of these informants, nine of twelve attributed the social separation between the two ethnic communities to social class differences. Their general description of the Mexican-origin population was that the majority were poor and either undocumented or first-generation immigrants. A few of these informants also added that the interethnic social separation in Santa Paula was a voluntary process on the part of the Mexican-origin community. Only three of my Anglo American informants offered insights similar to those provided by my Mexican-origin informants. They identified dominant group racism to be a major problem in the city. Santa Paula was characterized as a predominantly working-class community where bigoted ideas were common.

On the same issue of church segregation, my Mexican-origin informants offered alternative explanations. With the exception of Father Ignacio, sixty-three of my Mexican-origin informants concurred that Anglo Americans did not want to attend the Mexican churches because they were either afraid, uncomfortable, or did not want to associate with Mexican-origin people. These informants did not believe that social class was a major cause of interethnic social apartness in the churches or elsewhere. Social class differences were identified as significant only in explaining why part of the Mexican American middle class had changed parishes. Miriam, an accountant and one of my informants, describes in her own words why Anglo Americans do not visit the East Side. Miriam states:

> *There is tension between the citizens of Santa Paula. . . .*
> *The Anglo Americans view the* barrios *as an area where*
> *poor people live and where there is a high crime rate. They*
> *are afraid to come to our churches and neighborhoods. . . .*
> *I think these are racist stereotypes because there are many*
> *Okies [poor Whites] who live in worse neighborhoods. . . .*
> *When I was a teenager, many Anglos did not want to*
> *associate with me because I lived in the* barrio. *They*
> *assumed I was inferior. . . . The Okies tried to make fun*
> *of me.*

In sum, my field research of the churches indicates that there are interethnic divisions, and these divisions are apparently more rigid among the Protestants. In the case of the Catholics, Saint Peter's has become an ethnically mixed parish, suggesting that ethnic biases have slightly decreased. The continuous ethnic isolation of Our Lady of Guadalupe Church, however, also suggests that Anglo Americans have the power to determine the proper times for both groups to meet. That is, Mexican-origin people are welcomed at the Anglo American parish, yet the interethnic boundary at Our Lady of Guadalupe Church remains because Anglo Americans refuse to cross the line and integrate this parish.

THE EFFECTS OF SOCIAL APARTNESS IN THE EAST SIDE NEIGHBORHOODS

The Mexican East Side provides another example of the practice of social apartness. Anglo Americans continue to view this area as a place where only Mexicans live. Although part of the Mexican-origin population has gradually dispersed itself throughout Santa Paula, and currently 33 percent live outside of the East Side, only a few Anglo Americans have broken with tradition and currently reside in the Mexican neighborhoods. Only 5 percent of the Anglo American population live on the East Side (United States Census Bureau 1983b:66).

This residential practice has adversely affected the Mexican-origin community in various ways. For example, in a survey I conducted on the East Side business sector, I found that Anglo American businesspeople seldom invest money in East Side businesses and thus fail to contribute to the growth of this commercial sector. Anglo American businesses are concentrated on the West Side where several shopping centers have been established. Currently, on the East Side there are only three businesses owned by Anglo Americans, two of which are a pesticide plant and an oil-tank farm, both located near Barbara Webster School. The pesticide plant is located one block and a half from the school, and the oil tank farm was constructed across the street. Neither business generates jobs or services for the Mexican-origin community. Both businesses are storage places for pesticides and oil. The third business, a citrus packing house, has been located on the East Side since the early 1900s. This is the only Anglo American business that generates jobs for the local residents. All other types of businesses, such as grocery stores, auto repair shops, restaurants, and convenience stores, are owned by Mexican-origin people.

Besides the unbalanced commercial growth of the East Side, the city government has failed to construct recreational facilities outside of the West Side. With the exception of Las Piedras Park, none of the other six city parks are located on the East Side (Santa Paula Chamber of Commerce 1986). Furthermore, the only youth community center in Santa Paula is also located on the West Side. Why the city government has funded the recreational facilities in this lopsided manner is unclear. It is obvious, however, that council members demonstrate a blatant disregard for the needs of the East Side residents. Several of my Mexican-origin informants alleged that, because Anglo Americans do not reside on the East Side, the city council is not interested in constructing recreational facilities there for Mexican-origin youth. This is unfortunate because the majority of the elementary youth of Santa Paula are of Mexican descent and do not reside on the West Side (California State Department of Education 1985). In 1985, over 67 percent of the youth (K–6 grades) in Santa Paula were of Mexican origin and 32 percent were Anglo American (California State Department of Education 1985). And, by the mid-1990s, the Mexican-origin youth population is projected to exceed over 72 percent of the total elementary student population. Yet the city government continues to neglect the recreational needs of the Mexican-origin youth (Menchaca and Valencia 1990).

The ethnic isolation of the East Side has also affected the way city services are provided in Santa Paula. Although slightly over 50 percent of Santa Paula's total residents live on the East Side, the city's two fire stations were constructed on the West Side (Santa Paula Chamber of Commerce 1986; United States Census Bureau 1983b:149).[10] In the area of electoral politics, as mentioned earlier in my review of the at-large electoral system, the city government continues to neglect the Mexican-origin population (see chapter 5). Also, following a long-established tradition, the city government opens only one polling place on the East Side during election time, while on the West Side several polling places are open.[11] The city government has traditionally justified the location of the electoral polls by advancing two rationales: (1) the majority of the votes are cast on the West Side, therefore more polling places are needed there, and (2) a large percentage of the residents of the East Side are immigrants and are not eligible to vote. Jesús, one of my informants, and several Mexican-origin activists have repeatedly asked the city government to open more voting polls on the East Side, but their requests have been ignored. According to these political activists, the underlying motive for retaining the current polling pattern is to ensure that more votes are cast on the West Side, thus ensuring the continuation of Anglo American dominance in city government. Jesús also alleges that the unbalanced provisioning of city services on the East Side is related to the fact that the West Side is overwhelmingly Anglo American. Therefore, city council members and city administrators are concerned with improving the living conditions only on the West Side. According to Jesús, Santa Paula is separated into a predominantly Anglo American West Side, which is adequately represented by the city government, and a Mexican East Side, which is neglected. He comments:

Due to the city's political procedures, the politicians in
office elect the city's administrators, resulting in members of
their own social class and ethnic background getting the
administrative positions. These administrators, being from
the West Side and representing West Side interests,
authorize their opinions to be incorporated into the city's
decisions, resulting in the West Side monopolization of the
city. The West Side, in running the city, makes decisions
that affect the barrio, *negating the possibility of socially*
approved strategies. . . . Their decision to rezone the
barrio *from residential to industrial not only created health*
problems, but poses a constant danger from blow-outs,
especially from the oil, electrical, and chemical plants in the
neighborhood. . . . Comparing the two sections of town
[West and East sides], one can scarcely believe such
contrasting conditions exist. One is more inclined to believe
the two sections are living under apartheid. (Ornelas
1984:17–21)

Jesús' underlying critical view reveals that the Mexican East Side is neglected by the
city government and has become a dumping ground for industrial projects. The city
council, in order to maintain the clean appearance of the West Side, has permitted
the zoning of undesirable industrial projects in East Side neighborhoods.

RULES OF SOCIAL COMPORTMENT IN SHARED SPACES: DEFERENCE AND DOMINANCE

Areas where social apartness is temporarily suspended
in Santa Paula are the commercial zones of the West Side. These areas are
composed of shopping centers, restaurants, gasoline stations, liquor stores, clinics,
doctors' offices, a hospital, and a library. These places have become shared spaces
where Anglo Americans and Mexican-origin people come into contact. Although interethnic contact occurs in these places, it cannot be considered
integration. Quite the contrary. My ethnographic observations have revealed that
in shared spaces interethnic relations of domination persist. Ethnic mixing occurs,
yet the social boundaries remain in place because Anglo Americans continue to
control the interethnic interaction in these spaces. For example, Anglo Americans

decide when to greet, acknowledge, or speak to Mexican-origin people. In this way, Anglo Americans control their surroundings. On the surface, in shared spaces there is a peaceful ambiance where people go about their daily business. However, when Anglo Americans and Mexican-origin people come into contact, there are rules of social comportment that are followed. The proper etiquette is for Mexican-origin people to defer to Anglo Americans and to accord them privileged social roles. And when this protocol is not respected by a member of the subordinate culture, interethnic conflict erupts, and the peaceful ambiance is temporarily suspended.

Based on my field observations and interview data, when interethnic conflict erupts it is usually related to a Mexican-origin person's refusal to accord an Anglo American a privileged social role. When this happens, the Anglo American reacts to the alleged faux pas with indignation because an interethnic protocol rule has been broken. That is, a person of Mexican descent has refused to obey the rules that are practiced in shared public space. On the other hand, rules of social protocol also apply to Anglo Americans. They are permitted to publicly humiliate Mexican-origin people but not to physically abuse them. It is unacceptable and a sign of ungracious public behavior for Anglo Americans to physically abuse Mexican-origin people. Physical abuse is not tolerated by anyone. For example, spitting on or pushing a person of Mexican descent is considered improper. Mexican-origin people are expected to defer to Anglo Americans but not to tolerate physical violence. For the Anglo American, the proper method for commanding respect is by the use of cultural norms and not violent strategies.

Furthermore, based on several ethnographic observations in fast-food restaurants and in the ball park, I found that when interethnic conflict erupts in public it usually commences when the persons involved face and stare at each other. I call this a "visual duel." The confrontation proceeds to an exchange of epithets, which I term a "verbal duel." Exchanged words are often racial in content and attempt to associate the individuals involved in the altercation with the most discredited and stigmatized groups of Santa Paula. Anglo Americans often call Mexican-origin people "wetback Meskins" in order to associate them with the undocumented workers of Santa Paula and thereby negate any sense of legitimacy. In essence, this is the perpetuation of the old stereotype that Mexicans are foreigners and should be thankful that they are tolerated in this country. The equivalent racial insult is what Mexican-origin people call Anglo Americans: "White Okie trash." In Santa Paula the term "Okie" distinguishes a White person as a social failure and an outcast among his or her own kind. It also connotes laziness and ignorance. Usually, after words are exchanged, the individuals involved in the conflict turn their faces away from each other and seek comfort among their own kind. At this point the whispering begins among the observers.

In private conversations, people voice derogatory terms about members of the opposing culture and act as if they cannot be heard by the other group. In most cases the conflict ends when the persons who commenced the confrontation leave the scene.

While conducting my ethnographic interviews, I was also told by many of my Mexican-origin informants that not all Anglo Americans agree with Santa Paula's interethnic rules of social comportment. However, they did comment that in shared public places it is the norm for Anglo Americans to expect people of Mexican descent to defer to them. I personally experienced the pressures of these unwritten rules when I collected my field research. I, too, was expected to defer to the Anglo Americans because I am of Mexican descent. To elucidate this analysis, I would like to offer a few ethnographic examples from my field observations and interview data. The intent of this section is to illustrate that although ethnic mixing takes place in shared public places, Santa Paula's interethnic social boundaries do not diminish. And the purpose of maintaining these boundaries is to ensure that Anglo Americans be treated as a privileged group. My first set of ethnographic examples will focus on events in stores and restaurants. My next ethnographic example will examine gender and ethnic discrimination. My last set of illustrations will focus on the clubs and examine a social event in which I unwittingly committed a social blunder.

In regard to my first set of ethnographic examples, the majority of my Mexican-origin informants reported that the stores and restaurants are the places where they are most commonly discriminated against. The discrimination is subtle, yet humiliating. For example, let us examine what sometimes transpires in stores. If a Mexican-origin person arrives at the cashier's booth either at the same time as or seconds before an Anglo American, the clerk will first attend the Anglo American. It is also common for an Anglo American customer to stand in front of a Mexican-origin person to ensure that she or he be assisted first. On occasion, when the clerks are of Mexican descent, they will attend to the persons who arrived first. Most of my informants reported, however, that Mexican-origin clerks often behave the same way as Anglo American clerks do. I agree with my informants' observations that Mexican-origin people are discriminated against in the stores, as I personally observed and experienced similar incidents. I noticed that most of the stores in which I shopped on the West Side employed rude clerks. The clerks were polite and greeted me with a smile when business was slow. If the cashier lines were busy, however, I was generally treated as a second-class customer. For example, in Drifty's drugstore, I observed that if several Anglo Americans were waiting in line, the cashier would request that another checkout stand be opened. In contrast, when I and other Mexicans were waiting in line, the same courtesy was not extended.

According to my informants, for Mexican-origin people to be discriminated against in restaurants owned by Anglo Americans is also common. These types of restaurants generally cater to Anglo American customers and offer a southern cuisine or traditional Anglo American dishes (e.g., pea soup, chicken-fried steaks, Danish meatballs). In these restaurants it is an unwritten rule for a waiter to attend to the Anglo American customers first, regardless of whether they arrived after the Mexican-origin customers. Mexican-origin people generally only complain when the services are severely inequitable. For example, in a busy restaurant a waiter often serves several Anglo Americans within ten or fifteen minutes after their arrival yet takes at least forty-five minutes to attend to his Mexican-origin customer. Mexican-origin people often react by walking out or complaining to the manager of this extremely insulting situation. Many of my Mexican-origin informants, however, responded that they often accept inequitable treatment in restaurants that cater to an Anglo American clientele because otherwise they would constantly be arguing with the waiters. Unfortunately, I have to admit that when I conducted my research in Santa Paula I also had to accept being treated as a second-class customer. I had to. Otherwise, I would not have been able to conduct my ethnographic observations in these restaurants. At first, I was angry and hurt. I thought: "Why are they treating me rudely? I'm dressed well. I speak English. I have money. Why don't they like me?" After a couple of months, I learned that I had to either be tolerant or not go to the restaurants. These were my only two choices. I therefore decided to be patient. My favorite restaurant was Sally's Chili Hut because it was located half a block from the library where I was studying Santa Paula's archives. My relatives advised me not to go there because Mexicans weren't welcomed. I decided to go anyway, because during my study breaks I would be able to eat lunch or dinner there and then walk back to the library. The first week I sat in a booth so that I would be able to write notes while I ate. At this time I noticed that the waitresses were not friendly and that I had to wait a long time before being served. I didn't mind. It gave me time to observe the action. During the second week, I decided to sit by the counter and next to the exit door because several customers were making me feel nervous. They were intimidating me by staring. I thought, "Maybe I should eat fast and leave." When I changed seating locations, however, I noticed that Sally, the shop owner, became very friendly and started to treat me well. After that experience, I decided to sit by the counter because there I was treated cordially on a regular basis. Also, once I moved locations, I felt accepted and safe, as Sally would tell me, "You come back." In sum, I was accepted as long as I sat by the counter.

Several of my informants commented that there were some occasions when they would not tolerate discriminatory behavior in the restaurants. They felt that for most people of Mexican descent there was a tolerance-breaking point. When this happened, the outcome was usually a public display of interethnic conflict, or what I earlier called the "visual" and "verbal" duels. According to Iris and Miriam, two of my informants, the individuals who were most discriminated against by clerks and waiters were Mexicans who did not speak English. Both alleged that for most people of Mexican descent these situations made them feel indignant and angry. Based on my personal observations, I concur with Iris' and Miriam's analysis. Apparently, the places where monolingual Spanish speakers were commonly discriminated against were the fast-food restaurants. On several occasions I also observed that when a line was long in a fast-food restaurant and several Anglo Americans were waiting behind a Mexican customer who did not speak English, the clerk often asked the Mexican to step aside until the other customers were served. The clerk was reluctant to take the time to translate the order and preferred not to inconvenience the Anglo American customers. In these cases, when an Anglo American clerk intentionally and blatantly debased the Mexican customer, I observed that often a Mexican American would step in and demand that the Mexican customer be assisted. I noticed that the responses of the clerks often differed. When the clerks accommodated the Mexican customers and none of the Anglo Americans complained, the confrontations ended. However, when the clerks refused to accommodate the Mexican clients, conflicts usually followed, and an exchange of racial epithets ensued until the altercations were resolved. In these cases, the conflicts ended when the store manager stepped in or when Mexican-origin clerks assisted their co-workers and took the orders.

A second type of circumstance in which Mexican-origin people were discriminated against and expected to defer to Anglo Americans occurred when interethnic contact took place between men and women. For example, in stores, the library, and the post office, I observed that when an Anglo American male and a woman of Mexican descent approached the front door of a building, in most cases the Anglo American male did not open the door for the woman. When the gender and ethnic roles were reversed, however, the Mexican male opened the door for the Anglo American woman. The only times I noticed that this courteous practice was not followed by Mexican-origin males was when teenage boys were part of the group. In these cases, however, the Anglo American women tried to avoid the young boys.

In my ethnographic field research, I also identified a third type of situation when Mexican-origin people were discriminated against and were not allowed to interact with Anglo Americans. I found that a few social clubs were exclusively Anglo American. These clubs were the Daughters of the American Revolution, Eagles Lodge, Loyal Order of the Moose, Women of the Moose, and the Masonic Lodge. Three Anglo Americans and five Mexican-origin people informed me that most of these clubs were controlled by the families of the citrus growers. In order to obtain more information on these clubs and to see if I could attend their meetings, I contacted Natalie, a prominent citizen of Santa Paula and the wife of a wealthy farmer. I was referred to her by several of my Anglo American informants and the librarian of the Ventura County Museum of History and Art.

Natalie was very polite and gracious when I met her. According to Natalie, several clubs in Santa Paula continued to have exclusive Anglo American membership because that was the consensus of the groups. On occasion, however, they invited Mexicans to their meetings. For example, a few years ago the Daughters of the American Revolution honored and invited to their reunion the descendants of the first Mexican families who picked citrus in Santa Paula. Natalie also offered to invite me to one social event if I wrote a paper on Santa Paula's citrus industry and presented it to the group. I agreed and left her my phone number and address, but unfortunately I never received an invitation.

Later, I contacted the Women of the Moose and the Eagles Club to find out when club meetings were to be held. I was treated politely but told that meetings were not currently scheduled. I was also informed that I would be contacted about future meetings. As could be expected, no one called.

As I was not invited to any Anglo American social club activity, I decided to wait and see if any public fund-raising events would be held. One day, I read in the *Santa Paula Daily Chronicle* that several organizations were sponsoring a dinner-dance for the local hospital's cancer fund-raiser. It was a social affair open to all citizens. The entrance fee was fifteen dollars per person, and I decided to invite my fifteen-year-old nephew as my escort. On the day of the fund-raiser, we arrived at the restaurant where the event was being held. When we entered the building, we were met by a hostess who informed us that the restaurant was closed and only guests who were attending the fund-raiser were permitted to enter. I informed the hostess that I had come to attend the event. Quite surprised that we were there for the fund-raiser, she reluctantly directed us toward the entrance of the hall where the tickets were being sold. When my nephew and I were about to enter the hall, an usher stopped us and politely guided us to a booth hidden in a corner. As this isolated location did not provide us with a good view of the activities, and because it appeared that the waitress was not going to serve our beverages, we decided to move to a table near the center of the hall. Unwittingly, we must have broken protocol, as no one spoke to us throughout the entire evening nor did any waitress approach our table. We also noticed that many Anglo American senior citizens gave us vicious stares and attempted to make us feel uncomfortable. We decided to ignore them and move to the lounge. There we noticed that several people were staring at us and whispering behind our backs. They were speaking in a low tone, yet intentionally loud enough so that we could hear them. Their remarks were: "Who are they?" "What are they doing here?"

"Some people just don't know." "Does she work for the hospital?" We finally left when the band started playing country music. My nephew asked to leave because he was sad and afraid.

After this incident, I decided not to attend any more social club events where I was obviously unwanted. Although I knew I would not be physically injured at these events, I did not want to place myself in a situation in which I would be humiliated. I resented being treated as a worthless person merely because I was of Mexican descent. Thus, through this experience I once again observed and felt the manifestation of social apartness. I, like other people of Mexican descent, learned through this type of encounter that there were certain social clubs and public events where Mexicans were unwanted. Entrance into such social club events was permitted only when Anglo American residents invited us.

This type of social exclusion, however, cannot be considered segregation because physical violence is not used to deny people of Mexican descent entrance to the clubs or the Anglo Americans' public social events. Furthermore, in these types of contexts there is occasionally interethnic social mixing, such as when Mexican-origin people are honored at or invited to attend special club events. In the past, when Santa Paula was a segregated society, this type of social mixing did not occur, for the racial/ethnic boundaries were clearly delineated and trespassing those borders was not permitted. Moreover, if one argues that the clubs in Santa Paula are today segregated, one must account for the occasional interethnic mixing that occurs in most clubs. In a segregated society, such interethnic mixing is not tolerated, while in a community that practices social apartness it is. For example, I found that interethnic mixing is tolerated in the professional organizations (e.g., accountants, veterans), the recreational clubs (e.g., 4-H, Boys' Club, Girl Scouts, Boy Scouts), and the Democratic and Republican clubs. I unfortunately was unable to find out why Anglo Americans permit ethnic mixing in these contexts. Perhaps it is due to the fact that these clubs are local chapters of national organizations which do not practice racial-ethnic membership restrictions.

These ethnographic examples from the stores, restaurants, fast-food restaurants, clubs, and other public places indicate that, in a community where social apartness is practiced, Anglo Americans determine the social contexts in which interethnic mixing is allowed or prohibited. Interethnic norms and social protocol rules are used to ensure that the community's social boundaries are respected. Mexican-origin people, however, have the freedom to trespass these boundaries if they are prepared to confront the individuals who establish and maintain those bounded social spaces.

CONCLUSION

Based on my ethnographic field research, I found that past segregative practices in Santa Paula have been reformed and Mexican-origin people are not forced by local laws, physical violence, or their employers to remain among their own kind involuntarily. Nonetheless, segregation in Santa Paula has evolved into a system of social apartness. Anglo Americans determine the places and times when interethnic mixing can take place. They also practice a cultural system of correct social comportment in order to accord themselves social privileges.

On the surface, this system of social apartness may not appear to be harmful because no one is physically injured and it is a peaceful way to maintain cordial interethnic relations. The problem, however, is that it serves to debase Mexican-origin people and ascribe to them an inferior social position, while concurrently conferring special privileges upon Anglo Americans. As I have previously discussed, some of the outcomes of this system are that: the majority of Mexican-origin elementary students attend segregated schools, the city council continues to favor the West Side in funding city projects, the East Side has become a zone for industrial storage, Anglo Americans continue to humiliate people of Mexican descent, Mexican-origin people are not welcomed in the Protestant churches, and Mexican-origin people are discriminated against in the provisioning of public services.

NINE   *The Impact of Anglo American Racism on Mexican-Origin Intragroup Relations*

In concluding this historical account, I need to present a critical analysis of how a history of discrimination and marginalization has affected the intragroup relations within the Mexican-origin community of Santa Paula.[1] This analysis is based on a composite of seventy-four interviews with people of Mexican descent. Indeed, this issue is of major significance, as my Mexican-origin informants explained that Anglo American racism has at times served to generate ethnic cohesion, while at other times it has promoted intragroup conflict and social distance. Apparently, during times of crisis, racism generates political activism and serves to unify the Mexican-origin community for purposes of self-defense. In the daily lives of the Mexican-origin population, however, racism has subtly affected personal self-worth and cultural identities. Within this ethnic community, a history of Anglo American intolerance toward the public expression of Mexican culture has apparently served to generate a cultural ranking system. Anglo American culture is considered by many people of Mexican descent to be the prestigious culture and worthy of replication. In contrast, Mexican culture has been stigmatized. In other words, many members of the Mexican-origin community of Santa Paula place pressure upon themselves to appear and to identify as Americans. Sadly, these acculturation pressures (i.e., to adopt the culture and norms of the Anglo Americans) have generated intragroup conflict, as many individuals maintain close ties with Mexico and prefer to identify as Mejicano.

Currently, acculturation continues to be a source of intragroup conflict in Santa Paula because some Mexican traditions are considered by many Mexican-origin people to be improper forms of public behavior, such as speaking Spanish or playing Mexican music. Some individuals view this form of accommodation to be positive, while others consider it a shameful practice. Those who are critical of this Americanization norm believe that Mexican practices should not be censored in any situation.[2] They disagree with the belief that there are proper times when Mexican traditions should be expressed, as well as with the view that certain agrarian Mexican practices should be shed. Unfortunately, conflicting perceptions toward acculturation are often manifested in intragroup social distance. Apparently, also, intragroup cultural conflict is more intense between those individuals who were born in the United States and those who were born in Mexico. It is primarily a native-born and Mexican-immigrant conflict.

Interestingly, I found that although intragroup conflict is part of the daily lives of people of Mexican descent, it is often suspended. During periods of stress, when Anglo Americans confer upon them social, economic, or political disadvantages, intragroup conflict is temporarily suspended in favor of their common interest. In situations of this kind, they act as a political ethnic unit. Therefore, before I provide a description of how dominant group racism generates both conflict and cohesion within the Mexican-origin community, let me first briefly describe the people who compose this ethnic community.

SELF-REFERENCE LABELS: NATIVE-BORN, OLD IMMIGRANTS, NEW IMMIGRANTS, AND MIGRATORY FARM WORKERS

Ethnic self-reference labels gathered in interviews with my Mexican-origin informants suggest that they consider themselves to be a culturally diverse people, and for various reasons use these labels as ethnic markers. In illustrating this point, many of my informants stated that they were "Juntos pero no revueltos" (We are one people, yet not the same). This proverb indicates that they are aware of their cultural diversity. For example, for second- and third-generation American-born families to consider themselves "the old families" is common. They are very proud of their ancestry, and they claim to be descendants of the Mexicans who migrated to Santa Paula during the nineteenth century. Some of these families also claim to be descendants of Spanish pioneers who colonized California in the eighteenth century. They generally distinguish themselves from first-generation Mexican Americans, who are the children of immigrants. Nonetheless, regardless of generational residence, people who are born in the United States and are of Mexican descent are referred to as the "native-born."

Intragroup labels are also applied to Mexican immigrants and are used to distinguish them from other Mexican-origin residents. Immigrants who have resided permanently in Santa Paula between 1942 and 1964 are considered to be the "old immigrants," and those who migrated afterward are labeled "new immigrants." Mines and Anzaldúa (1982), in their study of Santa Paula, identified the usage of the same ethnic labels. Apparently, the years of the bracero program are used to categorize the Mexican immigrants. The old immigrant families settled in Santa Paula during the bracero period (1942–1964) (Menchaca 1987; Mines and Anzaldúa 1982) (see chapter 6). The majority are believed to have settled during the late 1950s, and a large part of them are rumored to have acquired legal residence with the assistance of the growers. Many of the old immigrants continue to work in farm labor and have acquired seniority within the agricultural industry. They are employed as cannery workers, truckers, crew leaders, and farm mechanics. They also receive among the best farm wages, vacation pay, and health insurance.

The new immigrants settled in Santa Paula after 1964, following the termination of the bracero program. They are considered to be the newcomers (Mines and Anzaldúa 1982). This group is primarily employed in agriculture, and the majority are year-round harvest pickers. They are permanent residents of Santa Paula. Their seniority within the company depends on how many years they have worked for the industry. Based on my ethnographic observations and interview data, the old and new immigrants can be described as follows: the majority are employed in the agricultural industry, their language is Spanish, they attend Our Lady of Guadalupe Church, and they take part in the same recreational activities (e.g., patronize Mexican bars or participate in the Mexican immigrant baseball league).

Another group of Mexican descent resides in Santa Paula and is considered to be different from the permanently settled immigrants. They are Mexican nationals and seasonal migratory farm workers. The majority of them are men who come to harvest lemons during the summer months. They also live in Santa Paula, but they are not considered part of the Mexican-origin community. Rather, they are viewed as visitors until they acquire year-round employment at Santa Paula farms. They are also easily distinguishable by their dress, language, and residential location. For example, the women wear braids and the men wear straw *sombreros* (hats), they maintain the dialect and intonation pattern of the sending region of Mexico, and they reside in the slum areas of the East Side *barrio* or in labor camps. This group is highly stigmatized and often ostracized by the native-born.

Although there are five major groups within the Mexican-origin community, the main distinction is made in reference to nativity, and the social division is between the native-born and the Mexican immigrant. We will now turn to this topic.

Native-born male.

Native-born female.

Native-born teenagers.

Old immigrants.

New immigrants.

Seasonal migratory male farm worker.

ACCULTURATION AND
INTRAGROUP CONFLICT

For the most part, acculturation among Mexican-origin groups in Santa Paula has been expressed by following the Anglo Americans' rules of correct social comportment. Through this process Mexican-origin groups have acquired the cultural knowledge to peacefully coexist with the dominant culture (see chapter 8). The most common rules of correct social comportment adopted by most Mexican-origin groups include speaking English in public, socially deferring to Anglo American people, celebrating American holidays, developing a U.S. nationalist identity, and not playing Mexican music in public. Ironically, the effect of this acculturative process on the perceptions of self-worth among the Mexican-origin population has been the development of intragroup cultural conflict. Such conflict is expressed in intragroup stratification between the "acculturated individuals" who conform to the culture of the Anglo elite and those who prefer to express their "Mejicanismo" (Mexican culture) in public. Second- and third- generation native-born people have conformed to the public culture of the Anglo American elite and expect Mexican immigrants to follow their example. If immigrants do not, the native-born maintain socially distant relations as a means of disassociating themselves.

Apparently, the intragroup conflict within the Mexican-origin community is also accompanied by negative stereotyping. The native-born, who are American-ized, often view Mexican immigrants as culturally backward. The former consider the latter to be distant kin who have not accommodated to the practices, norms, and values of the Anglo American elite. Mexican immigrants are often stigmatized as foreigners, since a large part of the adult Mexican population does not adopt the English language or Anglo American cultural practices. In particular, for many native-born, the Mejicanismo of the immigrants is a source of embarrassment. Although the Mexican immigrants resist the negative stereotyping, they react differently to such hostility. Some immigrants attempt to escape the stigma of being foreigners by acculturating, while others refuse to change their ethnic identity and seldom interact with the native-born. Also, attitudinal differences toward acculturation appear to be more pronounced among adults than in immigrant youth. Adult immigrants are often reluctant to acculturate, in contrast to immigrant children who often demonstrate a receptive attitude toward the new cultural norms.

The acculturation of the children of immigrant parents appears to be associated with the schooling experience and their school peers. That is, if the youth acculturate, they resolve the conflicts between themselves and the native-born. Three schoolteachers, a counselor, and several community members offered the following explanation regarding the acculturation process of the youth: in school, these children who are born in the United States or are raised from childhood in this country experience strong pressures to behave like Americans and to shed their Mexican identity. Younger children of immigrants who are schooled in the United States often prefer to identify themselves as "Chicano" or "Mexican American." The change in identity is triggered because first-generation and Mexican immigrant students are socialized in United States schools and are taught to become more independent from their families. In the schooling context, they acquire the tastes, norms, and lifestyle of the Mexican Americans. Furthermore, because many children of immigrant parents also form close friendships with their native-born peers, Mexican students develop personal ties with non-immigrant families. The common outcome is that, upon leaving school and becoming young adults, Americanized Mexicans prefer to be identified as members of the more prestigious native-born social networks. Moreover, a Mexican teenager's desire to be considered "normal" by school peers also explains why the individual may not choose to identify as Mexican. Within a youth's social circle, being an ethnic minority person is not a source of embarrassment, but being a foreigner is. Therefore, a need for normalcy pushes the young person to attempt to acculturate and pass for native-born. Because a Mexican student can pass for native-born, many youths choose to rid themselves of the newcomer label. The stigma attached to farm labor exerts additional pressure on the children of immigrants to enter native-born social networks. In rural communities like Santa Paula, the label "Mexican" is synonymous with being a farm worker, whereas the terms "native-born," "Chicano," and "Mexican American" have no strict accompanying occupational classifications.

In most cases, older immigrant children who settle in the United States as teenagers do not adapt to their new environment in the same manner as their younger siblings. This probably occurs because they have received most of their early childhood socialization in Mexico and are less willing to adopt a new ethnic identity. Also, because older children often supplement the family income by working alongside their parents in the orchards, their social environment is often restricted to that of other Mexican farm workers.

Among the Mexican-origin adult population, intragroup conflict is expressed by the maintenance of socially distant relations. As mentioned earlier, this social distance is associated with acculturation differences. The social separation, however, is different from that imposed by the Anglo Americans upon the Mexican-origin community. In the case of the Mexican-origin people, immigrants and native-born share the same social spaces. They live in the same neighborhoods, their children attend the same schools, both groups patronize Mexican businesses, and they attend Our Lady of Guadalupe Church. Moreover, one group does not control the other economically or politically. In essence, there are no economic or political relations of domination or subordination. However, as occurs in other Mexican-origin communities with large immigrant populations, the native-born impose social and cultural rules upon the immigrants (De la Garza and Flores 1986; Rodríguez and Nuñez 1986). If the immigrants reject the rules, social ostracization is typically the outcome.

MANIFESTATIONS OF ACCULTURATION CONFLICTS: VOLUNTARY AND INVOLUNTARY SOCIAL DISTANCE

While conducting my ethnographic research in Santa Paula, I observed that Mexican-origin adults voluntarily and involuntarily separated themselves into two social spheres. On a daily basis the native-born and the Mexicans were cordial, yet they retained their social distance. A common response of my informants further indicated that two intragroup social circles were organized to set forth the groups' cultural differences. Adult immigrants and Americanized native-born typically belonged to different social clubs, preferred different types of leisure activities and music, and maintained most of their close friendships within their respective ethnic sphere. Apparently, also, it was the long-term native-born residents who set the social boundaries and expected Mexican immigrants to keep their social distance. For example, I was often told that because the native-born have been socialized to accommodate to Anglo American culture, they acquired many of the tastes, norms, and prejudices of the dominant culture and they preferred to interact with their own kind. They also expected the Mexican immigrants to conform to certain cultural expectations and down-play their Mejicanismo in public. If the immigrants refused to conform, often the native-born would avoid all contact with those persons. The following four ethnographic examples, based on the comments of Roger, Raúl, Jorge, and Miriam, illustrate the conflicts that develop with respect to native-born and Mexican attitudes toward acculturation. Their comments also indicate that the native-born use intragroup social separation to pressure Mexicans into acculturating.

Roger Aranda, an attorney and a member of the old families, reported that the social snobbery displayed by the native-born toward the immigrant appears to be based on cultural differences. Many Mexicans wear agrarian clothing in public, and this is a source of embarrassment to the native-born. They consider these Mexican immigrants to be backward peasants. Aranda stated:

> There is social snobbery between the native-born and the rest of the Hispanic community. Many of the native-born do not want to associate with the immigrants because they think immigrants are rancheros [peasants]. . . . You see social distance in the restaurants and the clubs. . . . For example, there are two baseball leagues. One is composed of Mexican immigrants and the other of native-born. . . . You also see social distance in the restaurants.

Aranda's statement suggests that it is the native-born who do not want to associate with the immigrants because they are ashamed of them.

Raúl, an old immigrant who settled in Santa Paula during the bracero program, gave a similar account. Raúl is a middle-class and successful self-employed businessman. He owns a small auto repair shop that primarily provides services to seasonal farm workers and citrus labor contractors. He also owns an apartment building. Raúl felt that the native-born assumed an air of superiority because they considered themselves to be sophisticated, for they were Americanized, whereas the Mexican immigrants were not. He did not understand why many native-born held this view. For example, Raúl contended that, compared to the native-born, the Mexican immigrant has a stronger work ethic. He also alleged that, unlike the native-born, Mexicans were not part of the drug culture. Raúl offered the following comments about the native-born:

> *The native-born feel superior to the immigrant and the*
> *undocumented, yet the undocumented and the immigrant*
> *get along well. The native-born and the immigrant don't*
> *get along at all. . . . In the work place . . . the native-born*
> *is lazy and unproductive. That's why the immigrant and*
> *the undocumented have to work harder, just to make up for*
> *the native-born's laziness. At work they [the native-born]*
> *try to act as if they are friends [of the immigrants and*
> *undocumenteds], but it's another story in the social circles.*
> *. . . For example, it's rare when a native-born family*
> *befriends and visits an immigrant family. . . . The native-*
> *born excludes the immigrant, but not at work. That's*
> *because the majority of them [the native-born] are lazy,*
> *substance abusers. . . . When they get to work they have a*
> *hangover, and because they are also lazy the rest of the*
> *workers have to cover for them. In the workplace [the*
> *native-born] are very friendly, but not in any other place.*
> *[My translation]*

Jorge, a third-generation native-born and also a member of the old families, shared the same observations as Roger and Raúl did. Jorge is part of the working class. He is a Ventura County government employee and works outside of Santa Paula. He also recently started a small business. Jorge commented that intragroup social distance was primarily a result of the native-born's refusal to be around unacculturated Mexicans. Jorge was proud of being Mexican American but believed that there were times when their ancestral culture should not be displayed. Therefore, he preferred to stay away from people who did not share his views. Jorge offered the following comments regarding why he did not associate with Mexican immigrants.

> *I don't associate with Mexicans. . . . For example, the*
> *Mexicans are preparing an event for the Pope. They asked*
> *me to participate [and I did not accept]. Other than that, I*
> *don't associate with them. . . . Many of my friends and*
> *their kids don't want to have anything to do with*
> *Mexicans because they are embarrassed of them. When*
> *they hear Mexican music they don't feel anything*

> *inside. . . . They would rather not deal with Mexicans.*
> *. . . This irritates me.*

The three comments suggest that intragroup cultural differences are a major source of conflict within the adult Mexican-origin population. The native-born prefer to distance themselves from Mexican immigrants who display Mexican practices in public.

In response to the native-born's social snobbery, the immigrant has developed a defense mechanism. Often, Mexican immigrants generate antagonistic stereotypes about the native-born, while concurrently attributing to themselves positive images. Miriam, an accountant and an immigrant who moved out of Santa Paula to attend college, summarized several native-born stereotypes commonly perpetuated by immigrants. Miriam commented that the native-born had drug problems, they were welfare recipients, and they had lost the hope of improving themselves. Conversely, Miriam attributed positive traits to the immigrants, such as the immigrant work ethic. Miriam began her account by recalling how she was discriminated against by some native-born students when she attended high school.

> *They don't identify with each other. The native-born think that all the immigrants are wetbacks, and the immigrants think that all the native-born are pochos [not real Mexicans or Anglo Americans]. For example, when I was in high school I was popular with a lot of the native-born, but then some of them found out I was an immigrant. . . . They stopped talking to me. . . .*
>
> *A major difference between the immigrants and the citizens [native-born] is the absence of a drug problem among the immigrants. . . . Drugs are a big problem among the native-born. . . . Within the native-born there is a group who, for generations, have been on welfare. . . . They have no ambition [native-born on welfare]. They are satisfied with the little they have. . . . In contrast . . . in the immigrant community there is a dream of progress. The immigrants are motivated to progress, and most of them avoid being on welfare. . . . They came to the United States to better themselves and to improve their standard of living.*

Miriam's intraethnic perceptions suggest that the immigrants believe they are morally superior to the native-born (e.g., most native-born are lazy or substance abusers). She also believes that some American-born Mexican Americans are experiencing downward mobility, while some Mexicans are moving up. She attributed the Mexicans' upward mobility to their work ethic.

Stories told among immigrants also reveal how they defend themselves from the native-born's presumed airs of superiority. Flavio, a first-generation Chicano youth who is part of both native-born and immigrant social circles, reveals in a comical story the tensions within his community. Flavio's story also indicates that some first-generation youth from immigrant backgrounds empathize with the plight of the undocumented. What follows is one of the stories of the adventures of "Ignacio and Ramón," two characters who in several stories mock the American system and outsmart the Anglo Americans and the native-born. In this story, Ignacio and Ramón outwit an immigration officer and make fun of three native-born youth waiting for a city bus. This story is bilingual, and for the joke to be understood, the double meaning in the word "one-way" must be translated from English to Spanish. "One-way" in bilingual Spanish sounds like "one buey," which in figurative English means "one jackass." The story begins with Ignacio and Ramón crossing the U.S.-Mexico border in a Greyhound bus.

> *Ignacio y Ramón acaban de llegar a Los Angeles después de haber cruzado la frontera de Tijuana en El* **Grei-ja-und.** *Ya son tan aguzados en cruzar la línea que se vienen en el bus de primera clase. La migra ya no los molesta. Nada más se ponen la cachucha de Fernando Valenzuela y le dicen a la migra—"Dodgers y hotdog."*
>
> *En esta vuelta Ignacio y Ramón vienen a jalar en Los Angeles, y andan buscando un domicilio de un amigo, que les va a rentar un apartamento. El amigo vive cerca de un callejón de un sentido.*
>
> *Bajándose del* **Grei-ja-und,** *cogen un mapa, y se suben en el transito público. Se bajan en una calle en East Los Angeles.*
>
> *Buscando el domicilio, Ramón sees an alley with the name of the street next to a* **one-way** *sign. Under the sign there are three cholos waiting for a bus. Puntando al* **one-way,** *Ramón le dice a Ignacio, "Vamos allá, ahí está el address." Ignacio le pregunta a Ramón "En dónde está?" Ramón responde, "Ahí, debajo del* **one-way.**" *Ignacio contesta, "yo no veo* **one way,** *veo* **tres bueyes.**
>
> *Ignacio and Ramón arrive by Greyhound [El Grei-ja-und] in Los Angeles after having crossed Tijuana's border.*

They are already so experienced at crossing the border that now they come in a first-class bus. The border patrol doesn't bother them anymore. [When the border patrol inspects the bus] they just put on a Fernando Valenzuela baseball cap and tell the immigration officer, "Dodgers and hotdogs."

On this trip, Ignacio and Ramón come to work in Los Angeles, and they are looking for the address of a friend who will rent them an apartment. The friend lives near a one-way alley.

Getting off the Greyhound, they look at a map and board a public transit bus. They get off the bus in East Los Angeles.

Looking for their friend's address, Ramón sees an alley near a One-Way sign. Under the sign there are three cholos [native-born] waiting for a bus. Pointing at the One-Way sign, Ramón tells Ignacio, "Let's go over there, there's the address." Ignacio asks Ramón, "Where did you say you saw it?" Ramón answers, "There, under the One-Way sign." Ignacio responds, "I don't see One-Way, I see three bueyes [figuratively, three jackasses]."
(My translation)

Although the Mexican immigrants defend their cultural ways by generating jokes such as this one or considering themselves to be morally superior, the native-born have been successful in pressuring them to acculturate. This pressure is effective because if Mexicans do not acculturate they are not invited to join the native-born's social clubs or festivities. We now turn to why the native-born are able to convince many Mexicans to conform.

In Santa Paula, public leisure activities center around a bowling alley, a few restaurants, and parks. There are no theaters, and "respectable" citizens do not go to the *cantinas* (Mexican bars) or to the "Okie bars." Local social conventions dictate that the "night action" must end by 7:30 P.M. on weekdays and by 10:00 P.M., when the restaurants close, on weekends. After these hours all "respectable" citizens are expected to be off the streets. Therefore, the provincial recreational atmosphere in Santa Paula constrains an individual to satisfy all recreational and social needs within his or her kinship network or in club meetings that typically are held at a friend's home. In this setting, the native-born control the social life of their community because they have resided for longer periods in Santa Paula, and thus over the years they have formed clubs and social networks to keep themselves entertained. Mexican adults who want to enter the social circles of the native-born must conform to the cultural standards of the long-term residents. They must speak English or be bilingual, avoid displaying agrarian tastes in clothes, and find employment outside the citrus industry. This social context tends to pressure many adults to shed the practices of their homeland and begin behaving in public like the Americanized native-born.

Generational residence in Santa Paula also appears to contribute strongly to the native-borns' social dominance over their Mexican counterparts. Both groups have different referent groups and social networks. Because generational residence determines the size of an individual's kinship and social networks, second- and third-generation native-born have had considerable time to establish civic and recreational clubs as well as to form large family support networks. As a consequence, the native-born residents control the social life in Santa Paula's Mexican-origin community by deciding who is allowed to enter their social circles. In the eighteen genealogies that I collected in Santa Paula, I found that ten of the second- and third-generation respondents of Mexican descent had relatives from at least six families residing in town. In contrast, my eight immigrant respondents indicated that they had fewer relatives living in Santa Paula. Either all their relatives lived outside of the city, or they were related to only two local families. This finding was corroborated by Keefe's studies conducted in Santa Paula and the nearby cities of Oxnard and Santa Barbara (1979, 1980; Keefe and Padilla 1987). Keefe's research indicates that the social and kinship networks of Mexican Americans grow with increasing generations in the United States. Third-generation Mexican Americans form large social and kinship networks, while immigrants have small social networks because their kinship system is largely based in Mexico. Therefore, in Santa Paula if adult Mexican immigrants want to expand their recreational networks, they must enter the social circles of the native-born. To do so, Mexican immigrants must learn the practices and traditions of their American-born ethnic members, or else they will not be invited to enter those social circles.

For example, holiday celebrations appear to be social contexts in which intragroup social distance is clearly distinguishable. Mexican immigrants who are not Americanized are not invited to participate in the festivities of the native-born. On these occasions I often observed in the parks family picnics attended by large groups of people who appeared to be native-born. These family picnics often included from 75 to 150 people. In these contexts, English was the dominant language, and "oldies" and rock the preferred music. In other sections of the park, however, Mexican immigrants formed small family gatherings commonly composed of a couple with their children and several single males. In these places Spanish was spoken, and Mexican *ranchera* music was loudly played.

Mexican immigrants are also excluded from Mexican American social and civic clubs. Most of these clubs are organized, managed, and controlled by the native-born, and seldom do Mexican immigrants participate. In Santa Paula immigrants, who are agrarian in cultural style and Spanish monolingual, either do not join or are not recruited to join native-born clubs. Instead, immigrants have formed religious clubs centered around Our Lady of Guadalupe Church.

In sum, the social exclusion of Mexican immigrants has become an effective method used by the native-born to pressure some Mexicans into conforming to Anglo American public culture. Apparently, the acculturation of Mexican-origin groups is associated with the long-term effects of the Anglo Americans' cultural intolerance toward the public expression of Mexican culture. That is, in an attempt to maintain peaceful interethnic relations in public, the native-born down-play their ethnicity and conform to Anglo American cultural norms. In turn, they pressure or encourage their Mexican counterparts to acculturate.

SOCIAL CLASS DIFFERENCES WITHIN A CULTURALLY STRATIFIED MEXICAN-ORIGIN COMMUNITY

Unlike most people's conflicting perceptions toward acculturation, my Mexican-origin informants reported that social class differences are not a major source of group conflict within their community. In most cases, upper-class and middle-class families retain close ties with their working-class ethnic members. Social class snobbishness, however, does occur among the youth. Many of my informants reported that the children of wealthy businessmen flaunt their wealth and are conspicuous consumers. For example, upper-class youth often show off their new cars by driving around Santa Paula and blasting their expensive stereos. In this manner they attract attention. I agree with the observations of my informants, as I also witnessed similar incidents. During two city festivals, I saw several upper-class Mexican American teenagers driving around the city park while they honked their horns and waved to people. They were obviously showing off their expensive Volvos and BMWs. At the festivals, upper-class male youth were particularly demonstrative of their wealth. Several of them drove around the park to show off and to display their popularity with young women, as their cars were fully occupied with Anglo American and Mexican American teenage girls. And, when these young men walked through the park, they were usually accompanied by girls at their sides. It was also common for them to take out their billfolds and publicly display their money by paying for their friends' food and entertainment.

My informants reported that the social class snobbishness displayed by wealthy Mexican American youth is uncommon among the adult population and that the public conspicuous consumption of goods by the latter is unheard of. Three main reasons were offered for this behavior. The first involves kinship relations. Because most upper-class Mexican Americans are related to working-class family members, such as grandparents, aunts, uncles, and cousins, they prefer not to socially alienate their relatives. Keefe (1979) corroborates this analysis, as she found that first- to third-generation Mexican Americans in Santa Paula are related to at least seventeen families in town, and they maintain close ties with their extended kin. A second explanation is related to Santa Paula's past history of social segregation. In that most upper-class adults were raised on the East Side and attended segregated schools, they have formed long-term friendships with their working-class peers. Social class differences have not ruptured those friendships. Third, there is the issue of interethnic conflict. Because racial tension exists between the Anglo American and Mexican-origin communities, it has been necessary for the upper class to maintain formal and informal relations with their working-class ethnic members. This is a subject that I will momentarily elaborate.

In reference to the role that social-class differences exert on the cultural division between the native-born and Mexican immigrants, my informants commented that economic conflicts are insignificant because the majority of both groups are working-class people. To investigate these perceptions, I interviewed Rina Valdivia, the manager of the Employment Development Department of Ventura County. I was primarily concerned with my informants' assertion that the immigrant and native-born working-class sector earn similar wages. Rina corroborated my informants' analysis. She stated that farm labor wages and most service occupations in Ventura County pay comparable wages. People are paid either minimum wage or a couple of dollars above this scale. Rina added that as a result of unionization activity in Santa Paula farm labor wages have steadily increased and Mexican immigrants are paid decent wages.[3] In 1986, farm worker hourly wages ranged from $4.25 to $7.17 (Ventura County Agricultural Association 1986; Employment Development Department Research Division 1986). In her opinion, many Mexican immigrant families who are year-round farm workers earn stable incomes. To illustrate her statement, Rina offered the following analysis. In many cases, when a Mexican immigrant family combines the individuals' farm labor income, they can be economically stable. In such a family often both the father and the oldest son are employed as lemon pickers, and each receives wages of $6.00 an hour, while the mother works in the cannery and is paid $4.45 an hour. The rest of the children are not expected to work. Consequently, a nuclear family may live on a combined income of $16.45 per hour. Though these wages are low in comparison to American middle-class standards, they place many Mexican immigrants in an economically stable working-class category.

My informants also commented that income differences are not the basis of the native-born–Mexican immigrant conflicts because neither group is concentrated in one social class sector. Although most people of Mexican descent belong to the working class, there are individuals from both groups who are part of the upper and middle classes. In their analysis, my informants contended that native-born–immigrant conflicts are based on different perceptions of acculturation. In substantiating this observation, several of my informants identified the Mexican-origin merchants as an example of a group of people who share common socioeconomic interests but are set apart by cultural beliefs. Therefore, I decided to investigate this observation by conducting a survey of the Mexican-origin business sector. In the survey, I asked merchants where they were born, where they lived, and what they perceived to be major sources of group conflict and cohesion within their ethnic community. I also noted the type of business that each merchant owned (e.g., a large supermarket, jewelry store, or small cafe). I was able to interview seventy-seven (93 percent) of the eighty-three individuals who owned businesses (six people declined to participate). My survey data indicated that 63 percent were first to fourth generation and 37 percent were Mexican immigrants (22 percent old immigrants and 15 percent new immigrants). Approximately, 40 percent of the businesses were small scale, primarily "mom and pop" grocery stores or cafes. Most businesses, however, were mid- to large- scale. These included businesses such as supermarkets, auto repair shops, restaurants, real estate offices, liquor stores, clothing stores, and a hotel. Furthermore, 88 percent of my respondents stated that they lived in either middle- or upper-class neighborhoods located on the West Side or the East Side. After completing the survey, I confirmed my informants' observations. I found that, although the merchants account for a significant portion of Santa Paula's middle- and upper-class strata and share common economic and social class interests, cultural differences between the native-born and the immigrant businesspeople generated conflicts. For example, each group held stereotypical views of the other. Mexican immigrants considered the native-born to be provincial and ignorant of Mexican history. Likewise, a common response of the native-born was that Mexican immigrants should be satisfied with being Americans and stop thinking about returning to Mexico.

In sum, social-class conflicts within the Mexican-origin community appear to be mild. Middle- and upper-class adults have retained close ties with their working-class ethnic members and prefer not to flaunt their social-class status. Most conflicts among the adult population appear to be related to different cultural perceptions. Among the youth, however, there appears to be a developing social-class stratification. Many middle- and upper-class youth are conspicuous consumers and are glad to display their privileged economic positions.

ETHNIC COHESION WITHIN A CULTURALLY STRATIFIED MEXICAN-ORIGIN COMMUNITY

Despite the conflicts over attitudinal differences toward acculturation, Mexican immigrants and the native-born in Santa Paula have been able to maintain a sense of peoplehood and, during periods of crisis, mobilize such collectivity for their mutual benefit. In their everyday life, ethnic differences generate social cleavages, but during crisis periods they are able to temporarily suspend their differences and act as a cohesive group. Their sense of peoplehood emanates from both a common ethnic heritage and a shared subordinate ethnic minority group status. They have in common an indissoluble and intimate historical identity and an ethnic experience that is not shared by the larger society. As an ethnic minority group they have been discriminated against by the dominant society. Also, they voluntarily choose to identify as an ethnic group and distinguish themselves as a people of Mexican descent.

Interethnic conflict is pervasive and encourages the maintenance of the ethnic unit. Dominant group racial prejudice often forces the Mexican-origin community to involuntarily distinguish themselves from the Anglo Americans who attempt to confer upon them social disadvantages (see Despres 1975). The native-born and the Mexicans recognize that they must often mobilize themselves as a unified, political ethnic group if they are to share the resources that the Anglo American elite control; at other times, they need to become a cohesive front to defend themselves against dominant group racial discrimination (see Siegel 1970). Farm worker strikes are common examples of how racial discrimination forces them to behave as a competing ethnic unit. On one side are the Anglo American growers who owe their wealth to citrus, and on the opposing side are the Mexican laborers and the Mexican-origin community. Although the demand for higher wages and improved employment benefits has been the basis of the labor strikes, a closer analysis of the disputes in Santa Paula reveals a historical pattern of racial and labor tension. By tradition, the growers have economically dominated the Mexican-origin population as their employers. Also, in the past and until the mid-1960s, growers and other Anglo Americans subjected the native-born and Mexican immigrants to residential segregation (Menchaca 1987; Menchaca and Valencia 1990; Santa Paula property tax assessment records 1902–1957). Although the native-born no longer work in the orchard groves, memories of past farm worker strikes trigger recollections of economic deprivation and social injustice and thus temporarily activate a united native-born–Mexican immigrant political front (see chapter 7).

On a daily basis, less volatile forms of interethnic conflict also encourage the maintenance of the ethnic unit. For example, dormant interethnic tensions were activated in 1986 when the city government and the Chamber of Commerce accused Mexican-origin youth of vandalizing and destroying private property. The conflict began when a group of Mexican-origin teenagers formed a gang that they called the Crimies. For the most part, the Crimies served as an emotional support group that held meetings, wore Crimies jackets, hung around together in school, cruised the East Side streets, held parties, drank beer in parks, and occasionally painted graffiti on abandoned buildings. Gradually, the membership of the Crimies increased as many working-class Mexican and native-born teenagers joined the club. Subsequently, the Crimies' territorial influence expanded throughout the East Side *barrios*. Almost every street in the *barrios* had at least one *placa* (graffiti) stating: "Los Crimies de la 12th Rule C/S" (C/S = *con safos,* a retaliatory warning to anyone who defaces the graffiti). In response to the growth of the Crimies, many Mexican-origin teenagers who were not part of the gang organized an opposing group called the Party Boys, to counter the Crimies' territorial expansion. When the Party Boys challenged the territorial expansion of the Crimies, the latter responded by increasing their graffiti spray painting in the *barrios* to demonstrate that they were in control. In retaliation, the Party Boys defaced the Crimies' graffiti and replaced it with statements such as "Kill the Crimies—Party Boys Rule, C/S."

The graffiti conflict continued, but it took on a new direction. It was rumored that the leader of the Party Boys, who resided in a predominantly Anglo American neighborhood of the West Side, defaced the Crimies' *placas*. The Crimies responded by "bombing" (a term used to connote graffiti writing in an enemy's neighborhood) the West Side and the downtown area. One evening, the Crimies clandestinely invaded the West Side and spray-painted graffiti in several middle-class neighborhoods where the Party Boys resided and on several walls in the shopping centers and the downtown business district.

The city government immediately responded to this crisis. City administrators called a council meeting to investigate who the Crimies were and, in particular, to determine who spray-painted the West Side walls. Also, Anglo American businessmen offered rewards to anyone with information leading to the arrest of the Crimies' bombers. Immediately, a group of political activists who were part of Lucha (Struggle), a Chicano civic organization, attempted to diffuse the anticipated escalation of an interethnic confrontation. They asked parents to attend the city council meeting and to help them stop the council from harassing the Mexican-origin youth. At the meeting the political activists represented the Mexican-origin community. Daniel, the spokesperson, argued that the bombing was the result of the mischievous actions of a few teenagers and not the manifestation of an uncontrollable youth delinquency problem on the East Side, as the city government alleged. In his assessment of the graffiti conflict, Daniel contended that the underlying problem was not the youth but rather the city government's reluctance to establish recreational programs in the *barrios*. He also identified inherent contradictions in the city government's response to the graffiti bombing. Daniel questioned why the city government responded immediately to the bombing of the West Side neighborhoods when for months the city administrators did nothing about the graffiti on the East Side walls. Apparently, Daniel's presentation was effective and the presence of Mexican-origin people at the meeting diffused the conflict, for the city council dropped their charges and had the walls cleaned in both the East Side and the West Side neighborhoods.

Thus, the group unity displayed in this context indicates that during a crisis the Mexican-origin community temporarily sets aside its ethnic differences and acts as a political unit. Other cases in which similar cohesive actions were displayed include the farm worker housing movement, the movement to dismantle social segregation, political activists' protection of the social rights of the braceros, and everyday practices such as Mexican Americans' defense of the rights of Mexicans who are discriminated against because they do not speak English.

CONCLUSION

Using Santa Paula as an example, it can be argued that any acculturation process is the outcome of some form of dominance relation. In this ethnic environment, where relations of domination and subordination developed over the decades, the Anglo Americans did not allow the Mexican-origin people to influence Santa Paula's institutional cultural norms. The acculturation experience of the Mexican-origin community, therefore, has been historically conditioned by Anglo American intolerance toward cultural difference. This practice first set forth a culturally ranked social order in which Mexican culture was stigmatized and subsequently generated conditions for native-born–Mexican immigrant conflicts. As the Americanized native-born have been operational in the culture of the Anglo Americans, they ascribed themselves higher cultural prestige over the Mexican immigrants and in turn pressured their unacculturated group members to accept the cultural norms of the Anglo Americans.

Although dominant group prejudice toward the public expression of Mexican culture generated intragroup conflict, it also promoted cohesion during periods of stress. When the Anglo Americans attempted to confer upon the Mexican-origin community intolerable social disadvantages, dominant group prejudice served to maintain the ethnic unit. During heightened periods of interethnic conflict, the native-born and Mexicans temporarily suspended their differences and transformed themselves into a politically effective ethnic group.

TEN   *Historical*
        Reconstruction

In this historical account I have attempted to reconstruct the unwritten history of the Mexican-origin community of Santa Paula. I therefore documented their memories of marginalization and discrimination. In doing so, I relied on oral histories and on written documents to verify my informants' remembrances. I also conducted interviews and ethnographic field research to gather information about their intragroup relations and their civic, political, and economic status. In embarking on this study, my original aim was to write an ethnography about Mexican migration to the United States. However, as I read local accounts of Santa Paula's founding and development and compared these histories with the Mexican-origin community's oral histories, I became intrigued by the two dissimilar versions and, consequently, decided to conduct further historical research.

What I found was that one version was written by Anglo American elites and primarily focused on their families' accomplishments (Blanchard 1961; McFie 1944; Teague 1944; Santa Paula School District Board of Trustees 1963; Thille 1952, 1958). According to these accounts, Santa Paula was founded by their ancestors in 1872 (Belknap 1968; Teague 1944). With the exception of a few Native Americans, Santa Paula was uninhabited before the nineteenth century (Cleland 1957; Thille 1952, 1958). Allegedly, the Anglo Americans single-handedly built the town, overwhelmingly contributed to the success of the citrus industry, and were solely capable of governing the city. Moreover, plaques and portraits displayed in government buildings, Fourth of July celebrations, commemorative events (e.g., for the founding of the city, the oil museum, the citrus industry), and memorabilia enshrined in the city's oil museum attest to the validity of this historical account. This version had become Santa Paula's official and written history, safely guarded in the city's museum and in a special reading room located in the library.

On the other hand, when I spoke to people of Mexican descent, they offered a strikingly different version than that presented by the Anglo American elite. Their account, however, was not integrated within Santa Paula's official history. Nor were any of their written documents archived in the library or their memorabilia securely stored in the city's museum. Records about the people of Mexican descent can be found in the Mexican churches or held in trust by the secretaries of the Mexican American civic clubs. Interestingly, the Mexican-origin community's historical version of Santa Paula does not question the accomplishments of the Anglo American families, such as the founding of the citrus industry or the role of the elite families. Their account, however, was multicultural and dated back to the Native American occupation of Santa Paula. Also, their interpretation of the development of Santa Paula was somewhat unpleasant.

In my analysis, the main problem with Santa Paula's official history is the exclusion of information. That is, when I first began to gather ethnographic data and to review primary documents (e.g., autobiographies; city council, church, property tax, county, and school records), I found the history of Santa Paula, as remembered and immortalized by the Anglo Americans, to be distorted. The official version ignored the contributions of the Native Americans and people of Mexican descent. No significance was attributed, for example, to the fact that the Chumash Indians founded the city (see chapter 1). Santa Paula's official history also failed to report that the ancestors of the Mexican people, the Spanish and Mexican mestizos, subsequently colonized, renamed, and made structural improvements in the city. When occasional references were made to Mexicans, they were depicted as foreigners and outsiders (Belknap 1968; Heil 1983; Triem 1985). The Mexican-origin community in Santa Paula appeared to be a people without a history.

Subsequently, as I gathered further ethnographic data, a fuller and more realistic image of Santa Paula's history appeared. This led me to concur with my Mexican-origin informants that Santa Paula's history is indeed multicultural. In particular, interviews with elderly Mexican-origin people were especially useful in reconstituting parts of Santa Paula's unwritten history, as many of these people were descendants of Chumash Indians or of Mexican settlers who migrated to Santa Paula in the nineteenth century. Therefore, they were living proof that Santa Paula's official history was inaccurate. Their oral histories indicated that Mexicans were not newcomers to Santa Paula. In listening to their histories, and subsequently verifying them through a review of primary documents, I found it rather unfortunate that this history is forced to be part of an oral tradition rather than part of the city's official written history. In particular, I found it offensive that Santa Paula's public history presents an uncomplicated and eternally peaceful depiction of the city, while it omits all accounts of interethnic conflict. A history

of social segregation, Ku Klux Klan repression, the obstruction of labor unionization, and racial discrimination in everyday life were not included. Indeed, this is
an interethnic history that should not be forgotten or trivialized as unimportant.
Furthermore, the omission of these events has negated the fact that Mexican-
origin people have historically had to struggle to eradicate racist practices. These
obvious historical gaps have concealed the fact that Anglo Americans did not
altruistically accept the changes that brought about improved interethnic relations
in this community, for it was the people of Mexican descent—and not the Anglo
Americans—who converted Santa Paula into a more equitable society. Moreover,
Santa Paula's selective public history has served to perpetuate the myth that people
of Mexican descent have not contributed anything to their community and
therefore are not worth including within the historical records.

In my view, including Santa Paula's interethnic past as part of the city's official
history is necessary in order to provide a reflective account that also presents a
more comprehensive and realistic version of how community relations evolved.
That is, besides creating a more accurate public history, the inclusion of various
racially discriminatory events and facts would elucidate why there exists so much
social distance between the Anglo Americans and the Mexican-origin people. It
would also help to explain how Anglo Americans achieved the political power and
social privileges they enjoy today. Social segregation, dominant group violence,
the prohibition of farm workers to bargain collectively, and racism have been
effective means used to control and discriminate against people of Mexican
descent. Moreover, the inclusion of Santa Paula's interethnic history would
destroy the myth regarding how Santa Paula's public culture became Anglo
American. Anglo American culture achieved dominance and is considered to be
the city's most prestigious culture not because it is better, more modern, or more
functional but because for generations the Spanish language and Mexican
traditions have been stigmatized and pushed away, into the private sphere. In sum,
Mexican-origin people have been forced to conform.

I do not intend to suggest that this historical ethnography is generalizable to
other communities in the United States. Each community has its particular
history. This study, however, illustrates how dominant-subordinate relations
often emerge and are maintained and reproduced. It also illustrates that the
unwritten past of racial minority groups in the United States can be reconstituted.
These histories can shed light on national events, challenge elite histories, reveal
the tensions and sources of unity within multiethnic communities, and document
the social, political, and economic contributions of racial minorities in this
country.

Notes

INTRODUCTION

1. The term "Mexican-origin" refers to people of Mexican descent residing in the United States, regardless of whether they were born in Mexico or in the United States.

2. The names I use for my informants and the churches are pseudonyms. I also use pseudonyms in quoted texts when references are made to my informants.

CHAPTER 1

1. The Ventura County Superior Court records for the land case dispute *Santa Paula Water Works et al. v. Julio Peralta* 1893–1898 are currently titled and archived under *Water Works et al. v. Julio Peralta*. However, the original title of the case was recorded by the court as the former. I therefore use the title found in the original document.

Santa Paula Water Works et al. v. Julio Peralta was first litigated in 1893 and later was appealed to the California State Supreme Court in 1896. Although the state supreme court upheld the superior court's decision, the plaintiffs and the defendant continued arguing and submitting documents to the Ventura County Superior Court until 1898. A file was kept of these records and archived in the Ventura County Government Center. These records contain additional historical information not reviewed in the 1893 and 1896 cases. When I refer to these records, I use the dates 1893 to 1898.

2. Part of Santa Paula's Spanish and Mexican histories are based upon United States land case records and a judicial court case. These records include California Land Case No. 328 (1853), California Land Case No. 550 (1853), and Southern California district court case *Davidson et al. v. United States Government* (1857). In the land case documents, Davidson and other settlers claimed that they were the legal owners of Santa Paula y Saticoy. To support their case, their attorneys presented as evidence land grant documents dating back to the Spanish and Mexican periods, as well as the land tenure history of Santa Paula y Saticoy.

The purpose in presenting these documents was to prove that Davidson and the other settlers held perfect land titles because they were acquired from Mexicans who previously held legal title to Santa Paula y Saticoy.

The *Davidson et al. v. United States Government* case provides further historical information on Santa Paula's land tenure history and delineates the arguments used by the United States government regarding why the land inhabited by Indians belonged to the government and not to the Anglo American settlers.

3. In California, during the nineteenth century most Mexicans lost legal title of their property when squatters physically pushed them off it or when they were pressured to sell (Acuña 1972; Camarillo 1979). Mexicans sold their property in order to raise income to pay for land taxes or to pay for legal fees, often enormous. Hundreds of Mexicans hired attorneys to prove that they were the legitimate owners of the Mexican land grants. It was a no-win situation—they either sold their land to pay for legal fees or turned the property over to their attorneys in lieu of payment. The Carrillo family lost most of their property when they sold it to pay their attorney's fee and to raise money for the land taxes (Cleland 1957).

4. Refer to court case *Botiller v. Dominguez* (1889) for an account of the land displacement history of California's mission and *ranchería* Indians.

5. California's Spanish and Mexican land grant records are incomplete, for some have been destroyed and others are kept in private archives. Before the Mexican American War of 1846–1848, Manuel Jimeno Casarin was commissioned by the Mexican government to compile a central registry and holding archive for the Spanish and Mexican land grants. His project was interrupted by the outbreak of the war between Mexico and the United States. He subsequently turned over his incomplete registry and documents to the California Land Commission. The commission eventually used Casarin's records to confirm most California grants (Ross 1974).

6. Refer to the following United States Supreme Court cases for information on Mexican land grant litigation disputes: *Luco et al. v. United States* (1859); *United States v. Castillero* (1859); *United States v. Vallejo* (1861).

In my review of United States Supreme Court cases of the nineteenth century (volumes Howard, Black, Wallace) between 1859 and 1879, thirty Mexican land grant cases were litigated by the United States Supreme Court. Though at the state supreme court level the decisions were ruled in favor of the Mexican litigants, most of these cases were overturned at the United States Supreme Court level.

7. *SPDC* is an abbreviation for the *Santa Paula Daily Chronicle* and *SPC* for the *Santa Paula Chronicle*.

8. In 1917, the California State Supreme Court found the owners of Limoneira Ranch in contempt of water-use laws in *Limoneira Company et al. v. Railroad Commission of California* (1917). The charge was that the owners of Limoneira Ranch had formed two water companies to manage the water supply in Santa Paula and were using different water rates to charge its customers. Limoneira Ranch was given two hundred inches of water without charge and expected to pay only eight hundred dollars a year for the rest of its

annual water supply. Other ranchers, however, were obliged to pay two thousand dollars a year for less water. The California State Supreme Court ordered that Limoneira Ranch charge equitable rates to all its customers. The Railroad Commission of California was asked to monitor Limoneira Ranch's water company policies.

9. The following people were Mexican property owners in Santa Paula during 1902: Jesus Fernandez, Jesus Garcia, Concepcion Lopez, Petra Moreno, Luis Castaños, and Manuel Castaños ("Original Assessment Book, City of Santa Paula, 1902–1908").

10. Although the federal government did not stipulate what was meant by the racial category "White," district, state, and federal courts ruled that the term "White" referred only to Caucasians. To be considered Caucasian, a person could not be racially mixed with other races. For discussions of the term "White," refer to *In re Ah Yup* (1878), *In re Camille* (1880), *In re Rodriguez* (1897), *People v. De La Guerra* (1870), and *United States v. Wong Kim Ark* (1898).

11. There are various volumes containing Santa Paula's property tax records. For a complete list, refer to the bibliography under "City of Santa Paula." In the text, information dealing with Santa Paula's property tax records will be cited "Santa Paula property tax assessment records." The dates relevant to the discussion will be placed after the citations.

CHAPTER 2

1. The letter was written by George W. Caldwell, president of the Santa Paula Retail Merchant Association, to Rev. C. T. Harrison on March 21, 1922. Caldwell notes that the Mexican moral character was improving. A second letter was also written by businessman Howard Hubbs to Rev. C. T. Harrison expressing similar opinions as those of Caldwell and Shipley. The letters are archived at El Buen Pastor Methodist Church in Santa Paula.

2. Webster (1967) and the *Santa Paula Chronicle* report that Mexicans were actively participating in the literacy and Americanization programs during the 1920s (*SPC*, May 31, 1923, 135[13]:5).

3. Photographs of Mexicans attending mass in vacant lots are archived in Our Lady of Guadalupe Church. A photograph of such an event is also published in *Our Lady of Guadalupe Church, Santa Paula, California* (Los Angeles Archdiocese 1967).

4. Santa Paula's only newspaper underwent a name change several times. It was originally titled the *Santa Paula Chronicle* (*SPC*) in 1890 and retained the same name until 1914. Beginning in 1914 and until 1956, its name changed back and forth from the *Santa Paula Chronicle* to the *Santa Paula Daily Chronicle* (*SPDC*) (i.e., *SPC*: 1890–1914, 1915–1932, 1934–1955; *SPDC*: 1914, 1933, 1956 to present).

Between 1890 and 1908, the *SPC* was not published on a regular basis. Only a few issues were printed.

5. An embossed seal with the emblem and chapter number of Santa Paula's Ku Klux Klan is archived in the Ventura County Museum of History and Art (item no. 26036-93). It was used to stamp Klan documents.

6. News articles appearing in the *Santa Paula Chronicle* criticized the Klan in the early 1920s: *SPC,* May 1, 1922, 34[9]:1; *SPC,* June 1, 1922, 34[12]:1; *SPC,* January 4, 1923, 34[44]:5; *SPC,* February 8, 1923, 34[49]:6.

CHAPTER 3

1. Mrs. Isbell's memoirs indicate that she arrived in Santa Paula in 1872, and Webster (1967) reports that she arrived in 1865. This discrepancy may be associated with the fact that she first arrived in Ventura County in 1865, settling in Ojai. Webster may be referring to her arrival to Ventura County rather than to her permanent residence in Santa Paula.

2. The photograph for Isbell School was taken in 1990. Photographs taken of the school in 1926 are badly deteriorated and could not be reproduced for this book. The entrance view of Isbell School has not changed since 1925.

3. *De jure* school segregation refers to the establishment of laws to segregate racial minority students in separate schools.

CHAPTER 4

1. In California, the earliest mutual aid societies date back to 1849 (Camarillo 1979). They were organized by Mexican Americans as a form of "self-help," initially founded out of economic and political necessity because Anglo Americans were unwilling to extend loans or economic assistance to Mexicans.

2. Legislation exempted farm workers from union representation in the Wagner Act of 1935, the Taft-Hartley Act of 1947, and the Landrum-Griffin Act of 1959. Sosnick (1978:366) reported that farmers and agricultural lobbyists defended their anti-union position with four general points:

a. The extreme vulnerability of the farmer to strikes because of the perishability of most farm products

b. The inability of the farmer to control the price he receives for his produce

c. The economic inability of the farmer to increase wage rates, the only major cost factor primarily within his control

d. The place of farming as one of society's most useful and necessary enterprises supports the farmer's basic right to an adequate supply of inexpensive labor

3. Roney, José, and Isabel recall that living conditions differed substantially in the farm labor camps. For example, Limoneira Ranch was the largest citrus company in the county and provided its workers clean houses or apartments. The families were given adequate living space and were not placed in overcrowded rooms. The housing conditions on the small citrus ranches, however, were often deplorable and substandard. The houses were without heat or running water (Meany 1941).

4. In 1930, the United States Census Bureau reported that in Santa Paula 60 percent of the population was Anglo American and 40 percent Mexican-origin (United States Census

Bureau 1932:57). Between 1940 and 1960, however, the Census Bureau included Mexicans born in the United States as part of the White population and did not provide a separate category to count them (United States Census Bureau 1942:83, 91; 1963:6–384). The Census Bureau did designate a separate category, however, for people born in Mexico.

CHAPTER 5

1. Refer to Morin (1963) for a discussion of the type of discrimination experienced by soldiers of Mexican descent during World War II and the Korean War. Morin also discusses why Mexican veterans were treated as second-class citizens in their communities after they returned from military duty.

2. In Santa Paula the two main employment industries were agriculture and oil. Photographs at the Santa Paula Union Oil Museum indicate that Mexicans were not employed in the oil industry.

3. The name Daniel Guzman is a pseudonym.

4. Although the opening of opportunity structures allowed Mexican Americans to move out of farm labor, it is unclear how many of them were drafted during World War II and eventually survived to take advantage of the GI Bill. We do know that in 1940 there were 409 Mexican males registered for military service (*SPC*, October 19, 1940, 54[146]:4–6).

5. Early records of La Casa del Mexicano are in the possession of Raymundo. A similar account was told by José, Tony, and Linda.

6. The names Martin Morales and Henry Villa are pseudonyms.

7. Refer to Table 1, in Chapter 4, for estimates of the size of the Mexican population of Santa Paula from 1930 to 1980.

8. News articles in the *Santa Paula Chronicle* indicate that the Latin American Civic Organization (LACO) was primarily composed of Mexican American veterans (*SPC*, July 14, 1948, 62[63]:1; *SPC*, February 18, 1950, 63[118]:1). Also, a 1940 military draft registration list published in the *Santa Paula Chronicle* indicates that members of LACO were registered for military service (*SPC*, October 19, 1940, 54[146]:4–6).

9. Currently, only 5 percent of Santa Paula's Anglo American population resides on the East Side (United States Census Bureau 1983b:66). Most working-class Anglo American families reside in ethnically mixed working-class neighborhoods located on the West Side.

10. Santa Paula property tax assessment records for the years 1959 and 1960 are missing from the City Hall archives and the Ventura County Property Assessors Office. Therefore, I was unable to use these records to determine the number of Mexican-origin people that moved to the new housing developments in 1959.

CHAPTER 6

1. Sixty-four of my informants recall that by the late 1960s most of the West Side of Santa Paula was desegregated.

2. Mines and Anzaldúa's findings were corroborated by three interviews that I conducted with a former manager of the Ventura County Growers Association, with the executive manager of Limoneira Ranch, and with Ralph López (a former farm manager for the Santa Paula Growers Association [SPGA]). My three informants concurred that the entrance of a new labor force was expected to stabilize domestic farm wages.

3. This information was obtained from a former manager of the Ventura County Growers Association and Lencho Velásquez, a labor contractor. Lencho was asked by Limoneira Ranch to return to his village in Mexico and recruit workers to Santa Paula.

4. Phillip Martin in *Illegal Immigration and the Colonization of the American Labor Market* (1986) reported that a similar process occurred throughout California following the termination of the bracero program. Employers recruited Mexican labor to the U.S. regardless of whether the individuals had green cards or not.

5. To deal with the "undocumented status" of many farm workers, growers helped their employees secure green cards. In the first four years after the bracero program ended, a letter from an employer requesting that a worker be allowed to work for a grower was all that was needed to secure a green card (Mines and Anzaldúa 1982:37).

6. Agricultural associations in Ventura County were formed by independent growers after the termination of the bracero program. The associations functioned as cooperative harvesting companies. For example, a group of growers who did not want to hire directly or manage the farm workers who harvested their fields employed a management team to do this administrative work. The associations also became the legal buffers for independent growers. That is, if the growers were sued by the farm workers, the association rather than the individual grower would be responsible. In this manner, the growers' independent assets would not be liable. In the case of Santa Paula, the SPGA rotated the pickers as needed in the orchards of the growers. The SPGA also provided labor camp housing to its employees. I collected this information in several interviews with Ralph, the current executive manager of Limoneira Ranch, a former manager of the Ventura County Growers Association, and a public relations officer for the California Farm Bureau.

7. This information was obtained in fifty-seven interviews with Santa Paula residents.

8. Prior to the passage of the ALRA on June 5, 1975, farm workers could hold union elections only if employers allowed them and agreed to collective bargaining. If employers refused, workers could strike and thereby place pressure on the growers to enter labor arbitration talks (Decierdo 1980; Mines and Anzaldúa 1982).

9. This information was gathered from the following informants: five Limoneira employees, the current executive manager of Limoneira Ranch, the manager of the UFW office in 1986, Ralph, and Lencho.

10. This information was obtained from the former director of the Ventura County Agricultural Labor Relations office (in 1986) and from a former manager of the Ventura County Growers Association.

11. This information was obtained in interviews with the former director of the Ventura County Agricultural Labor Relations office (in 1986) and with Ralph. An article appearing in the *Santa Paula Daily Chronicle* (May 10, 1976, 89[133]:1) also summarized the results of the lawsuit.

CHAPTER 7

1. "Mexican American" is used here in reference to individuals who are eligible to vote.

2. The level of education of three of the Mexican American community leaders is as follows: José and Tony both obtained high school diplomas, and Tony also completed junior college; Robert obtained only two years of elementary education. Other community leaders whom I interviewed were also high school dropouts.

3. What follows are the main Chicano organizations that formed the first phase of the Chicano Movement:

a. The United Farm Workers union was led by César Chávez. Its goals were to (1) increase wages, (2) upgrade health benefits, and (3) lobby for federal legislation that would establish occupational safety laws, labor camp housing regulations, workmen's compensation, and unemployment insurance.

b. The Alianza Federal de Pueblos Libres (Federal Alliance of Free City States) of New Mexico was a civil rights organization led by Reies Tijerina. One of its goals was to return the Tierra Amarilla Spanish land grants to the descendants of the original pioneers. The Alianza also attempted to obtain the water rights for the residents who lived along the Tierra Amarilla River.

c. The Crusade for Justice was led by Rodolfo "Corky" Gonzalez. This was a civil rights organization based in Denver, Colorado.

d. The Brown Berets was a lumpen proletariat and juvenile ultra-leftist paramilitary movement. Its ideologies were separatist, Marxist, and ultra-leftist. Eventually it became marginal to the movement's process and disintegrated.

e. The Chicano Student Movement espoused class struggle and emanated from working-class college students. Eventually it spread to the high school level.

For further discussions of the Chicano Movement, refer to *Students por La Raza: The Chicano Student Movement in Southern California* (Gómez-Quiñonez 1978) and *Chicano Manifesto* (Rendon 1971).

4. Similar to what transpired in the 1940s when many people of Mexican descent changed their ethnic label from "Mexican" to "Mexican American," during the 1960s many Mexican-origin people elected to change their ethnic label to "Chicano." People who did so supported the ideology of the Chicano Movement.

5. *Cholos* are Mexican-origin youth who speak *caló* (bilingual slang) and wear clothing (e.g., khaki pants, bandannas, oversized shirts, dark outfits) to distinguish themselves from other people.

6. In 1978, a revival of the Chicano Movement occurred in Santa Paula. A group of Chicano professionals founded La Raza (*SPDC,* April 6, 1978, 90[256]:1). Most of La Raza's members were former residents of Santa Paula who had decided to return to their hometown and find employment in Ventura County. Jaime, Rolando, and Gary provided the information on the members' backgrounds.

7. Descriptions of El Campito were obtained from Mexican-origin residents. I also obtained part of these descriptions based on my previous years of residence in Santa Paula. As a child in the 1960s and a young adult in the 1970s, I visited farm worker families at El

Campito. When I was a child, I accompanied my brothers to visit friends in the camp. Later, as a young adult, I participated in a Catholic social service program that extended financial aid to farm workers in economic distress.

8. Information on the history of the Cabrillo Economic Development Corporation (CEDC) was provided by the director, the manager, and an analyst employed by the corporation.

9. This information was obtained in four interviews with a representative of the Ventura Legal Aid, the director and manager of the CEDC, and Ralph.

10. This information was provided by the same people cited in note 9, above.

11. I obtained the information on SAMCO's history and the second phase of the housing cooperative movement from Ralph and five farm workers.

12. In 1978, the UFW unionized over 80 percent of the citrus pickers in Ventura County, including those employed by Limoneira Ranch. By the early 1980s, however, most Limoneira employees who had voted for the UFW were discontented with the union and organized a committee to decertify it. They sent a committee representative to the state capital to ask that the union be decertified. The management of Limoneira Ranch reported that their employees voted against UFW representation because the union did not offer them any special benefits. Allegedly, pickers resented paying union dues for receiving the same benefits the company had offered them before the union was certified. The management of Limoneira Ranch also reported that union representatives were disorganized, unreliable, and unprofessional; therefore, the pickers were disillusioned.

In 1986, the manager of the Oxnard UFW office reported that the union was decertified at Limoneira Ranch as a result of the seniority system. Employees who had been working for Limoneira Ranch were treated fairly and therefore were loyal to the company. These workers consequently discouraged the newcomers from joining the union. Union organizers also accused Limoneira Ranch management of bribing several employees to head the decertification campaign.

CHAPTER 8

1. Census data do not provide information on the size of the households in Santa Paula. However, Keefe (1979), who conducted a statistical study of Mexican-origin and Anglo American households in the cities of Santa Paula, Oxnard, and Santa Barbara, found that on the average an Anglo American household was composed of both parents and three children and a Mexican-origin household contained both parents and four children.

2. Government records indicate that Anglo Americans also are dependent on the welfare system. In June 1985, the County of Ventura Public Social Services Agency reported that of 855 people on Aid for Families with Dependent Children (AFDC) in Santa Paula 66 percent were White and 34 percent of Spanish origin (Santa Paula Public Social Services District Office 1985). The statistical research analyst for the Santa Paula district office also reported that, on a monthly basis, Santa Paula's AFDC caseload has approxi-

mately the same percentages as described above. Furthermore, the director of Santa Paula's Housing Authority reported that in 1986 there were approximately 376 families receiving housing assistance on a monthly basis. Of these people, 47 percent were White and 53 percent of Mexican origin (Jay 1986).

3. In 1978–1979, the Santa Paula School District used a common statistical formula to determine if a particular school was segregated. The district's average of minority students in kindergarten through grade 6 (in this case, 67 percent) served as the anchorpoint. Fifteen percent over or under the district average identified the ceiling or floor range to determine racial/ethnic balance or isolation (i.e., 67 ± 15 percent). Any school in the district that had a minority student body of 52 percent to 82 percent was considered racially/ethnically balanced. Any school with less than 52 percent or greater than 82 percent combined minority was considered segregated.

4. McKevett School was founded two years before Olivelands School. Santa Paula school records provide very little information on the early history of the school. The only information that is available about its early days is the date that it was opened, the ethnic composition of the school, and that it received an award in 1911 for being the best-planned school built in the United States.

5. This information is based upon my observations as a previous resident in Santa Paula and on interview data collected while conducting my field research.

6. Between 1920 and 1963, White students who resided in Santa Paula's northeast section did not attend Barbara Webster School, regardless of the fact that it was located near their homes. The northeast is separated from the East Side by groves of oak trees. This information was obtained from two schoolteachers and one administrator.

7. The percentage of non-White and non-Hispanic minority students at Glen City is 2 percent and at Thelma B. Bedell 5 percent.

8. In 1990, I spoke to two teachers, several residents, and one of the former members of the 1979 school desegregation advisory committee. I asked them if any desegregation plans had been implemented, and they all informed me that to their knowledge the board of trustees had not enacted any changes.

9. Father Ignacio was born in Spain and is not a Mexican citizen.

10. In 1986, one of the firehouses located on the West Side of Santa Paula was closed down. It had been there for almost thirty years.

11. This information was reported by the organization Mexican Americans for a Democratic Society. Moreover, in 1986, when I conducted field research in Santa Paula, I observed that only one polling place was opened on the East Side.

CHAPTER 9

1. Sections of this chapter were previously published in an article entitled "Chicano-Mexican Cultural Assimilation and Anglo Saxon Cultural Dominance," *Hispanic Journal of Behavioral Sciences* 1989, 11(3):203-231.

2. "Americanization" is defined for this period as the process by which an individual becomes operational in Anglo American customs, speech, and traditions.

3. The hourly wage scales earned by packing house workers and lemon pickers were obtained in interviews with several informants. Included among the informants were the manager of the Employment Development Department at Oxnard, a manager of Limoneira Ranch, a manager of the Ventura County Agricultural Association, a labor contractor, and several agricultural and cannery workers.

Bibliography

Acuña, Rodolfo. 1972. *Occupied America*. San Francisco: Canfield Press.

Aikens, Melvin C. 1978. "The Far West." In *Ancient Native Americans,* edited by Jesse Jennings, 131–181. San Francisco: W. H. Freeman and Company.

Alatorre, Zenovich, Dunlap, and Berman. 1975 (June 5). *Senate Bill No. 1, Agricultural Labor Relations Act.* An act to add part 3.5 (commencing with section 1140) to division 2 of the Labor Code, relating to agricultural labor. Sacramento: Government Printing Office.

Almaguer, Tomás. 1979. "Class, Race, and Capitalist Development: The Social Transformation of a Southern California County, 1848–1903." Ph.D. diss., University of California, Berkeley.

Alvarez, Robert, Jr. 1986. "The Lemon Grove Incident: The Nation's First Successful Desegregation Court Case." *Journal of San Diego History* 32 (2):116–135.

———. 1988. *Familia: Migration and Adaptation in Baja and Alta California, 1800–1975.* Berkeley: University of California Press.

Barth, Fredrik. 1969. *Ethnic Groups and Boundaries*. Boston: Little, Brown, and Company.

Belknap, Michael. 1968. "The Era of the Lemon: A History of Santa Paula, California." *California Historical Quarterly* 47 (2):113–140.

Black, Bill. 1983. "Builder Reaps Rewards from Housing for Farm Workers." *Builder* (October):1.

———. 1984. "Converting Renters into Homeowners without Displacement." *Home Again* (Spring):14–15.

Blanchard, Sarah. 1961. *Memories of a Child's Early California Days*. Los Angeles: Ward Ritchie Press.

Blum, Jeffrey. 1978. *Pseudoscience and Mental Ability: The Origin and Failures of the IQ Controversy.* New York: Monthly Review Press.

Brown, Alan K., trans. 1983. *Gaspar de Portolá, Explorer and Founder of California.* (Journal compiled by Fernando Boneu Companys). Lerida, Spain: Instituto de Estudios Ilerdenses.

Burgess, Robert. 1982. "Personal Documents, Oral Sources, and Life Histories." In *Field Research: A Sourcebook and Field Manual,* edited by Robert Burgess, 146–151. Boston: George Allen and Unwin.

Cadena, Gilbert. 1987. *Chicanos and the Catholic Church: Liberation Theology as a Form of Empowerment*. Ph.D. diss., University of California, Riverside.

Caffrey, Margaret M. 1989. *Ruth Benedict: Stranger in This Land*. Austin: University of Texas Press.

Caldwell, George W. 1922. Letter written by George W. Caldwell to Reverend C. T. Harrison. Letter is located at El Buen Pastor Methodist Church in Santa Paula, California. The letter was also published in the *Santa Paula Chronicle* on March 24, 1922.

California. 1849. Constitution of the State of California, 1849. (Reprinted in original form in 1949). San Marino, Calif.: Friends of the Huntington Library.

"California Fair Employment and Housing Act." 1980. In *Laws Affecting Farm Employment in California,* compiled by Robert Shulman, 1986, 12, 28. North Highland, Calif.: Cooperative Extension, University of California Division of Agricultural Resources.

California Land Case No. 328. 1853. "For the Place Named Santa Paula y Saticoy." United States District Court, Southern California. California land cases compiled by Mr. Guadalasca. Archived at Bancroft Library, University of California, Berkeley.

California Land Case No. 550. 1853. "For the Place Named Santa Paula y Saticoy." United States District Court, Southern California. California land cases compiled by Mr. Guadalasca. Archived at Bancroft Library, University of California, Berkeley.

California State Department of Education. 1929. "California School Code, Section 1.12." In *California School Codes*. Sacramento: State Government Printing Office.

―――. 1985. *California Basic Educational Data System*. Reports compiled by the Santa Paula School District and submitted to the California State Department of Education.

Camarillo, Albert. 1979. *Chicanos in a Changing Society: From Mexican Pueblos to American Barrios in Santa Barbara and Southern California 1848–1930*. Cambridge: Harvard University Press.

―――. 1984. *Chicanos in California: A History of Mexican Americans in California*. San Francisco: Boyd and Fraser Publishing.

Casa del Mexicano. 1946. Original documents of the first meeting and founding of the Casa del Mexicano in Santa Paula, Calif., August 26. Archived by the secretary of La Casa del Mexicano in Santa Paula, Calif.

Castañeda, Carlos, comp. 1956. *The Mexican Side of the Texan Revolution [1836]*. (Memoirs of Antonio López de Santa Anna and other participants). Dallas: P. L. Turner Co.

Castetter, Edward, and Willis H. Bell. 1951. *Yuman Indian Agriculture: Primitive Subsistence in the Lower Colorado and Gila Rivers*. Albuquerque: University of New Mexico Press.

City of Santa Paula. 1908. "Original Assessment Book, City of Santa Paula, 1902–1908." Santa Paula, Calif. Archived in Santa Paula City Hall.

―――. 1915. "Assessment Roll 1909 to 1915, City of Santa Paula." Santa Paula, Calif. Archived in Santa Paula City Hall.

―――. 1928. "Assessment of the Property of the City of Santa Paula, Ventura County, 1928." Santa Paula, Calif. Archived in Santa Paula City Hall.

―――. 1932. "Assessment Book of the Property of the City of Santa Paula, Ventura County, for the Years 1931–1932." Santa Paula, Calif. Archived in Santa Paula City Hall.

―――. 1953. "Assessment Roll Zones A-B-C-D, City of Santa Paula, Tax Roll 1945/ 1946 thru 1953." Santa Paula, Calif. Archived in Santa Paula City Hall.

―――. 1957. "Assessment Roll, City of Santa Paula, 1953–1957." Santa Paula, Calif. Archived in Santa Paula City Hall.

———. 1986. "Assessment of the Property of the City of Santa Paula, 1986." County Assessors Office, vol. 072–107. Ventura, Calif. Archived in Ventura County Government Center.

———. 1914–1989. "Minute Book." Santa Paula, Calif. Archived in Santa Paula City Hall.

Cleland, Robert. 1930. *A History of California: The American Period.* New York: Macmillan.

———. 1957. *The Place Called Sespe.* Alhambra, Calif.: Braun and Company.

Cowman, Robert G. 1977. *Ranchos of California: A List of Spanish Concessions, 1775–1822, and Mexican Grants, 1822–1846.* Los Angeles: Historical Society of Southern California.

Craig, Richard. 1971. *The Bracero Program: Interest Groups and Foreign Policy.* Austin: University of Texas Press.

Decierdo, Margarita A. 1980. *The Struggle Within: Mediating Conflict in California Fields 1975–1977.* Berkeley, Calif.: Chicano Studies Library Publications.

De la Garza, Rodolfo O., and Adela Flores. 1986. "The Impact of Mexican Immigrants on the Political Behavior of Chicanos: A Clarification of Issues and Some Hypotheses for Future Research." In *Mexican Immigrants and Mexican Americans: An Evolving Relation,* edited by Harley L. Browning and Rodolfo O. de la Garza, 211–229. Austin: Center for Mexican American Studies, University of Texas Press.

De León, Arnoldo. 1987. *They Called Them Greasers: Anglo Attitudes toward Mexicans in Texas, 1821–1900.* Austin: University of Texas Press.

Despres, Leo. 1975. "Toward a Theory of Ethnic Phenomena." In *Ethnicity and Resource Competition in Plural Societies,* edited by Leo Despres, 187–208. Chicago and The Hague: Mouton Publishers.

Donato, Rubén, Martha Menchaca, and Richard R. Valencia. 1991. "Segregation, Desegregation, and Integration of Chicano Students: Problems and Prospects." In *Chicano School Failure and Success: Research and Policy Agendas for the 1990s,* edited by Richard R. Valencia, 27–63. Stanford Series on Education and Public Policy. Basingstoke, England: Falmer Press.

Employment Development Department Research Division. 1986. *Employment Development Department Oxnard-Ventura Labor Market Bulletin.* Los Angeles: Employment Data and Research Division.

Fagan, Brian. 1991. *Ancient North America: The Archeology of a Continent.* London: James and Hudson.

Feagin, Joe. 1989. *Racial and Ethnic Relations.* Englewood Cliffs, N.J.: Prentice-Hall, Inc.

Forbes, Jack D. 1973. *Aztecas del Norte: The Chicanos of Aztlan.* Greenwich, Conn.: Fawcett Publications.

———. 1982. *Native Americans of California and Nevada.* Happy Camp, Calif.: Naturegraph Publishers.

Forgacs, David, comp. 1988. *An Antonio Gramsci Reader: Selective Writings 1916–1935.* New York: Schocken Books.

Fraysier, James. 1968. "Place of the Lemon: History of Limoneira Ranch." Master's thesis, Pepperdine University.

Frisch, Michael H. 1981. "The Memory of History." *Radical History Review* no. 25:9–23.

Galarza, Ernesto. 1964. *Merchants of Labor: The Mexican Bracero Story.* Santa Barbara, Calif.: McNally and Loften Publishers.

———. 1972. "Mexicans in the Southwest: A Culture in Process." In *Plural Society in the Southwest,* edited by Edward Spicer and Raymond Thompson, 261–298. New York: Interbook, Inc.

García, José E. 1847. *Translated Manuscript of José García's Account of the Proposed Attack on the American Encampment in Sespe,* translated by Nellie Van de Grift Sanchez. Berkeley, Calif.: Bancroft Library of the University of California.

Gidney, C. M., B. Brooks, and E. M. Sheridan. 1917. *History of Santa Barbara, San Luis Obispo, and Ventura Counties, California.* Vol. I. Chicago, Ill.: Lewis Press.

Glazer, Nathan, and Daniel P. Moynihan. 1963. *Beyond the Melting Pot: The Negroes, Puerto Ricans, Jews, Italians, and Irish of New York.* Cambridge: MIT and Harvard University Presses.

Gómez-Quiñonez, Juan. 1978. *Students por La Raza: The Chicano Student Movement in Southern California, 1967–1977.* Santa Barbara, Calif.: Editoria La Causa.

Gonzalez, Gilbert. 1974. "The System of Public Education and Its Function within the Chicano Communities, 1910–1930." Ph.D. diss., University of California, Los Angeles.

———. 1985. "Segregation of Mexican Children in a Southern California City: The Legacy of Expansionism and the American Southwest." *Western Historical Quarterly* 16:55–76.

———. 1990. *Chicano Education in the Era of Segregation.* Philadelphia: Balch Institute Press.

Gonzalez, Juan. 1985. *Mexican and Mexican American Farm Workers: The California Agricultural Industry.* New York: Praeger.

Gordon, Milton. 1964. *Assimilation in American Life: The Role of Race, Religion, and National Origins.* New York: Oxford University Press.

———. 1971. "Assimilation in American Life: Theory and Reality." In *Majority and Minority: The Dynamics of Racial and Ethnic Relations,* edited by Norman Yetman and C. H. Steele, 261–282. Boston: Allyn and Bacon.

———. 1978. *Human Nature, Class, and Ethnicity.* New York: Oxford University Press.

Gossett, Thomas. 1953. "The Idea of Anglo-Saxon Superiority in American Thought, 1865–1915." Ph.D. diss., University of Minnesota.

———. 1977. *Race: The History of an Idea in America.* New York: Schocken Books.

Greenwood, Roberta S., and R. O. Browne. 1969. *A Coastal Chumash Village: Excavation of Shisholop, Ventura County, California.* Ventura, Calif.: Memoirs of the Southern California Academy of Sciences, Vol. 8, October 1, 1969.

Hall, Stuart. 1986. "Gramsci's Relevance for the Study of Race and Ethnicity." *Journal of Communication Inquiry* 10(2):5–27.

Heil, Grant. 1983. *Of California's First Citrus Empire: A Rainbow of Arches from Maine to Ventura County.* Pasadena, Calif.: The Castle Press.

Heizer, Robert F., and Alan F. Almquist. 1971. *The Other Californians: Prejudice and Discrimination under Spain, Mexico, and the United States.* Berkeley, Calif.: University of California Press.

Hendrick, Irvine. 1977. *The Education of Non-Whites in California, 1849–1970.* San Francisco: R and E Associates.

Hull, Elizabeth. 1985. *Without Justice for All: The Constitutional Rights of Aliens.* Westport, Conn.: Greenwood Press.

Hull, Frank L. 1974. "The Effects of Braceros on the Agricultural Labor Market in California, 1950–1970: Public Law 78 and Its Aftermath." Ph.D. diss., University of Illinois at Urbana-Champagne.

Hutchinson, Cecil Alan. 1969. *Frontier Settlement in Mexican California: The Hijar-Padrés Colony and its Origins, 1769–1835.* New Haven: Yale University Press.

Jay, Ramsey. 1986. "Santa Paula Housing Assistance Report, July 1986." Santa Paula, Calif.: Housing Authority of the City of Santa Paula.

Keefe, Susan. 1979. "Urbanization, Acculturation, and Extended Family Ties: Mexican Americans in Cities." *American Ethnologist* 6(2):349–369.

————. 1980. "Personal Communities in the City: Support Networks among Mexican Americans and Anglo Americans." *Urban Anthropology* 9(1):61–74.

Keefe, Susan, and Amado Padilla. 1987. *Chicano Ethnicity*. Albuquerque: University of New Mexico Press.

Kibbe, Pauline. 1946. *Latin Americans in Texas*. Albuquerque: University of New Mexico Press.

Knights of the Ku Klux Klan (Santa Barbara and Ventura Counties). 1923a. "Many See Ceremonial." *Ku Klux Klarion* 1(1):1.

————. 1923b. "Mr. John J. Cordero." *Ku Klux Klarion* 1(1):1.

————. 1923c. "The Tidal Wave of Kluxism: A Tribute to the Ku Klux Klan." *Ku Klux Klarion* 1(1):2, 3.

Konvitz, Milton R. 1946. *The Alien and the Asiatic in American Law*. Ithaca: Cornell University Press.

Kroeber, Alfred. 1970. *Handbook of the Indians of California*. 3d ed. Berkeley, Calif.: California Book Company, Ltd.

Lafaye, Jacques. 1974. *Quetzalcoatl and Guadalupe*. Chicago: University of Chicago Press.

Lamar, Howard R. 1966. *The Far Southwest 1846–1912: A Territorial History*. New Haven, Conn.: Yale University Press.

Larson, Robert W. 1968. *New Mexico's Quest for Statehood, 1846–1912*. Albuquerque: University of New Mexico Press.

León-Portilla, Miguel. 1972. "The Norteño Variety of Mexican Culture: An Ethnohistorical Approach." In *Plural Society in the Southwest,* edited by Edward Spicer and Raymond Thompson, 77–101. New York: Interbook, Inc.

Lipe, William. 1978. "The Southwest." In *Ancient Native Americans,* edited by Jesse Jennings, 78–115. San Francisco: W. H. Freeman and Company.

Los Angeles Archdiocese. 1967. *Our Lady of Guadalupe Church, Santa Paula, California*. South Hackensack, N.J.: Custom Book, Ecclesiastical Color Publishers.

Los Angeles Times. 1972, 1975, 1983.

Madsen, William. 1964. *Mexican Americans of South Texas*. New York: Holt Reinhart and Winston.

Mamer, John W., and Donald Rosedale. 1981. *The Management of Seasonal Farm Workers under Collective Bargaining*. Davis, Calif.: University of California, Division of Agricultural Sciences.

Martin, Phillip. 1986. *Illegal Immigration and the Colonization of the American Labor Market*. Washington, D.C.: Center for Immigration Studies.

Mason, John. 1969. "The Aftermath of the Bracero Program: A Study of the Economic Impact on the Agricultural Hired Labor Market of Michigan from the Termination of Public Law 78." Ph.D. diss., Michigan State University.

McFie, Maynard. 1944 (October 7). "The Gay Nineties." Paper presented in a meeting of the Sunset Club at Los Angeles, California. Archived in the Santa Paula Dean Hobbes Blanchard Library.

McWilliams, Carey. 1968. *North from Mexico.* New York: Greenwood Press.

Meany, George. 1941. "Peonage in California." *American Federationist* 48:3–5, 31.

Menchaca, Martha. 1987. "Chicano-Mexican Conflict and Cohesion in San Pablo, California." Ph.D. diss., Stanford University.

————. 1989. "Chicano-Mexican Cultural Assimilation and Anglo-Saxon Cultural Dominance." *Hispanic Journal of Behavioral Sciences* 11(3):203–231.

————. 1993. "Chicano Indianism: A Historical Account of Racial Repression in the United States." *American Ethnologist* 20(3):583–603.

Menchaca, Martha, and Richard R. Valencia. 1990. "Anglo-Saxon Ideologies in the 1920s–1930s: Their Impact on the Segregation of Mexican Students in California." *Anthropology and Education Quarterly* 21(3):222–249.

Mines, Richard, and Ricardo Anzaldúa. 1982. *New Migrants vs. Old Migrants: Alternative Labor Market Structures in the California Citrus Industry.* Monograph 9. San Diego: University of California, San Diego, Program in United States Mexican Studies.

Montejano, David. 1987. *Anglos and Mexicans in the Making of Texas, 1836–1986.* Austin: University of Texas Press.

Morin, Raúl. 1963. *Among the Valiant: Mexican Americans in WWII and Korea.* Los Angeles: Borden Publishing Company.

Nathan, P. D., and L. B. Simpson, comp. 1962. *The Letters of Jose Señan, O.F.M. 1796–1823.* Ventura, Calif.: Ventura County Historical Society.

National Advisory Committee on Farm Labor. 1967. *Farm Labor Organizing, 1905–1967: A Brief History.* New York: National Advisory Committee on Farm Labor.

Newcomb, William W. 1986. *The Indians of Texas: From Prehistoric to Modern Times.* Austin: University of Texas Press.

Ornelas, Jesús. 1984. *Historical Development of Internal Colonialism in Santa Paula, California.* Unpublished paper submitted in partial fulfillment of a Master's degree for the California State University, Long Beach. Archived in Santa Paula, California, by Lucha, a Mexican American civic organization.

Padilla, Fernando. 1979. "Early Chicano Legal Recognition, 1846–1897." *Journal of Popular Culture* 13(3):564–574.

Paredes, Américo. 1973. *With His Pistol in His Hand.* Austin: University of Texas Press.

————. 1978. "The Problem of Identity in a Changing Culture: Popular Expressions of Culture Conflict along the Lower Rio Grande Border." In *Views across the Border: The United States and Mexico,* edited by Stanley Ross, 68–94. Albuquerque: University of New Mexico Press.

Pitt, Leonard. 1966. *The Decline of the Californios: A Social History of the Spanish-Speaking Californians, 1846–1890.* Berkeley, Calif.: University of California Press.

Ransford, Edward H. 1977. *Race and Class in American Society.* Cambridge: Schenkman Publishing.

Reisler, Mark. 1976. *By the Sweat of their Brow: Mexican Immigrant Labor in the United States, 1900–1940.* Westport, Conn.: Greenwood Press.

Rendon, Armando. 1971. *Chicano Manifesto.* New York: Macmillan.

Resources. 1984. "California Project Converts Farmworkers to New Homeowners." November (4):4–5.

Richardson, Rupert N., Ernest Wallace, and Adrian N. Anderson. 1970. *Texas: The Lone Star State.* 3d ed. Englewood Cliffs, N.J.: Prentice-Hall.

Riles, Wilson. 1978. "Plans to Alleviate Racial and Ethnic Segregation of Minority Students." Letter sent to the Santa Paula School District Board of Trustees by Wilson Riles, superintendent of education of the state of California. Letter archived at the State of California Department of Education in Sacramento and by the Santa Paula School District Office.

Robinson, William W. 1948. *Land in California.* Berkeley: University of California Press.

———. 1955. *The Story of Ventura County.* Los Angeles: Title Insurance and Trust Company.

Rodríguez, Nestor, and Rogelio Nuñez. 1986. "An Exploration of Factors that Contribute to Differentiation between Chicanos and Indocumentados." In *Mexican Immigrants and Mexican Americans: An Evolving Relation,* edited by Harley Browning and Rodolfo O. de la Garza, 139–181. Austin: Center for Mexican American Studies, University of Texas Press.

Ross, Ivy B. 1974. *The Confirmation of Spanish and Mexican Land Grants in California.* San Francisco: R and E Research Associates.

Salas, Victor, Jr. 1984. "Chicano Representation in the City of Santa Paula, 1971–1980." Paper submitted in partial fulfillment of a Bachelor's degree in Political Science, University of California, Davis. Archived in Santa Paula, California, by Lucha, a Mexican American civic organization.

Salinas, Guadalupe. 1973. "Mexican Americans and the Desegregation of Schools in the Southwest." In *Voices: Readings from El Grito,* edited by O. I. Romano V, 366–399. Berkeley, Calif.: Quinto Sol.

Samora, Julian. 1971. *Los Mojados: The Wetback Story.* Notre Dame: University of Notre Dame Press.

Sanborn, Colonel W. J. 1959 [1873–1875]. "Memories of a Santa Paula Sheepherder." *Ventura County Historical Society Quarterly* 5(2):1–16.

Santa Paula Chamber of Commerce. 1986. *Community Economic Profile for Santa Paula, Ventura, California.* Santa Paula, Calif.: Santa Paula Chamber of Commerce.

Santa Paula Chronicle 1910–1914, 1915–1932, 1934–1955.

Santa Paula Daily Chronicle 1914, 1933, 1956–1986.

Santa Paula Public Social Services District Office. 1985. "County of Ventura Public Social Services Agency, Monthly Staffing Report, June." Statistical Research Unit, Jan Butler. Santa Paula, Calif.: Santa Paula District Office.

Santa Paula School District Board of Trustees. 1963. "Santa Paula School District Development." Unpublished report. Archived in the Santa Paula School District Office, Santa Paula, California.

———. 1979. "1979 State of California Department of Education Desegregation Report." Unpublished report. Archived in the Santa Paula School District Office, Santa Paula, Calif. The report was also submitted to Wilson Riles, superintendent of education of the State of California.

Santa Paula Water Works et al. v. Julio Peralta. 1893–1898. Reel no. 38, case no. 001458. Superior Court, Ventura County, Calif.

Sheridan, Solomon. 1926. *History of Ventura County, California.* Chicago: S. J. Clark Publications.

Shipley, F. A. 1922. Letters and a report written by F. A. Shipley and addressed to several businessmen in Santa Paula. Archived in El Buen Pastor Methodist Church, Santa Paula, Calif.

Shulman, Robert, comp. 1986. *Laws affecting Farm Employment in California.* North Highland, Calif.: Cooperative Extension, University of California Division of Agricultural Resources.

Siegel, Bernard J. 1970. "Defensive Structuring and Environmental Stress." *American Journal of Sociology* 76 (1):11–32.

Siegel, Bernard J., Evon Z. Vogt, James B. Watson, and L. Broom. 1954. "Acculturation: Social Science Research Council Summer Seminar." Stanford University, 1953. *American Anthropologist* 56(6):973–1002.

Signal 1871.

Sosnick, Stephen. 1978. *Hired Hands: Seasonal Farm Workers in the United States.* Santa Barbara, Calif.: McNally and Loftin, West.

Spicer, Edward. 1962. *Cycles of Conquest: The Impact of Spain, Mexico, and the United States on the Indians of the Southwest, 1533–1960.* Tucson: University of Arizona Press.

Spier, Leslie. 1933. *Yuman Tribes of the Gila River.* Chicago: University of Chicago Press.

Stuart, James. 1879. *Arguments and Points and Authorities on Appeal to the Honorary Secretary of the Interior: In the Case of the Southern Pacific Railroad Company vs. The Settlers on Land.* San Francisco: Bacon and Company Book and Job Printers.

Surace, Samuel. 1982. "Achievement, Discrimination, and Mexican Americans." *Comparative Studies in Society and History* 24:315–339.

Swanton, John R. 1984. *The Indian Tribes of North America.* 4th ed. Washington, D.C.: Smithsonian Institution Press.

Takaki, Ronald. 1987. "Reflections on Racial Patterns in America." In *From Different Shores,* edited by Ronald Takaki, 26–37. New York: Oxford Press.

Takash-Cruz, Paule. 1990. "A Crisis of Democracy: Community Responses to the Latinoization of a California Town Dependent on Immigrant Labor." Ph.D. diss., University of California, Berkeley.

Taylor, Ronald B. 1975. *Chávez and the Farm Workers: A Study in the Acquisition and Use of Power.* Boston: Beacon Press.

Teague, Charles. 1939. *Ten Talks on Citrus Marketing.* Los Angeles: California Fruit Growers Exchange.

———. 1944. *Fifty Years a Rancher.* Los Angeles: Ward Ritchie Press.

Thille, Grace. 1952. *Day before Yesterday.* Archived in the Santa Paula Dean Hobbs Blanchard Library. Santa Paula, Calif.: Published by author.

———. 1958. *Yesterday.* Archived in the Santa Paula Dean Hobbs Blanchard Library. Santa Paula, Calif.: Published by author.

Triem, Judith. 1985. *Ventura County: Land of Good Fortune.* Northridge, Calif.: Windsor Publications.

United States Census Bureau. 1922. *14th Census of the United States, 1920: Volume 3, Composition and Characteristics of the Population by State.* Washington, D.C.: Government Printing Office.

———. 1932. *15th Census of the United States, 1930: Population Bulletin, Second Series, California, Composition and Characteristics of the Population.* Washington, D.C.: Government Printing Office.

———. 1942. *16th Census of the United States, 1940: Population, First Series, Number of Inhabitants, California.* Washington, D.C.: Government Printing Office.

———. 1952. *Census Population, 1950: Volume 2, Characteristics of the Population, part 5, California.* Washington, D.C.: Government Printing Office.

————. 1963. *Census Population, 1960: Volume I, Characteristics of the Population, part 6, California.* Washington, D.C.: Government Printing Office.

————. 1973. *General Social and Economic Characteristics 1970, California.* Washington, D.C.: Government Printing Office.

————. 1983a. *Census of Population 1980, General Social and Economic Characteristics of California.* Washington, D.C.: Government Printing Office.

————. 1983b. *Census of Population and Housing 1980, Oxnard-Simi Valley, Ventura, California.* Washington, D.C.: Government Printing Office.

Valencia, Richard, and Sofia Aburto. 1991. "The Uses and Abuses of Educational Testing: Chicanos as a Case in Point." In *Chicano School Failure and Success: Research and Policy Agendas for the 1990s,* edited by Richard R. Valencia, 203–251. The Stanford Series on Education and Public Policy. Basingstoke, England: Falmer Press.

Vansina, Jan. 1985. *Oral Tradition as History.* Madison, Wis.: University of Wisconsin Press.

Ventura County Agricultural Association. 1986. "Farm Labor Wage Survey in Ventura County." Survey conducted by Walley Haven, director of the Ventura County Agricultural Association. Available at the Ventura County Agricultural Association.

Ventura County Agricultural Commission, comp. 1921–1986. "Ventura County Crop Reports, 1921 to 1986." Reports available at the Office of the Ventura County Agricultural Commission in Santa Paula, Calif.

Ventura County Historical Society Quarterly
    1955. "Dr. and Olive Mann Isbel, Pioneers of 1846" 1(1):1–5.
    1956. "Candalaria" 2(1):1–8.
    1957. "Our Schools" 2(4):1–13.
    1958. "The Sespe School District" 3(2):12–13.
    1959. "The Briggs School Story" 4(4):13–16.
    1961. "Pioneer Country Doctor" 6(2):1–20.

Ventura County Magazine. 1985. "Santa Paula Farmworkers Become Homeowners." May–June, 41.

Ventura County Star Free Press 1972, 1983.

Weber, David. 1975. *Foreigners in Their Native Land.* Albuquerque: University of New Mexico Press.

————. 1982. *The Mexican Frontier, 1821–1846: The American Southwest under Mexico.* Albuquerque: University of New Mexico Press.

Weber, Debra. 1973. "The Organization of Mexicano Agricultural Workers in the Imperial Valley and Los Angeles, 1928–1934: An Oral History Approach." *Aztlan* 3:301–347.

Webster, Daniel. 1967. *A History of the Santa Paula Elementary School District.* Master's thesis, University of Southern California.

Weinberg, Meyer. 1977. *A Chance to Learn: The History of Race and Education in the United States.* Cambridge: Cambridge University Press.

Wollenberg, Charles. 1974. "Mendez v. Westminster: Race, Nationality, and Segregation in California Schools." *California Historical Society Quarterly* 53(4):317–332.

————. 1976. *All Deliberate Speed: Segregation and Exclusion in California Schools, 1855–1975.* Berkeley, Calif.: University of California Press.

Zambrano, Ariel. 1982. "A History of 'El Buen Pastor' United Methodist Church." Unpublished report archived in El Buen Pastor United Methodist Church, Santa Paula, Calif.

CASES

Botiller v. Dominguez, 130 U.S. 238–256 (1889).

Chirac v. Chirac, 2 U.S. (2 Wheaton) 259–278 (1817).

Davidson et al. v. United States Government, United States District Court of Southern California. County of Santa Barbara, no. 328. Archived at Bancroft Library, University of California Berkeley (1857).

Independent School District v. Salvatierra, 33 South Western Reporter, 2d Series 790–796 (Texas Court of Civil Appeals 1930).

In re Ah Yup, 5 Sawy 155–160 (Federal Cases 1878).

In re Camille, 6 Federal Reporter 256–259 (Circuit Court, District of Oregon 1880).

In re Rodriguez, 81 Federal Reporter 337–356 (District Court, W.D. Texas 1897).

Limoneira Company et al. v. Railroad Commission of California, 162 Pacific Reporter 1033–1037 (Supreme Court of California 1917).

Luco et al. v. United States, 23 U.S. (23 Howard) 515–543 (1859).

Lueras v. Town of Lafayette, 100 Colorado State Supreme Court 124–127 (1937).

Mendez v. Westminster School District, 64 Federal Supplement (S.D. Cal) 544–554, (1946); aff'd 161 Federal Reporter 2d Series 774–785 (9th Circuit Court of Appeals, San Francisco, 1947).

People v. De La Guerra, 40 California 311–344 (Supreme Court of California 1870).

Plessy v. Ferguson, 163 U.S. 537–564 (1896).

Robinson and Wife v. Memphis and Charleston Railroad Company, 109 U.S. 3–62 (1883).

Santa Paula Water Works et al. v. Julio Peralta, case no. 001458 (Superior Court, Ventura County, California 1893).

Santa Paula Water Works v. Peralta, 5 California 239 (Supreme Court of California 1895).

Santa Paula Water Works et al. v. Peralta, 113 California 38–45 (Supreme Court of California 1896).

Terrel Wells Swimming Pool v. Rodriguez, 182 South Western Reporter, 2d Series 824 (Texas Civic Appellate, San Antonio 1944).

United States v. Castillero, 23 U.S. (23 Howard) 464–469 (1859).

United States v. Vallejo, 1 U.S. (1 Black) 541–565 (1861).

United States v. Villato, 2 U.S. (2 Dallas) 370–373 (1797).

United States v. Rogers, 4 U.S. (4 Howard) 567–574 (1846).

United States v. Wong Kim Ark, 169 U.S. 649–730 (1898).

"Water Works et al. v. Julio Peralta," 1893 to 1898. Superior Court, case no. 38. Ventura County Government Court House, Ventura, California.

Index